Lour
Portillo: *The*
Devil

Never

Sleeps

and

Other

Films

Leticia
Buena Suerte !

Lourdes Portillo

CHICANA MATTERS SERIES
Deena J. González and Antonia Castañeda, editors

Chicana Matters Series focuses on one of the largest population groups in the United States today, documenting the lives, values, philosophies, and artistry of contemporary Chicanas. Books in the series may be richly diverse, reflecting the experiences of Chicanas themselves, and incorporating a broad spectrum of topics and fields of inquiry. Cumulatively, the books represent the leading knowledge and scholarship in a significant and growing field of research and, along with the literary works, art, and activism of Chicanas, underscore their significance in the history and culture of the United States.

Lourdes Portillo: *The Devil Never Sleeps and Other Films*

Edited by Rosa Linda Fregoso

University of Texas Press Austin

Interview with Lourdes Portillo (1994) was originally published in "Sacando los Trapos al Sol (Airing Dirty Laundry)
in Lourdes Portillo's Melodocumystery, *The Devil Never
Sleeps,*" in *Redirecting the Gaze,* ed. Diana Robin and Ira Jaffe
(Albany: SUNY Press, 1999), 307–330.

A modified version of Chapter 4 appeared in *Wide Angle,*
vol. 20, no. 4 (2000).

Library of Congress Cataloging-in-Publication Data
Lourdes Portillo : The devil never sleeps and other films /
edited by Rosa Linda Fregoso.—1st ed.
     p.   cm. — (Chicana matters series)
   Includes three interviews with Lourdes Portillo.
   Includes bibliographical references and index.
   ISBN 0-292-72524-8 (cloth : alk. paper) —
   ISBN 0-292-72525-6 (pbk. : alk. paper)
   1. Portillo, Lourdes.   2. Diablo nunca duerme.
I. Fregoso, Rosa Linda. II. Portillo, Lourdes.
III. Series.
PN1998.3.P675 L68   2001
7*1.43'0233'092—dc21   00-061516

For Herman and Jasim

Contents

Acknowledgments

This book took final shape in the "Summer of Jasim," as we often refer to the summer of 1999, when our grandson came to liven our house and spirits for a few months. I count among my main sources of inspiration Jasim's warm smile, charisma, and exuberance, even though he made it difficult for me to work at home that summer. Fortunately, three dear friends came to my rescue, providing me with a refuge to write and gather my thoughts: I thank Lata Mani and Ruth Frankenberg for once again offering their home as my writing retreat while they were overseas, and B. Ruby Rich for lending me her office for the same purpose. I owe many thanks to Reneé Tajima-Peña and Angela Fregoso for their insightful comments on the introduction. Two dedicated research assistants, Erin Maya Higgins and Kim Owyoung, helped with bibliographic research and worked hard at transcribing the interviews from audio- and videotapes. Funds for this project came from the Office of the Dean of Humanities, Arts and Cultural Studies (College of Letters and Sciences), and from the Chicana/Latina Research Center at the University of California–Davis. I appreciate the support of editors Jim Burr and Theresa May at the University of Texas Press. In many ways, this work would not have been possible without the love, encouragement, and inspiration of my students, family, friends, mentors, and colleagues in Women and Gender Studies at UC–Davis. Finally, I thank Herman Gray for being there—and here—always.

Lourdes Portillo: *The Devil Never Sleeps* and Other Films

Introduction

TRACKING THE POLITICS OF LOVE

Lourdes Portillo and I first met during the screening of her unforgettable film *Las Madres: The Mothers of the Plaza de Mayo* in 1987, a year after it received an Academy Award nomination for Best Documentary. I was living in Santa Barbara at the time, writing a dissertation on telecommunication policy and teaching a course on Chicano/a cinema. The organizers of a UC–Santa Barbara-sponsored conference on Third World cinema had asked me, the resident Chicana film "expert," to introduce the Chicana filmmaker and highlight the significance of her work. What I hadn't anticipated then was the extent to which *Las Madres* represented a turning point in Portillo's career as a filmmaker, winning twenty international awards and expanding the audience for her films beyond the U.S. borders. Nor did I realize until years later how that evening in Santa Barbara marked my life in fundamental ways.

Twenty-one years later, as part of my research for this book, I accompanied Portillo to the world premiere of *Corpus: A Home Movie for Selena* in Chicago. As I sat in that Chicago movie theater with an audience of mostly Latinas and Latinos, I was struck with how much things had changed. *Las Madres* had screened in an academic venue; *Corpus* with a general audience. *Las Madres* documented the struggle of social activists; *Corpus,* the legacy of a celebrity. The former was international and political in focus; the latter, local and cultural. At first glance, this seems like a contradiction, and if one is not familiar with her work, *Las Madres* and *Corpus* appear to be made by entirely different filmmakers. But then I too had changed in the span of two decades. My own analysis of Portillo's work had evolved from nationalist political concerns to a multilayered understanding of the production process. I no longer viewed films primarily through the detached lens of scholarly discourse. I was now interested in how emotions, love, audiences, and compassion play a part in the production process. In the following pages I aim to take you on what Renée Tajima-Peña reminded me is my "intellectual process of discovery," that is, how I discovered the evolution of Portillo's aesthetic and thematic concerns and, in the process, discovered my own intellectual approach and methodology as a critic.

The international aperture for Portillo's films was a logical extension of her work. From the beginning, Portillo's scope and vision have been much broader than the orthodox view of artistic genres or social identities allows for. Her films demonstrate how one's cultural or social identity need not limit the choice of the subject matter. Her first two films depict women of different national and cultural identities: *After the Earthquake/Después del terremoto* deals with the plight of a Nicaraguan domestic worker in San Francisco, while *Las Madres* documents the struggle of the mothers of the disappeared in Argentina. Just as she crosses the borders of ethnic and cultural identities, so too are her films and videos genre-benders, crisscrossing various genres, like documentary and fiction, experimental and docudrama, melodrama and mystery. Her work refuses to be pigeonholed into one category or filmic style. Each film or video is a hybrid, a blend of stylistic elements and combinations of, for instance, noir and telenovela (as in *The Devil Never Sleeps/El diablo nunca duerme*); telenovela with neorealism (*After the Earthquake/Después del terremoto*); and political satire with experimental video (*Columbus on Trial*). If anything, Portillo's stylistic signature is this defiance of categories and borders.

The idea for writing this book came to me ten years later, after conducting research and publishing a book on the Chicana and Chicano film movement. Portillo was one of a handful of early 1970s filmmakers who were still making films in the nineties. And even though she had remained on the fringes of the Chicano/a film movement, working instead out of the multicultural, multiracial sensibility of the Bay area, I included her in my study of Chicana/o cinema. Part of the reason I did so was because she self-identified as Chicana, thus meeting one of the criteria of Chicano/a cinema, which I defined then as "by, for, and about" Chicanas and Chicanos. More important, by making films for the Chicano/a community, Portillo met my second criteria. It wasn't until her third production (*La Ofrenda: The Days of the Dead*) that Portillo decided to make a film about the Chicana/o experience.

While I situated her within a nationalist-based tradition, the Chicano/a art movement, I was mostly drawn to the ways in which her work complicated the definition of Chicana/o cinema by not conforming to the movement's nationalist ideology. Her films are about a whole range of topics (not just Chicano/a ones), and she works with multiracial production crews and casts across ethnic, class, gender, and sexual alliances—despite the fact that, as Portillo explains, her films are made "in the service of the Chicano community first." During the 1990s I wrote a book chapter and several articles addressing this hybrid complexity, partially because her work on the borders between two or more cultures and cinematic traditions has profoundly altered my thinking about the nature of social and artistic boundaries.

Shortly after relocating to the Bay area, I came in contact with the circle of friends and network of artists, intellectuals, and activists that Lourdes belonged to and eventually befriended her. This friendship has forced me to struggle continually with my own motivation for writing about her work, and has raised questions of professional integrity as well. After all, my formation as an intellectual is to some extent influenced by Modernist notions of scholarly work—the objectivity issue—but also the idea that the search for "truth" requires detachment and distance from the subject matter. Even though recent theories in the natural and human sciences make claims about scientific detachment and objectivity suspect, especially given the impossibility of separating the analyst from the object of analysis, somehow this theoretical insight—the idea that the act of observing itself affects the phenomenon observed—strikes me as too much of an abstraction to apply to daily life because it doesn't, for example, adequately cover the realm of human relationships. After all, a molecular biologist and a cell don't actually hang out and enjoy each other's company in a Berkeley cafe.

So I am often plagued with internal conflicts, anxieties, and self-doubts around notions of scientific objectivity and detachment, repeatedly questioning whether my ability to think critically about Portillo's work is compromised by our friendship. Would I write a similar analysis if I didn't know her personally, or if she had lived in the nineteenth century? Has my love and respect for Portillo as a friend clouded my ability to be truthful? Do my feelings for her compromise an honest critique? Do they get in the way of a critical analysis of her recent film? Am I like those baby boomer parents who, for fear of affecting their child's self-esteem, tell her how well she did, no matter how poorly she sang in the school play or how many times she kicked the soccer ball off-side during the tournament? But then again, I do keep reminding myself that this is not the case with Portillo. She does not need me to boost her self-esteem or to prove her merits. As her innumerable awards make evident, Portillo is legitimately talented, independent of any favorable analysis I may offer. Nonetheless, I have decided to be up-front about my relationship with Lourdes because

I don't know how to get around this except by naming my own investment, but also because I cringe at the thought of someone dismissing my analysis for this reason, especially since friendships between artists and their critics are fairly commonplace.

Similar to the insider's knowledge of a culture, my relationship with the artist can prove especially valuable for readers precisely because I have observed intimate aspects of Lourdes' life, those subjective and emotional dynamics which inevitably come into play in artistic creation. While I am not in favor of psychologizing the work of art or of analyzing an artist's intentions, I still maintain that an artist's personal life and subjectivity undeniably inform her creativity. In writing about Lourdes' work, I allowed myself to be what the anthropologist Ruth Behar calls a "vulnerable observer," to make my emotional connection to her as a friend not only evident to readers but also a central part of my study.[1] I did so because it is precisely this vulnerability, this emotional engagement with Lourdes, which allows me to bear witness to some of the psychic dimensions to her art.

A witness is someone who provides testimony about something they have seen, and in nonsecular traditions bearing witness refers to the act of testifying about elements one may not necessarily encounter with the naked eye, the mind, or cognition, but may observe through other ways, such as through feelings, through the heart. Friends can bear witness to each other at deeper, more profound levels than persons who are strangers. Friends bear witness to intimate details, faults, or strengths in character: to private, vulnerable moments. As a friend, I know Lourdes in both public and private settings, perceive the difference between her public persona and her private self when her guard is down, pay close attention to those passions and fears which influence her choice of subject matter and editing decisions. In the past few years we have shared the tribulations of our professional lives as well as the uncertainties and joys of motherhood. As a "vulnerable observer" I bear witness to her incessant devotion to creative endeavors and to the life of an artist. This personalized, emotive connection to Lourdes and her work is something I learned not from theory, but from Portillo's example as a practitioner of "vulnerable" filmmaking.

I write to introduce readers to an internationally acclaimed Chicana filmmaker who has given voice to the realities, cultures, and perspectives of people who are neglected or misrepresented in the media, as much as she has worked to push the documentary form forward. Portillo is a political filmmaker who first made films during the early 1970s as a member of the Marxist collective Cine Manifest, first working as Stephen Lighthill's assistant in the collective's feature, *Over, Under, Sideways, Down* (1972). Nearly thirty years later, she remains motivated by the political ideals of that early formative period. While Portillo has expanded her perspective to include other forms of social analysis besides class (i.e., antiracism, sexism), she still maintains an old, relentless allegiance to the underdog, the downtrodden. Portillo's images represent a complex, assorted, and endlessly astounding world, offering viewers new, multilayered ways of seeing which speak to the amazingly intertwined, multiplex realities of the twenty-first century. She presents viewers with a vision of an intricate world in which life is not just a matter of good versus evil. Portillo's films depict a journey, paralleling the filmmaker's, of constantly struggling with questions. She is unique in her perspective, for unlike most political artwork, her films do not provide definitive answers. In many ways, the cinema of Lourdes Portillo challenges our normal assumptions about the nature of political cinema, continually pushing the boundaries of conventional models.

She began testing the limits of artistic codes and conventions with *After the Earthquake/Después del terremoto,* a film she made with Nina Serrano in 1979. Not only did the film actively push the boundaries of political film with its syncretic style—the blend of neorealism and telenovela aesthetics—but it was also ahead of its time in telling the story of the Nicaraguan diaspora in dramatic form at a time when most political films used documentary formats. The story in *Las Madres,* on the other hand, is told in the familiar political style, yet, unlike the distanced tone of documentary films of the eighties, the intimate, personal, lyrical narration in *Las Madres* brings viewers into the subjective reality of the interviewees. She tests the limits further in *La Ofrenda.* A documentary which at first glance appears to be about cultural tradition, its poetic, meditative lyricism masks a submerged engagement with the politics of sexual repression and mourning around AIDS deaths in the gay community. And the older Portillo gets, the more audacious, adventurous, and gutsy she becomes, boldly trying out avant-garde techniques and styles. In *Columbus on Trial,* she mixes witty political satire with novel experimental video techniques. Portillo breaks with documentary codes in *The Devil Never Sleeps* by making contact with the audience and even questioning the documentary's premises and criteria for truth and accuracy, including its reliance on visual evidence. Beyond these tangible, material elements observable in her films, there is another important way in which the filmmaker tests the

Lourdes Portillo, camera assistant to cinematographer Stephen Lighthill, *Over, Under Sideways, Down* (1972). Courtesy of Lourdes Portillo.

limits of the realist political genre. Portillo makes herself "vulnerable" as a filmmaker, and she does so not simply by inserting the "I" of the filmmaker into the text, but by making films that call for an intellectual and emotional engagement from the viewer. She elicits this emotional response from her viewers by insisting on an emotional connection between producers and the subject matter. Rather than conform to conventional models, Portillo fundamentally alters our perceptions of political documentaries with her approach to making films.

The cinema of Lourdes Portillo deals with a wide range of themes—from gender politics to culture, state repression to AIDS; however, the leitmotiv in all of her work is love and compassion—qualities one does not usually associate with political documentaries. Conventional wisdom assumes that documentaries are supposed to educate, inform, offer analysis, and—in the case of political documentaries—move us to act upon the world. As viewers, we divide the cognitive from the emotional, expecting documentary filmmakers to present their audiences with logical pro and con arguments and analysis. Rarely do we think of the filmmaker's relationship to her subject matter in emotive or spiritual terms, for that would be too subjective, stretching the limits of objective analysis. For valid historical reasons (i.e., the populist legacy of fascism), the Left has been wary of linking politics with emotions or the realm of the psyche. As in Che Guevara's notion "sin amor no hay revolución" (without love there can be no revolution), Portillo uses the idea of love in its spiritual rather than romantic sense to redefine and reaffirm her commitment to social change.

"Politics is about your heart," she tells me. "It's about charity—it's love. That's what politics should be." Love is the guiding principle in her work, one of the criteria for hiring the members of her production team: "I need to love them in a very profound and accepting way," she says. And, in turn, Portillo demands love from each crew member who is hired, not in terms of racial or sexual criteria, but for "receptivity, heart, compassion, ability to communicate and to forgive." In relating to the subject matter—the theme, interviewees, actors—a loving, emotional connection is, for Portillo, the most crucial element at every level. "Even the production assistants have to have a heart," she explains. "They have to have feeling for the subject matter and they have to be open to it. I can't bear to work with anyone who is deeply cynical and critical of whatever it is that we are doing. We have to kind of really bow down to the subject, you know." Portillo has in many ways succeeded in translating this strong desire to bond emotionally with the subject matter into her final product, the film, which captivates audiences even more because the way she touches viewers' emotions enhances their intellectual responses.

In many ways, Portillo's work responds to a growing awareness about the limits of analytical thinking for altering and changing consciousness. I am now convinced that in order to raise awareness or to eliminate the ideologies of ignorance like racism and sexism, reaching the mind is insufficient. One must touch the heart along with the mind. As the politics of love at work in her films and videos shows, Portillo seems to have figured this out early on in her career as a filmmaker. I have seen all of her films dozens of times, in film festivals, theaters, and in the courses I teach on cinema. Years ago, I remember discovering with my students that one of the distinguishing features about her films is that they have a "heart center," what in T'ai Chi is called the "dan tien"—the site where all the energy of the body comes together. As I look back at the essays I published on Portillo's films, I realize that I was writing about this heart center, even though I didn't call it that. I had identified a center of bodily energy, a susceptible dimension in her film form, a love inscribed through the treatment of the subject matter—the camera's framing which gently caresses people and scenery; the lighting which softly touches them. Portillo makes every attempt to expose her own vulnerability, her emotional attachments, rendering subjects lovingly, with respect, compassion, and dignity. This heart center is itself a product of her commitment to a life connected to deeper, more profound forces than the demands of the capitalist market.

In tracking the politics of love and emotion in her work, I came upon the various social and artistic movements that left their imprint on Lourdes Portillo. She moved to the San Francisco Bay area during a vibrant moment in history: the 1960s. While I would not necessarily characterize her sensibility as countercultural—even though the icon of counterculturalism himself, the late Jerry Garcia of the Grateful Dead, once gave her money to finish a film—Portillo's lifestyle would be considered countercultural to some people. She believes in spiritual enhancement and in the power of exploring the inner psyche, often consulting a Jungian psychotherapist who has guided her personal enhancement and growth through various film projects. The importance of Portillo's unyielding investment in self-exploration should not be underestimated. The various therapeutic and spiritual practices she employs have helped her to break down the imaginary barrier between her internal and external worlds, the distance between the self and the subject matter. They have exposed her and made her vulnerable, which has allowed her to bridge the gap between the filmmaker (observer) and the phenomenon (observed). They are practices of the heart, which soften the heart, keeping Portillo focused on efforts to render justice to the world she lives in and grounded in a political mission which she characterizes as "channeling the hopes and dreams of a people."

Another influence is the impact of Third World struggles for liberation and the new social movements on the development of leftist approaches to filmmaking. Portillo came of age as a filmmaker at a time when the avant-garde, the new Latin American cinema and the feminist and Chicana/o film movements, made their mark as alternative cinemas. As a bilingual and bicultural filmmaker, Portillo was uniquely poised at the crossroads of these various artistic currents. She openly acknowledges the new Latin American (especially Cuban) cinema and the political avant-garde as her primary influences, however, I would also connect her evolving stylistic approach to the feminist and Chicano/a film traditions, for reasons that will become evident.

Portillo was drawn to radical cinema's emphasis on linking artistic innovation with the revolutionary struggles of the Latin American Left because she too sought to combine her art with politics. Along with many of her generation, Portillo rejected the elitist notion of art for art's sake. She was also among a cadre of filmmakers who opposed the distinction between artistic experimentation and political commitment, which some on the Left, suspicious of the bourgeois individualism of the avant-garde, subscribed to. Artists like Portillo were determined not to sacrifice their artistic self-expression for politics or divorce their politics from art. She drew her vitality and creative inspiration from Latin American filmmakers, many of them working out of Cuba's ICAIC (Instituto Cubano del Arte e Industria Cinematográfica), who were reimagining alternative ways of seeing and being in the world by breaking with the Hollywood model. Radical filmmakers in Latin America were proving that one could use highly innovative techniques and still deliver a progressive political message.

Influenced by Italian neorealism, Latin America's radical filmmakers skillfully assembled masterful works of art, volatile and spirited indictments of the ruling order and its complicity with U.S. imperialism and colonialism. They disrupted Hollywood's goal of entertainment as much as they disturbed the viewing expectations of the film audience with alternative schemes. While Hollywood films were designed to distract audiences from knowing the real problems of the world, radical filmmakers sought to enlighten and inform their viewers. They countered dominant cinema's legitimation of the status quo with a revolutionary focus on the oppressive forces in society. In the face of Hollywood's rendering of passive consumers of meaningless images, Latin American filmmakers attempted to transform their audiences into social agents who would act to change the world.

Yet their contempt for Hollywood was really a minor part of the equation, for these filmmakers were waging an ideological war against the forces of U.S. imperialism incarnated in the Studio system. In so doing, they were practicing "concientization," a revolutionary principle first alluded to in liberation theology and then in the various manifestos coming out of Latin America (e.g., "For an Imperfect Cinema" by Julio García Espinoza; "Aesthetics of Hunger/ Violence" by Glauber Rocha; "For a Nationalist, Realist, Critical and Popular Cinema," by Fernando Birri). Concientization entailed decolonizing the mind—liberating the image, and hence the imagination, from Hollywood's colonial hold. It was a principle that guided cultural workers fighting against the powerful economic, political, and social institutions running the artistic and social world of the times. Latin American revolutionary filmmakers like Sara Gómez, Tomás Gutiérrez Alea, Humberto Solás, Glauber Rocha, and Patricio Guzmán deployed concientization within highly self-conscious film styles, making artists like Portillo aware that one did not have to sacrifice artistic experimentation for politics.

Portillo came to this understanding early on in her career. After working with leftist filmmakers in Cine Manifest for several years, she earned an M.F.A. from the San Francisco Art Institute, studying film as an art form, with special emphasis on its vanguard and experimental aspects. The New Left's investment in realism had proven to be a limitation for Portillo, who turned to the avant-garde as a way out of the confining mantle of a realist aesthetics. Fusing the avant-garde techniques she had studied at the Art Institute with the aesthetic practices of Latin American filmmakers, Portillo broke out of the straitjacket of realism, venturing beyond the U.S. cinema verité and French avant-garde legacy of the seventies. Yet despite the liberating influence of the vanguard, it soon became dismally evident that neither of these two pillars of alternative cinema were sympathetic to the concerns raised by feminists. It was precisely this widespread disregard for and total indifference to the gravity of women's oppression within capitalism, among activists in the New Left and the various nationalist and anticolonialist movements, which sparked the formation of the feminist film movement.

Portillo was not directly involved in, nor did she associate with, the early feminist film movement of the seventies, yet she has much in common with the project of "cinefeminism." While her early work did not directly embrace the incipient feminist goal of combating patriarchal capitalism, her first film, *After the Earthquake/Después del terremoto,* did in fact tackle the thorny issue of women's oppression within Latino patriarchy. Portillo once remarked that she has never considered herself a feminist, but I would qualify her statement by pointing out that she is rather a different kind of feminist, a Third World organic feminist whose take on feminism is not informed by the consciousness-raising groups of the women's liberation movement, much less by feminist academic theory. She has more in common with Mexican women who similarly frown on the label "feminista," even though they actually practice a form of feminism that Sonia Saldivar-Hull calls "femenismo popular."[2] Theirs is a feminism honed in the trenches—on factory floors and in sweatshops, in the marketplace and in the fields, in the bedroom and in the streets; fine-tuned while they clean floors and cook, caring for wealthy homes and children, for their own children; living alone, with a loving partner, with an abusive husband. Theirs is not a feminism learned from books, but culled from the micro details and practices of everyday life. From her own experience as a wife of a traditional husband, a mother of three sons, a lesbian in a homophobic culture, a woman in a male-centered world of cinema, Portillo developed her own brand of feminist consciousness.

In making films, she responded much like other feminist filmmakers, realizing early on that woman as woman was not represented on the screen—neither did she have a voice nor was the female point-of-view visible, and not just in Hollywood but in the progressive and avant-garde cinemas. With *Las Madres* Portillo breaks bread with feminist filmmakers, heralding her strong commitment to women's struggles. So too does *La Ofrenda* partake in the feminist film movement's desire to document women's everyday lives on-screen. And with *Vida, Columbus on Trial,* and *Corpus: A Home Movie for Selena,* Portillo furthers the feminist goal of rendering meaningful portraits of women—recovering the heroes in women's history, their voices, perspectives, and points-of-view. Similar to filmmakers in the feminist film movement, Portillo inordinately attends to the details of interior spaces, the domestic sphere, family dynamics, and gender relations. Like it or not, Portillo wears the legacy of cinefeminism on her sleeve.

In all fairness, Portillo's resistance to the feminist label is in part related to the preponderance of whiteness and classism in women's liberation and the feminist film movement, which has undoubtedly kept many women of color at bay. Even so, Portillo's disavowal of feminist identity may be more related to cultural reasons. For a Chicana with strong roots in Mexican Catholicism, feminism is tantamount to Malinchismo, a betrayal of the culture, of the race, of all that is sacred to the *familia,* the Holy Family of God and Nation. Being a feminist is a heavy cross to bear for a Chicana, more so if she is a lesbian.

This is probably why Portillo was not arrantly embraced by her counterparts in the Chicana/o film movement during its heyday. Few today would admit the contempt they felt then for women's struggle or the machismo they expressed, which was called to my attention by one of the few women filmmakers working out of Los Angeles in the early days of the movement. Fortunately, we now have access to the writings of Chicana feminists working in other sectors of the Chicano/a art movement, who bear witness to the pervasive sexism in Chicana/o cultural identity politics. From my own research, I can certainly testify to the many ways in which the early Chicana/o movement filmmakers "disappeared" Chicanas: through an aesthetics of objectification, narcissistic preoccupation with male heroes and history, and neglect of female voices and perspectives. And when it came to film festivals and conferences on Chicano/a cinema, women filmmakers were rarely invited to the party. While it must be recognized that Portillo and Sylvia Morales (another early Chicana filmmaker) were in fact included in the first anthology of Chicana/o cinema, published in 1982, one of the authors erroneously referred to Portillo as a Nicaraguan filmmaker and the editor failed to mention the instrumental role she played as cofounder of Cine Acción— one of the oldest Latina/o media arts organizations in existence to this day. Throughout those formative years of movement politics, Portillo remained on the periphery of the Chicano/a film movement, in part because her ideological perspective was broader than that of Chicano nationalists, but also because she, along with many other women filmmakers, was marginalized in the canon of Chicano/a cinema. It wasn't until I wrote an essay recognizing the significance of the works by three pioneering Chicana filmmakers (Portillo, Sylvia Morales, and Esperanza Vásquez) that Portillo's imprint on the Chicana/o film movement was finally acknowledged.

When I decided to write this book about Portillo, I soon recognized my own limitations in that I knew little about the nuts and bolts of making films. More than anything else, I was driven to understand what Julia Lesage refers to as the "filmic milieu"—the whole process of film production rather than just the film text.[3] I felt the need to immerse myself completely in the making of a film, to observe first-hand its evolution from beginning (the concept) to end (the product). In the world of film criticism, we critics write mostly about the meaning of the text, in some cases relating our analysis to the social context or to pertinent historical issues. Rarely do we analyze films from the perspective of the production process. Few critics provide a first-hand account of how a film is made, of how it is filmed, how the shooting and production schedule is assembled, the length and duration of a film shoot. Nor do we take into consideration how those least glamorous parts of documentary filmmaking—the grueling eighteen-hour days; the hours of waiting for an interview or an event to happen; the canceled interviews; the arrangement of lights, cameras, and sound recording; the technical malfunctions, difficulties with battery-packs; or the weathering of climatic hardships—affect the mean-

Portillo traveled to Israel shortly before the War of 1967. Pictured here with a friend, José Barak (left), during the war. Courtesy of Lourdes Portillo.

ing of the final product. It was in the context of gaining a broader under-standing of this "filmic milieu" that I asked Lourdes if she would let me participate in her next production. The opportunity would come soon enough, a little over a year after the death of Tejana singer Selena Quin-tanilla.

Portillo considers her Selena documentary, *Corpus: A Home Movie for Selena,* to be one of her minor films, even though in the following discus-sion I dedicate a substantial amount of space to the video. Certainly *Cor-pus* is not in the same league as *Las Madres, The Devil Never Sleeps,* or *Colum-bus on Trial* in terms of budget or aesthetic achievements. The reason I have chosen to spotlight *Corpus* has more to do with the role it played in my own formation, the fact that my intimate involvement with the making of *Corpus* influenced my own intellectual process of discovery and evolution as a critic. Through *Corpus* I came to reject the conventional academic method of analysis as too one-dimensional and limiting, and instead brought all my resources—my scholarly knowledge, understanding of the subject, on-site witness of and participation in the production process—to bear in conveying more fully the filmmaker's motivations, intentions, aesthetic choices. Thus, my involvement with *Corpus* is how I came to this point.

In July of 1997, I spent a scorching week participating in and observing the shooting of *Corpus*. In many ways, *Corpus* felt like my own home movie. Not only was it shot mostly in my hometown of Corpus Christi, but it was I who had introduced Portillo to Selena's music a month or so before she died. Not that I was a fan of her music (though several of my siblings were), but I was interested in the singer's growing popularity in the Tejano music scene. After visiting my family in early 1996, I shared with Portillo details of my trip to Corpus Christi, including my mother driving me to the Selena boutique, a largely desolate store where the singer sold her collection of tinselly apparel and beauty products. Portillo had never heard Selena's music, so I played her an old cassette compilation of Tejana singers, which included Selena and "la reina de la canción tejana," Laura Canales. A few weeks later, Portillo would once again hear Selena's name, this time during a visit with her own family in L.A. on the weekend Selena was killed.

For months after Selena's death, Portillo toyed with the idea of making a film about the Tejana icon and applied for funding to produce a documentary. As part of my ongoing research on Latina representation, I continued to collect all the Selena material I could get my hands on, including newspaper clippings, videos, English and Spanish language magazines (of reputable and tabloid variety), books, articles on the Internet. Portillo and I apprehensively awaited the upcoming (March 1997) release of Greg Nava's film *Selena,* and as I had anticipated, we were both extremely disappointed.

Mostly we lamented the film's missed opportunity, the weakness of a plot held together loosely by a series of spectacular musical performances. Dramatic tension in the story was also weak, focused around Selena's relationship with the men in her life: her father and husband. The best thing about the film was Jennifer Lopez' uncanny resemblance to Selena. But apart from that, the film was not particularly engaging. It was also really not about Selena but about the family patriarch, Abraham Quintanilla (played by Edward James Olmos)—the only character portrayed with any depth. Viewers hardly got to know Selena; as a character she remained enigmatic, a cardboard Barbie-doll figure. Most of my distress centered around the way in which the film sugarcoated the hard life of performers—those grueling rehearsal schedules, fatiguing nights on the road, and exhausting back-to-back performances. To quote filmmaker Renée Tajima-Peña, who accompanied me to the prerelease screening in San Francisco, "This film is *People* magazine's version of Selena's life."

Later Portillo and I discussed at length the looming presence of the patriarch in Greg Nava's version of Selena's life. Portillo decided then to make an alternative film, one that would follow the story into places where Nava had refused to go, filling in the gaps of his sappy tale and providing details that had been published in recent books written by journalists close to the story. The initial focus for Portillo's version of Selena came later in March, when I attended the screening of Nava's film in Corpus Christi during its national release.

My second viewing of Selena differed, not so much in my perceiving a different message, but in my witnessing how the film touched her hometown audiences. I attended the screening with my mother, brother, and sister-in-law in a theater filled to capacity, with more than six hundred people—a cross-generation of Chicanos, Chicanas, Tejanas, and Tejanos: babies, young adults, children, and the elderly. As the film ended, I witnessed and connected with an overpowering feeling of despondency looming throughout the theater, a sadness so thick one could slice it with a knife, a sentiment so contagious it made me cry along with many who filed silently out of the aisles, miserably broken-hearted. My sister-in-law, Sylvia, poignantly captured the mood when she said, "The movie made us relive her death all over again—the tragedy, the sadness." I found myself bearing witness to her observation even as I continued to lament the gaping hole left by Nava's film. Fortunately, others in Corpus Christi also felt something profoundly lacking in the film. I met with my brother's friend Anissa Rivera, a reporter for the *Corpus Christi Caller-Times* who had recently written a story about audience reactions to *Selena*. "Even those who liked the film," she told me, "felt that it failed to capture the soul of Tejano music," and Anissa went on to explain the film's most obvious omission: "The fans' point of view."

Here was what Portillo's documentary needed, a way to construct the story from an entirely different angle. Rather than focus on Selena's life, she could make a film about Selena's fans. Also, on this trip I had also heard stories from several local residents about the monopoly control that Abraham Quintanilla ("Mr. Q," as locals called him) exerted over the use of Selena's name, no matter how innocuous—as, for example, when Mr. Q obtained a court order for a police raid of a flea market to confiscate "unauthorized" Selena T-shirts, or when he filed suit against the guy who rented a tour bus he bought from Mr. Q to the Nava group making the Selena film. The focus on Selena's fans would be a way of avoiding Abe Quintanilla's meddling interference. Even though fan worship contributes to the enrichment of the Selena estate, fans have an autonomous existence, residing outside the commercial purview of the Selena trademark. As I sat with Anissa Rivera in a Mexican restaurant, eating my favorite kind of Tex-Mex enchiladas, in walked "the Devil himself" (as I referred to Abe Quintanilla in my journal), foreshadowing things to come for Portillo's documentary.

That summer I took on the job of associate producer (though I later decided to forfeit the credit), which involved lining up interviews, looking for places and events to shoot, setting up the crew's one-week schedule in Corpus, and acting as their tour guide. Portillo came into town a few days later and, with her all-female crew (Imiko Omori, Sarah Chin, Anya Portillo), charmed her way into the hearts of many Corpus Christi Tejana/os, including my family and friends, many of whom appeared in the film or served as contacts for other interviews. The focus of the film at that point remained solidly fixed on the fans, along with some of the more sordid details of Selena's life, such as her rumored love affair with a plastic surgeon in Mexico; the singer's obsession with her body, cellulite, and weight; Abe Quintanilla's purported sexual assault on Yolanda Saldivar and his threat on her life; and the lesbian subtext. High on our list of priorities for the film shoot was an interview with Yolanda Saldivar, who was then serving a life sentence in prison.

In the course of making this documentary, the focus began to shift, in part because some of our production plans fell through. For instance, Yolanda Saldivar's interview never materialized due to her lawyer's refusal to grant his permission, since there was an appeal pending; one interview took longer than expected, forcing cancellation of the filming of a Tejano dance; and some subjects failed to show up for their interviews, while others did not work out. Of course, these problems are not unheard of in the course of making any documentary. However, the most disconcerting shift came from Portillo herself, who midstream in the editing process changed the course of the documentary, which in and of itself is also a common occurrence in any creative project. The reason I have chosen to spotlight this as a disconcerting shift in Portillo's thinking is because I believe there is a lesson here for all of us about the social, political, and economic constraints of filmmaking, as well as about the limits of artistic independence and creativity.

I consider Portillo to be a model for younger filmmakers who want to pursue the independent route. Located on the fringes of commercial television and the Hollywood Studio system, Portillo has generally been able to make films on her own terms, with relative autonomy and freedom. To be sure, her life as an independent artist without the steady flow of a monthly paycheck has taken its financial toll, for as a single mother raising three sons, she has usually lived from grant to grant, often mortgaging her house to finance her next project. Nonetheless, her freedom from the constraints of private commercial media is what allows her to maintain her integrity as an artist, to develop an innovative and experimental style that subverts conventional aesthetics—qualities which I expected would continue to inform her Selena documentary.

A little over a year after the filming in Corpus Christi, Portillo invited me to an editing session of the Selena documentary at the Lucas production facilities on the Skywalker Ranch. Portillo has edited several of her films there, and after driving up there I can understand why. The Skywalker Ranch is ensconced in the Santa Rosa Mountains, forty-five minutes away from the major interstate, in a breathtaking valley. Portillo and Vivien Hillgrove (her editor) shared an editing room in a building designed like a Mexican hacienda, with a large interior patio and its own cafeteria. They were in the final stage of editing, and toward the end of the day Portillo showed me an almost-final cut of the documentary. I was very touched by how Portillo had succeeded in capturing the spirit of my Corpus Christi paisanos—their down-to-earthness and their quirkiness—and at the same time avoided being condescending, as has too often been the case in documentaries about working-class folks (e.g., Michael Moore's films). Later that evening I wrote in my journal: "This is such a female-centered story, not at all spectacular, but plain and simple folks. She captures the down-home, down-to-earthness of people telling stories of her [Selena's] death, their feelings, the meaning of Selena in their lives, how she inspires them to write poems, visit her grave, perform in her name, carry on in her legacy. Portillo captures the simple beauty . . . the ordinariness of Corpus."

It was during this editing session that Portillo also shared with me the difficulties she was having in obtaining the rights to Selena's music. Not only was the cost for the music rights well over the film's budget, but she had learned that Abe Quintanilla owned the rights to all of her music, including every one of her performances (even though Selena is a public figure, there is no fair use clause in this case). I cautioned Portillo about the potential for problems if she involved Mr. Q and suggested that she avoid dealing with him entirely. I also suggested she forget about the music, including the performances, since the news footage would provide viewers with the necessary historical context. Besides, the focus of this film, I reminded her, was on Selena's fans, not on Selena.

But it was also during my visit to Skywalker Ranch, observing Vivien and Lourdes in their editing mode, where I got a glimpse of the vulnerability in Portillo's style of filmmaking. I sat there watching both of them as they became profoundly enmeshed with the subjects on the screen, talking about them to each other as if they knew these people from Corpus intimately. The director and her editor were sitting before the editing screen, establishing an emotional bond, a loving connection with the fans who loved Selena. In the process of touching the hearts of her fans, Portillo would later convert into one of them, listening to Selena's music, admiring her talents, her beauty, her indigenous and African features, calling me on the phone several times to express a profound sadness over Selena's tragic end.

Her desire to include Selena footage in the documentary grew the more Portillo watched the singer's performances on video. Coincidentally, around the time Portillo's resolve solidified, she received a telephone call from Abraham Quintanilla, who expressed his willingness to help by providing music, including Beta video copies of performances, and footage of Selena unavailable elsewhere. Portillo then decided the documentary would be enhanced by an interview with Quintanilla, and she made plans to return to Corpus. But Quintanilla asked to see the latest cut of the film beforehand, so Portillo sent it to him. In confidence, one of the crew members told me that when they arrived to interview Quintanilla he demanded several changes, making it clear that if Portillo really wanted his help (i.e., use all the footage and all the contacts he had made available to her), then she was going to have to eliminate certain parts he disliked. According to my confidential source, Portillo objected: "But Abe, that's censorship." To which Quintanilla responded, "Yes, but who would know except the people in this room—and nobody's going to tell."

Eventually Portillo capitulated to several of his demands, cutting out some of *my* favorite footage, like the segment of an animated Tejano expressing in colorful descriptive terms his disappointment with Selena's modest tombstone (too critical for the patriarch). She also eliminated a scene that typifies Portillo's ironic montage style, one in which a fan's voice is heard off-screen while images of Catholic saints and virgins appear on-screen (offensive to Quintanilla's religious beliefs). Once she edited the final version of *Corpus,* inserting the interviews of Quintanilla and Selena's sister, the film lost its magic for me. Eventually I viewed this final (prebroadcast) cut during the film's premiere at the Mexican Museum of Chicago. It was well received by the Selena fans who packed the theater, but I sat there lamenting the loss of the irreverent, biting humor of the earlier version—a style she had cultivated over the years and perfected in *The Devil Never Sleeps.* The following year, after Abraham Quintanilla viewed the final version shortly before its national broadcast on public television's *Point of View,* he demanded even more edits. To Portillo's credit she refused, agreeing to only one of his demands even after he harassed her repeatedly, threatened to sue her for libel, and attempted to block the national broadcast. Even so, from my perspective the final version of *Corpus: A Home Movie for Selena* is Portillo's most conventional documentary. And although she would never admit it, Abraham Quintanilla's overbearing presence looms large in this film. (Quintanilla was insistent that Portillo edit out the part where he says, "In the end, it was all worth it," and she eliminated it from the broadcast version.) I often joke that while "The Devil never sleeps" serves as a guiding metaphor in her documentary about her Tío Oscar's murder, in this particular case Portillo ended up "sleeping with the Devil."

The point I am trying to convey is the degree to which my involvement in the making of this documentary allowed me to come to terms with those lessons we fail to teach in film courses about the creative process. We tend to freeze a filmmaker's aesthetics; however, as I learned, artistic innovation and experimentation do not exist in a vacuum or outside of a historical context. Economic and political forces often impinge upon the creative process, no matter how hard the artist tries to resist them. In this particular case, it wasn't so much the power of one individual, Abraham Quintanilla, but what he represented—the music industry's monopoly control over music and performance rights—that played a decisive role in determining the final product. As an independent filmmaker working within a limited budget (the Selena documentary cost $130,000), Portillo was forced into a position of compromise, into contending with powerful corporations who owned the music rights (EMI Latin) and news footage (CBS), into facing the reality that even the public image of Selena is owned by corporate America. In other ways, though, the filmmaker was not entirely a passive victim in the game of image making but complicitous in negotiating away her own artistic principles. What has become clear to me is that Portillo's experience is not unique but, on the contrary, quite common in the lives of independent filmmakers, who often have to contend with the threat of lawsuits over issues of fair use. As Portillo told me afterward, "It happens in every film—we are always wheeling and dealing. This notion that you can just make a film about any old thing and say anything you want is fantasy."

In the process, I too have learned a great deal about my own stakes, my own investment, in films that are nonconventional or countercultural. Eventually I came to the realization that my overinvolvement with the project mostly had to do with the nostalgic investment and love I harbored for my hometown of Corpus—and these emotions competed with Portillo's vision. It was, after all, her film and not mine. (Yes, somewhere along the way I had forgotten, as my companion, Herman Gray, pointed out, that I am a critic and not a filmmaker.) But more important, I confronted the reality that as a critic I had become too attached to Portillo's innovative, experimental, and ironic style without taking into consideration the conditions that make this style possible.

As is usually the case, critics like myself are often out of touch with the pulse of film audiences, for this "inexpensively" made video has proved to be one of Portillo's most successful works and received numerous invitations, including one from the prestigious Venice Biennale Film Festival in Italy. *Corpus* may indeed lack the innovation of a film like *Columbus on Trial* or the masterful ironic critique of *The Devil Never Sleeps,* but even the final (censored) version is a gem in its own right. *Corpus* is first and foremost a love poem to Selena and to her fans, depicting a warm and loving portrait of the young fans who so adored the singer. It is a film that conscientiously (and I would add reflexively) validates the bodies of brown women by purposely voicing and visualizing them as alternatives to the emaciated, light-skinned blondes populating the media. More important, the filmmaker doesn't shy away from the complexities surrounding Selena—her somewhat enigmatic legacy as a role model. During the parodic scene featuring a gathering of Chicana intellectuals, including writers Cherríe Moraga and Sandra Cisneros, Portillo forces us to grapple with the negative underside of the singer's image: its hypersexualization. And for all the compromises Portillo was forced to make, she managed to once again validate the experiences of her people, a community that is often ignored and misrepresented in the dominant media.

Ultimately I learned that artists like Portillo are complicated (and vulnerable) individuals motivated by a variety of factors, including love. This portrait of Selena started out as a gossip-driven concept and ended up a loving tribute to Selena. When I asked Portillo about her "love-affair" with Selena, she responded, "As a filmmaker I want to make people fall in love with her; that's my job. I fell in love with her, so why can't they? That's my treat to you." Yes, Portillo fell in love with Selena and, as is often the case, lost a part of herself in the process.

My current understanding and reading of her work in the end influenced the organization of this book. Divided into three parts, the book introduces readers to Portillo in Part One through a series of interviews conducted during the nineties. The first interview took place in Chicago on the evening before the premiere of *Corpus: A Home Movie for Selena* and deals with the collaborative nature of Portillo's work—a topic which actually originated months before, during an informal conversation in Mexico City. I had organized a panel on her films for the National Association of Chicana and Chicano Studies conference, and one day over lunch she discussed the process of improvisation and collaboration that informs her productions, which Herman Gray, who was sitting with us, characterized as a process typical of jazz bands. Portillo liked the idea of comparing her film crew to a jazz band, where no one instrument or musician dominates, because she prefers to view her crew as a collective rather than in terms of the traditional hierarchy in which the director is credited as the sole creative agent.

The second interview, on *The Devil Never Sleeps,* was recorded at Portillo's former office near Mission Dolores in San Francisco and originally published with an article I wrote on this documentary.[4] In the interview, Portillo discusses the making of the film, the construction of its audiences, and the critical reception, both negative and positive, that *The Devil Never Sleeps* has received.

Kathleen Newman and B. Ruby Rich conducted the third interview during the historic "encuentro" (gathering) of women film- and video-makers from both sides of the U.S.-Mexico border in Tijuana, Baja California. Of the three interviews published in Part One, this last one is the most comprehensive, covering most of Portillo's early career and providing details pertaining to her earlier films.

Part Two includes several essays which illustrate the application of a variety of theories and methodologies, often in combination, to the study of visual culture. These approaches include cultural studies, feminist film criticism, queer theory, discourse analysis, ethnographic studies, and spectatorship theory. The contributors are unified by a concern for the intersecting issues of social identities and differentials of power. My essay, "Devils and Ghosts, Mothers and Immigrants: A Critical Retrospective of the Works of Lourdes Portillo," is informed by a feminist cultural studies approach and explores the broad transnational focus of Portillo's films. By contextualizing her work within global capitalism, this article explores the ways in which Portillo positions women at the center of her stories and documents the effects of structures of domination on women's everyday lives.

Yarbro-Bejarano, Thouard, and Iglesias offer wide-ranging formulations and analyses of *The Devil Never Sleeps,* a film that has been instrumental in the evolution of the documentary genre of the 1990s. In "Ironic Framings: A Queer Reading of the Family (Melo)drama in Lourdes Portillo's *The Devil Never Sleeps/El diablo nunca duerme,*" Yarbro-Bejarano examines how the film "negotiates differentials of power" through its use of the cinematic apparatus. Informed by queer theory, the critic's incisive analysis focuses on the aesthetics of playful resistance and ironic critique in the film.

Thouard and Iglesias consider the relationship between the film and its audiences. Thouard's essay, "Performances of *The Devil Never Sleeps/El diablo nunca duerme,*" situates the film within the feminist performance and performative documentary traditions. Even though the author draws from feminist theory of spectatorship, Thouard eloquently critiques its commitment to one version of spectatorship. She examines the film within various performance contexts, in France and the United States, and highlights the film's role as a participant in the performance.

In "Who Is the Devil, and How or Why Does He or She Sleep? Viewing a Chicana Film in Mexico," Iglesias provides an ethnographic study of actual viewers in Mexico, highlighting the conjunction of reception studies with textual analysis. In this analysis as well, the author examines what the film does to audiences and how audiences modify the film's original intent and meaning. Iglesias' work yields valuable insights into the film's reception by Mexican viewers as well as their perceptions of a Chicana filmmaker and her relationship to Mexican cultural heritage.

McBane's essay, "Pinning Down the Bad-Luck Butterfly: Photography and Identity in the Films of Lourdes Portillo," explores the role of photographic images in *La Ofrenda, Las Madres,* and *The Devil Never Sleeps,* teasing out the formal and thematic links of still images to the filmmaker's "consistent interest in the subject of death," which has "frequently noted associations with both the ancient roots of Mexican culture and with photography." However, McBane skillfully goes beyond the study of the still image's relation to the moving image, for the author proposes new interpretations of Portillo's use of the photograph to map out social identities and make reference to marginal or "deviant" sexualities in her films.

In rare instances do readers or viewers have an opportunity to examine what I would call the "seams" of a film, that is, those elements which go into the making of a film but remain invisible or hidden in the final product. Some would say that the labor of those who work on a film is what gets hidden behind the director's authorship; however, even these individuals are recognized in the film's credits. My reference to the invisible elements of a film is to archival material—the written maps for making a film and guiding the filmmaker throughout the production process. Part Three of the book contains a sampling of such preproduction and production materials: a funding application; script notes containing technical details about camera takes in each scene; and storyboard and production notes with narrative, visual, and technical information. I have also included written texts of the Spanish and English narration for *La Ofrenda* and the screenplay/script for *Columbus on Trial*.

In closing, let me say that I was led to this place by Hannah Ngala's words. "Tracking isn't instinctual or natural," she explains. "It only begins when you start seeing the ground under your feet instead of just staring blindly at it; when you acknowledge the pain, accept the uncertainty of hope, feel the fear of being saviorless, yet insist on paying attention to the small details of one's life once again. Tracking means immersing yourself in signs and in the knowledge that none of us goes anywhere without leaving a trail behind."[5] I invite readers of this book to join me in tracking the trail that Lourdes Portillo's films and videos have left behind.

PART ONE

THE WOMAN BEHIND
THE CAMERA

Part one introduces readers to Portillo through three separate
interviews. Rosa Linda Fregoso's first interview with Portillo
takes place in Chicago on November 12, 1998, during the world
premier of *Corpus: A Home Movie for Selena* at the "Tribute to
Mexican Women" festival sponsored by the Mexican Fine Arts
Museum. On this occasion, Portillo discusses the production
process and the ways in which she works with members of her
production crew. Fregoso's next interview with Portillo was
recorded in San Francisco during the summer of 1994 and
focuses on the making of *The Devil Never Sleeps*. In December of
1990, Kathleen Newman and B. Ruby Rich interviewed Portillo during the conference, "Cruzando Fronteras/Crossing the
Border: Encuentro de Mujeres Cineastas y Videoastas Latinas,
Mexico—Estados Unidos." This final interview is the most comprehensive of the three and deals with the filmmaker's early career, including various artistic and social influences on her work.

Interview with Lourdes Portillo
by Rosa Linda Fregoso

CHICAGO, 1998

Rosa Linda: I wanted to pursue a line of thinking that we began in Mexico City, when you talked about the process of making films as teamwork. And I think you specifically referred to this as like a jazz band, this process. So I wanted to ask you how making a film is like playing in a jazz band, because one of the things we are trying to do—you made me see this in terms of your work—is to get away from this view of film as the product of one person, which is the director. The whole auteur theory in cinema. So can we begin by talking about that?

Lourdes: I think that whole theory of one person making a film exists . . . I think that there are people who make their vision and everything is in the service of that vision. Particularly, I think, in narrative films—you know, dramatic narrative films. Whereas in documentaries it's somewhat different: there is a visionary, there is a person who sees, like an architect, who sees the building before it's built. Everyone is in the service of that building. But at the same time, in documentaries, in my experience, in working I have a vision, but there's a lot of different people: masons that are doing things and engineers that have better ideas than I do while entertaining that vision. So I allow for that. I really work collaboratively with people in every aspect. I mean, the concept itself is always very much mine, and then in the course of making it, for example, the cinematographer adds to it. If I give him an idea of what it is that I want to convey, he has to process it through his own creativity and figure a way to tell it as best he can. One thing that is assumed is that you have to have these very close emotional relationships with people. They are not necessarily professional, but the bottom line for me is to know this man who is my cinematographer and this woman who is my cinematographer, and see where their heart is at and what it is that they feel. Do they feel the same way that I do about the subject, so that they can make a portrait of it, in a sense? I prefer to work with people that are very talented—very, very talented—and are very emotional. And I think in that way we can construct our dream at every level. Even the production assistants need to have a heart and they have to have a feeling for the subject and they have to be open to it. I can't bear to work with anyone who is deeply cynical and critical of whatever it is that we are doing. We have to kind of really bow down to the subject, you know? And we live the subject. When we shoot, we are all together, and after we shoot we talk about it: we throw ideas around, we figure out what the next step is. I'm very, very open in that way. Because I really believe that we are all doing it together. I don't believe that it's just my thing. It's my concept, but then ultimately the construction itself is made by all of us.

RL: So it's not that you just look for someone who is talented. You look for someone who is talented but also has affect—like you said, someone that has a heart in it. How is that decision made, to find someone like that? Do you have to get to know this person before you hire them for a project?

L: Well, generally what happens is I hire someone because they can do the job, because they are proficient at it. After they're proficient at it . . . It's very strange for me to talk about it this way, but it really is this way for me . . . I don't know that it's so for other people. I need to love that person, you know, I need to love them in a very profound and accepting way. And I think they need to feel the same way towards me and then we are a team. And it just happens like anything, like falling in love with someone, that's how it is. Like my editor said, she is my wife, my temporary wife. She temporarily becomes my wife for the duration of the editing. And when we finish, she goes off to her real wife. [*Rosa Linda and Lourdes both start laughing at this point.*]

L: And I think that we all feel that way—that we are all married together for that duration—so that we have to have a good marriage, all of us. Maybe it's a romantic view, I don't know . . . I'm sure it's very romantic because some people just make films and they say, "Well this guy can do it and he can climb the tree" and perhaps he can, and it's just like that. But I think that the product I want to come out with is something that has a lot of sentiment, a lot of feeling, and that's the reason why I work this way. I've worked the other way, which is fine, but it's just a job.

RL: You mean the other way, which is having more of a division of labor: so-and-so does this and so-and-so does that, and you just kind of . . .

L: Yeah. And if they screw up, you kick their ass. Stuff like that, yeah.

RL: Why is the heart or love so important to your subject manner?

L: Well, rather than try to convey political oppression, economic oppression, I think what I'm trying to do is, I'm trying to touch people's humanity with the humanity I'm trying to portray. So that people can look at these films and then feel something and not just intellectually try to conceptualize something. We want feelings and hope that, in creating this love and this feeling of humanity amongst the viewer, the film creates compassion. And then, therefore, my whole political purpose: I want to be able to live in this country with respect and with wholeness and some kind of integrity as a human being, where I'm not mistreated for who I am and neither is anyone else.

RL: So going back to the process of working with these people, talk to me a little bit about how decisions are made. Let's say with an editor—can you give an example with an editor? I know I've seen you and Vivien work together. How is it that the decision-making process comes about in this relationship?

L: Well, I think, for example, with Vivien, as you have seen, it's more like, there is my concept "Here is my baby" and I bring it to Vivien. Here is what I shot, right? What I want out of this film is for it to tell a story, which could ultimately be a very different story. It could be like a paragraph, what I want to tell. So that's her editing goal. Now, in the service of that we work together, make very small decisions, keep on making decisions all the time. It's incredibly collaborative. Sometimes I lose, kind of lose, myself . . . like fall in love with a piece of film or sound that I really, really like and maybe it's not that important, looking at the total picture. We always have to come back to the emotionality or the intent, the original intent. That's why Vivien is there. She is there to make it, to weave and to make it beautiful and to make it coherent. And I'm there making decisions about what's important, keeping each other on track. She has the skill of the editor, and basically I just throw ideas around and try to fulfill our original mission.

RL: So like in a jazz band, there is—or my sense is that there is—a lot of improvisation as this goes on or . . .

L: A lot, a lot. From the beginning to the end in documentary—and that's the beauty of it—you improvise even in the shooting, or even in the selection of your subjects. Someone may not be there—for example, in *The Devil Never Sleeps* Ofelia didn't pan out. So what do we do? So I dreamt up that we'll just film the telephone conversations. And that's how improvisation happens at the level of not getting your subjects or not being able to get the people you want and how fast you can think on your feet. And how fast you as a director can think on your feet and the cinematographer and the sound man because we all . . . we all work together and the conversations are . . . that would be interesting to make: a documentary about making a documentary. Because it's all about . . . for me, it's all

In 1993 Portillo wrote, directed, and produced *Mirrors of the Heart*, a sixty-minute documentary commissioned by WGBH in Boston for the PBS series "Americas." The film examines the complex issue of cultural identity within the synchretic cultures of Bolivia, the Dominican Republic, and Haiti. The program was broadcast nationally in 1993. Above, cinematographer Kyle Kibbe (left) checking the light meter before filming, while Portillo (right) observes. Courtesy of Lourdes Portillo.

about my interaction with my crew and how we move as an organism together. And if somebody has a better idea, we go with that better idea.
If I need to just pull rank and say I'm the boss, I do that. I would rather
not—I would rather just work together as a team, as a family.

RL: Organic, it's a very organic kind of thing. Now, you've worked with
Kyle Kibbe on *The Devil Never Sleeps, Columbus on Trial* . . .

L: And Derek Bell's little piece.

RL: Yeah, tell me about that process of you working with Kyle as well, a little
bit more. Be a little more specific about how you relate to the cinematographer.

L: For example, I am presented with a situation where I have to shoot, for
example, an intellectual, and I want to give it a different tone, not just

Cinematographer Kibbe filming a Haitian ceremony on the street in the Dominican Republic. Courtesy of Lourdes Portillo.

Cinematographer Emiko Omori in Bolivia. Courtesy of Lourdes Portillo.

Sound recordist
José Araujo (left),
Portillo (center),
and Emiko Omori
(right). Courtesy
of Lourdes Portillo.

Lourdes Portillo with her film crew in Bolivia. Courtesy of Lourdes Portillo.

make it pretty lighting or nice background. We want to give it a personality, we want to give it depth. So then I would say to Kyle, "This is what
I want with Rosa Linda. How can we get it?" And he'll say, "Well, we can
do this and we can do that." And he'll give me different choices. We just
pursue the choices that he might give me. I present him with a problem
and he comes up with a solution, in a way, but within that decision I also
have input. We go back and forth, always using his skill as a cinematographer. I throw things at him: What can you do with this? What can you do
with that? Then we proceed. I think a lot of it has to do with being chal-
lenged. It's a challenge for all of us. It's not only that we are presented
with something that we have to resolve; it's more like, how can we make
it better than better? And it's the same with José, the sound recordist, and
with Vivien, the editor.

RL: Who is José?

  L: José Araujo is the sound recordist. He himself is a filmmaker, a very talented one. He made *Landscapes of Memory.*

RL: Well, also I was able to see a lot of your shooting on this new film, *Corpus.* The new film, this is video?

  L: Video.

RL: On the new video with Emiko Omori and Sarah Chin, one thing I no-
ticed about when Emiko was shooting the performance by the little girls,

was that a camera in any kind of situation is very intrusive. I mean, it takes the subject a long time to forget that there is a camera right there—you know what I'm saying. But there was a way that Emiko was able to blend into the scenery. She just has this very unintrusive way of filming things.

L: Yes. Well, partly it has to do with the fact that she's a woman. Secondly, she's a very small woman and she's a very gentle woman—you know what I mean. And also she is somewhat distant from her subject. That is one of the things that Emiko does: she gives it a lot of distance. Sometimes with men, what they do is they come in really close.

RL: I want to talk about the work process. How do you prep your team? I know you've probably already said this, but I want to see if can I get it another way.

L: No, that's OK.

RL: How much flexibility do they have? But I'm really interested in the prepping of people because I don't know how much knowledge they need to have to be able to get your vision about the subject matter. I'm just trying to get it.

L: Well, I try to tell them. First of all, I give them all the documentation on paper, telling what the film is about. That's one thing. Then we talk about what the style is, then we talk about color . . . we're going to talk about light . . . we talk about all those things. Basically, one of the most important things is, what are the people like that we are shooting? That sort of thing, all that is deep conversation, but the greatest conversation that we have is about style. How do we develop a style? How is this film going to be different from the last film . . . the last film that we made? How are we going to create a style? How are we going to make it unique? So then we develop stylistic themes, dramatic stuff. For example, for *The Devil Never Sleeps* we said, "OK, it's going to be noirish. We're going to use a lot of mirrors and reflections. We're going to use very saturated colors, etc. And then we're going to use toys and we're going to do things with photographs." That's how we developed the style of *The Devil Never Sleeps*. But at the same time, when we were working, there would be a moment when—I remember distinctly—the crew would say, "Well, what are you doing?" I mean Kyle and José. "What are you doing, Lourdes? What is it that you are doing?" Because it was so wildly improvisational at times.

RL: What specifically did they say that for?

L: Well, I think. . . . I don't know how it was . . . it was just how we were proceeding. It was unclear to them.

RL: Incoherent for them or something?

L: Yes, it became like an incoherent way of telling the story. It was not. They asked because it wasn't the way that documentaries were being shot. A lot of it was like traditional documentaries, but then a lot of it wasn't. It was like we were treading new ground, so it was hard to know what we were doing.

RL: When you say "we," is it that you were telling them what the colors were, or were you making a collective decision about it?

L: Well, basically I do make decisions, but the others make suggestions. Ultimately, "I don't like that background" or "Why don't we use this other color?" and they will do the best that they can to please me. That's another thing: If I have an idea, their involvement in it is really intense. They will try to make things work, or try to see something the way I'm looking at it. But then, if it doesn't work and someone else comes up with another idea that works, then we'll just buy that.

RL: Now, most of your projects have not . . . I mean, you have had minimal funding on projects, so how is it that you get such talented people to work for you? And of course if they are that talented, they probably have shoots on other, more expensive projects.

L: Yeah, they do. They actually do. A lot of the people, most of them are filmmakers. The people that work with me want to work with me because I challenge them. I challenge their notions of documentary or challenge their notions of beauty or identity, whatever. They want to be associated with someone who is trying to do something new, something different, and something beautiful and meaningful.

RL: So what kind of projects do they work on—like, Vivien and Kyle?

L: Well, Vivien came from narrative film. She worked on *The Right Stuff, Amadeus, The Mosquito Coast*. She comes from the big Hollywood films, and slowly she gave that up to work on documentaries, because she became very disenchanted with the whole Hollywood machinery.

RL: What disenchanted her?

L: I think it was the lack of respect that was given to an editor, that was what was disenchanting to her. She wasn't getting the respect that she deserved, like in *Henry and June,* I think.

RL: Was it that they were seen more like technicians, as opposed to artists? Is that it?

L: Yeah, I think that that's part of it, but even as a worker she was not given sufficient respect.

RL: And Kyle, what kind of work has he done?

L: Kyle is . . . Kyle is very secretive about the kind of work that he does, but his wife tells me. What he does is music videos, advertising, like Calvin Klein and stuff like that. He works with other documentarians like Barbara Kopple and many others. So he's really out there working in New York, doing all kinds of different things.

RL: Well, there's another element of the postproduction process, which is the actual production facilities. Right?

L: Yeah.

RL: Can you talk a little about the relationship with the people in this production facility?

L: For the last one, two, three . . . for the last four films, we've worked at Lucasfilm, the Skywalker Ranch. Basically because Vivien had those connections from her feature work. But not only that, we have developed our own relationship with the facility and they have been incredibly generous with me through the years. I think that I am one of the few independents that they are really, really generous with, and I'm very grateful to them. They mostly get all the Hollywood films that come through there. I assume it's hard to have a lot of respect for things that are made solely for money. So they feel like they are actually doing something that will bring about some social change—they're committed to helping. And I'm very grateful to a lot of people that feel that way towards my work . . . I'm very grateful to all of them.

RL: So what do you think—why do you think that people are so generous with you?

L: In thinking about it—in our conversation this morning—I think people see me doing some kind of work . . . of Mother Theresa work, you know? [*Rosa Linda and Lourdes laugh*] Is this the reason they give the nuns free food? You know, because I'm doing social work and over the years I've proven to be doing this. It's not for my self-edification or my ego trip . . . I'm sure it's for my ego trip in some way, but I'm doing it for a greater good. I really am and I realize that . . . and I've actually just realized that recently. I never knew I was like a machine, just doing it. Not that it's true, that's what I do it for and that's the same reason I teach. I do it so that I can inspire kids to get into film and do things—people that are of my background. So I think that's the reason that people are very generous towards me. They see that I'm not getting rich off it. In fact, it's quite the opposite.

RL: Do you get more in debt with each film?

L: With each film it's worse and worse. My house starts peeling, my deck starts rotting. It's like all that money that could go into my house goes into my films.

RL: Explain how art can be very ego-invested. You said there is a way it is that for you—that brings you a kind of ego fulfillment.

L: Yes.

RL: But in the film world, egos are particularly big.

L: Yes.

RL: And there is a lot of self-promotion and there is a lot of self-interest in making—in having your name as the director or producer—of this particular project. How is that different for you? How is the ego investment or the process not so ego-invested for you?

L: Well I think it *is* ego-invested, it just depends on where I want my name and who I want to be associated with. I mean, I'm not particularly interested in being associated with big stars—that leaves me cold. They are people just like I am. I want to be associated with just causes. You know, I want to be associated with moral things, I want to be associated with beautiful things—and that's my ego investment. I want to be associated with a new idea, with a new concept, with a new way. Those, those are my conceits.

RL: But you were also saying earlier—if I can be so bold as to mention something that you have discovered recently in therapy about how you see your relationship to your subject matter, or what is maybe your mission or your purpose in life . . .

L: Yeah, I have spent a lot of years of my life in therapy, I mean, that's one of my luxuries, because I like to look inward a lot. I have this Jungian therapist, this friend of mine, this wonderful person. We talk about my work and my mission a lot. What is my work? What does my work mean? What is the sense of my work? And we discovered in the process of investigating this that really what I am is an artist—that is, just fulfilling the needs and the dreams and the visions and desires of a people. I'm channeling my people, and therefore the sense of mission that I have—this sense of purpose that goes beyond me. And that was very illuminating for me. It really contextualized a lot of the things that I had been feeling, because I always thought that I was a political filmmaker—like a social this and a social that. To put it into Jungian terms, it just seems like much more all-encompassing and beautiful and purposeful way of looking at my work.

RL: So to be a channeler, one has to be really be in touch the with soul of a people?

L: Right. Yeah. Therefore, why hire people who have no heart or be around people with no heart? Right? Therefore, the people that I work with, they could be any color, they could be any race, it doesn't matter. It has to be people that have an open heart, you know, because that's what we're all doing as a team.

RL: Channeling.

L: Channeling. [*Rosa Linda and Lourdes both start laughing*] That sounds weird, but I'm sorry.

RL: That's very Californian of you!

L: Well . . . well, maybe . . . I'm sure it does. I mean, I'm sure it does, but that's where I've arrived at in this point of my life, age fifty-four. Is it . . . is that what I am? I forget when my birthday . . .

RL: Yesterday you were fifty-four years old. Yeah, very wise, you are fifty-four. So your teams—you mentioned this—so your teams are not racially defined. Then you don't have a Chicano team?

L: No, I don't define anything by that kind of identity. Again, I define it by receptivity—by love, heart, compassion, ability to communicate and to forgive. All those things. I ask them to be like priests and nuns.

RL: So this multiracial aspect of it is in the service of a people who are racialized?

L: Right.

RL: Where does that . . .

L: Well, I think we are all in cahoots. I mean, we all believe that we are doing the right thing for the people we are doing it for. I don't think that . . . and people see the beauty . . . the crew sees the beauty of . . . what I'm trying to say . . . you know what I'm saying? So they're in agreement and part of . . . it's not so much the product . . . Also, what's important to them is the fact that in the process, which is us as a team, we're not recording what goes on between us, but we're creating a spirit. I sound like Don Juan here. [*Rosa Linda and Lourdes both start laughing at Lourdes' comment*]

RL: No. I think that this brings me to one of the errors—I don't know if it would be one of the big errors—of Chicano nationalism. That was to sort of occult or to hide the kind of multiracial alliances that are always at work in the process of social justice and in the process of social transformation. So in many ways your work kind of goes against the grain of that received wisdom of the Chicano movement.

L: Yes, I think so. I think. . . . Well, it's a replication. The Chicano movement sometimes is the nationalist replication of the things that they were precisely trying to fight against, so I don't see the point. You know, we live in a multicultural society where we are trying to accept each other—I think that that's the purpose. We are trying to get along, and I can't just hold all my grudges against everybody and say that my color or my identity is the perfect identity. And I will only buy bread from a Chicano, and only buy shoes from a Chicano. And I will only have friends that are Chicanos, and my lovers will have to always be Chicanos. I can't do that because the heart is not like that. If you are really trying to be a proponent of love and brotherhood and humanity, then, you know, you can't act like that.

RL: Well, in terms of your mission, you were talking about being a channeler. Yet are there other ways that you see your mission, in terms of our people?

L: Yeah. Well, I think one of the things that happened to me, that marked me, was the fact that I came to this country and I could speak some English. Because I had studied English, and I came here with my mother and father and my brothers and sisters, and I was the only one that spoke English. So I mean, in the course of having to live here, we had to make a lot of decisions and my parents did not speak English, so I had to become the translator. I became the translator when we bought a house. I mean, I bought a house when I was thirteen years old. I put my brothers and sisters in school. I don't think that this is unique. I mean, I don't think that I am a unique human being in any way, but I think that that's the role of the first-born that is an immigrant. That one becomes the translator of ideas or interactions and tries to kind of marry these two cultures together in some way so that they can communicate. And I think that is the root of my work, what it has become, that I am that translator. I am . . . I don't know if I want to use that whole idea of La Malinche, you know . . . I don't know that I am the betraying Malinche, but . . .

RL: But, Chicanas have rewritten the Malinche as not the betrayer . . .

L: Exactly. As a facilitator.

RL: Yeah. And so?

L: And therefore you know that's the kind of work that I do in an artistic type of modern way.

RL: So that would be as a translator. That would be to another audience, because you've said that you see in a lot of ways your audience—your primary audience—is the Chicana, the Latina audience . . .

L: Right.

RL: But your role outside of that community would be, then?

L: Yes, yes, would be the role of translator. So I'm always maneuvering two things . . . I'm maneuvering many things, I'm not just translating and trying to convey information. I'm trying to convey other things as well to both, so that they all feel that they are being spoken to. I don't want—I don't believe in—exclusion, as you already know. So it's inclusion, and inclusion of a dialogue that starts with the crew ends with the product itself, and ultimately when it comes to the audience speaks to them and they respond to it.

Interview with Lourdes Portillo
by Rosa Linda Fregoso

SAN FRANCISCO, 1994

Rosa Linda: How did the idea for the topic [investigating Tío Oscar's death in *The Devil Never Sleeps*] come about? Or why did you decide to do a film about this subject matter?

Lourdes: I've been making heroic, celebratory films about Chicano culture. So at first, I didn't even think about making a film about Tío Oscar's death; actually, I thought it was my personal life, but I was really obsessed with everything that was happening after he died. And I kept telling Ruby, "Oh, this happened today, and guess what happened, and so-and-so called, and somebody found this out." And that's all I talked about for days and days. And she said, "Well, you should make a film about that." And it had never really sunk in that that's the kind of film that I would like to make — that I had always wanted to make these other kinds of films that were celebratory and heroic. So I thought, yes this is my chance to do this. This needs to be done. Do something very, very subjective. So that's how it came about, with my own obsession with everything that was happening. And also — which is funny to me — because I think that there's a kind of distancing from the real subjective experience in terms of Chicano film, that there is that wall that you have to break. And you have to come to terms with your own existence and who you are. And that is as valid as, for example, a film that celebrates the Chicano Moratorium or what have you.

RL: Tell me about the preproduction elements that went into the shooting. What kind of obstacles or paths did you have to clear?

L: Emotional. The emotional obstacles were the biggest because I had to go back to Mexico, where I had not been in a long time, to my birthplace. I had not been to Chihuahua in the last fifteen years. And I had to be confronted with the past that I loved so much, and that was so much a part of everything that I ever aspired to. It was like heaven, going back to Mexico. But I also was very afraid, because I knew that I had to be confronted with the fact that my grandmother didn't live anymore, some of my aunts and uncles were dead. So I knew that there were going to be a lot of painful things. More painful even than finding out who my uncle was, because who my uncle was, was a known. But what was unknown to me at first was what my emotional reaction to my birthplace would be.

RL: How did you prepare in order to be able to face these emotional aspects?

L: One of the things I did was I made phone calls to make contact with my cousins, especially one of them who I had never met. And it was exciting and it was distressing at the same time. Basically, I spoke to my mother and father at length. They prepared me, they would go over many things for me that would enable me to cope with it once I got there. Other than that I didn't have any other preparations. I think the thing with my parents was the most significant. They talked to me, they reminded me of places, they reminded me of my childhood.

RL: You are a central character in the film. And that used to be considered an avant-garde technique. Now it seems to be more common in film, especially in documentaries, to center the producer of the film. It's what Mike Nichols terms the "self-reflexive" style in the documentary form, a style that is more in use today. Could you talk about the function of the filmmaker's presence in the film?

L: Within the framework of my entire work and the importance of bringing forth Chicano filmmakers, I felt that it was important for me to be a part of the film at this point. I never felt that I would be one of the central characters of the film, so this was the first time. I was encouraged by the crew and by my friends who said, "Just go ahead and do it, put yourself in the film." It's important to have that image for many reasons: a middle-aged woman with gray hair, a Chicana. That's not what you see, that's unusual, it's not what you typically see in films.

RL: How did it come about, the decision to insert yourself in the film? Did you plan it? Or was it something that came about organically?

L: Before I shot, I went to Mexico. I went to see all my family, and I did pre-interviews to determine who I was going to interview on film. And I tried to reach my uncle's widow, and she said, "OK, well, I'll think about it." She basically gave me a tenuous answer. And my cousin who knows her quite well said, "Come on, Ofelia. It's gonna look bad if you're not in the film. You should be a part of the film." And Ofelia responded, "Well, I'm going to think about it. And when she comes back, by then I'll have decided." So I knew at that moment that she wasn't going to be a part of the film. So when I came back and I proposed to her, "Why don't you be a part of the film?" she said, "Absolutely not. I will not be in the film." So at that moment I realized that she was not going to be in the film, so I was going to put her in the film by hook or crook. And, in fact, I would put myself in the film talking to her. So that's when the decision was made, very much at the beginning of the filming.

RL: When you talked to your family in Mexico, what did you tell them you were doing? What kind of a film? How did you present the subject matter?

L: I told them that I was going to make a film about my uncle. My uncle was a very much admired character in the whole familial scene. And they imagined that I would just make a film about all the great things that he did and all the wonderful things that he was. And they all agreed to do it. Some of them, the more intelligent ones, looked at me with a jaundiced eye and said, "Hmm." [Lourdes laughs]

RL: Did you find out things during the process about your uncle that you didn't know before? I mean he was your favorite uncle, and when we have favorite uncles, we tend to idealize them. And I'm just wondering if you found out some things, in the process of filming, that you didn't know about before?

L: I felt that I found out that my uncle, at the same time that he was very intelligent and able, was also very disabled, very ineffectual, as an emotional human being. That he really lacked a lot of things. And it enabled me to see a lot of the frailties of the upbringing that he had, and that generation had. So it was hard to see that. It was hard to see that a man who was so strong was at the same time so weak. That was one of the things that I discovered that made me feel, I guess you grow up and you find these things out. Aside from that, the whole thing about him being gay, I don't know if he was or wasn't, it's really kind of irrelevant. I think that men who have a lot of power are really polysexual. I mean, they are avaricious in terms of the things they want to have, not just in terms of money but in terms of sexual things.

RL: My next question has to do with the overall structure of the film. Were there any major changes in terms of the way you perceived your subject matter, because we all have a general idea about what our finished product will look like, but in some cases, something happens to alter our perceptions drastically. Did you experience a similar situation?

L: No. What I set out to do, to make a film about family interactions, to make a film about gossip, about hearsay, a person's rise and demise, I pretty much expected that. The only thing that was a surprise was this whole thing about my uncle being gay. That was totally unknown to me. And also the willingness of some of the members of my family to kind of sell him down the river, that was surprising.

RL: Were you ever frightened during the making of the film?

L: Oh yeah, I had a lot of fear. I felt like—I really believe that—some people are innately bad and that there is evil in the world. And somehow I was always overshadowed by my own fear of his widow, because she was so unwilling to cooperate and she had such a bad reputation within my family. So I had the notion that she was capable of doing anything. And I was actually afraid of her and her willingness to harm me, but she didn't know what I was doing really.

RL: Ofelia to me is a pitiful character. And I identity with her, not because I'm that way, but because I feel like she is being set up by you, the film-maker, and by some of the other family members. Because she's from a different class and she comes off as a person who is manipulative, but at the same time there's a way that I kind of understand that person. I feel sorry for her. And I remember at the Pacific Film Archive's screening, talking to Jerry Garcia of the Grateful Dead, and he said to me that he liked Ofelia too. So I wonder if you ever foresaw that you would have people in the audience sympathetic to her. That some people would like her.

L: Oh, when I met her she was immensely likable. I have good memories of her. She was really exciting and lots of fun. I can't entirely dismiss the experiences that most of the members of the family had over the course of twenty years with her. Aside from being a family that has the natural prejudices of people of their class, they are also compassionate human be-ings. If this was a woman that came from a humble birth and was a good woman, and you knew it, there's nothing in the world that would stop them from liking her. The whole notion of class would be totally thrown out the window. My family never mentions that she is from a different class. I mention it, and I don't think that that is their point. The bottom line is that she was not a good person to my uncle and she was not good to his children.

RL: Let's turn to style and form. You coined the term "melodocumystery" to describe the film.

L: Well, I didn't want the film to be a documentary in the traditional, North American documentarian tradition. I wanted it to be a documentary that incorporated my whole national culture, and my national culture incor-porates the melodrama into their everyday life, for whatever reason, I don't know—from seventeenth-century Romanticism . . . I couldn't say what it is because I'm not a scholar, really. But, I wanted melodrama to be a part of my film, and I knew that in some way it would turn some people off because that's not what Americans like. Americans don't like this kind of melodrama. But I was bent on doing it. And it's a mystery be-cause there are things that I don't know, that we try to discover. And it's *docu* because it's documentary. One of my main objectives was really to make melodrama a part of a documentary, which is really not done. It's kept separate. In traditional documentaries, there's a sense of objectivity in documentary where you're not supposed to feel strong feelings. And that's what melodrama is about, the exaggeration of drama.

RL: How do the storytelling techniques of *The Devil Never Sleeps* differ from others?

L: Deviating from the norm. What I've seen and what my experience has been in the United States is that the storytelling is always very logical, and one thing follows another so that ultimately you come to some conclusion. Well, I had the privilege of meeting a Mauri filmmaker in New Zealand, Maurita Mita. And she saw the film and she adored it, she really loved it. She told me that one of the things she loved about the film was that the storytelling is not linear or horizontal; it's a vertical story, the way we tell stories. A story can go on for years, you can be telling a story by not only directly linking fact to fact, but also by branching out and telling other stories, and then coming back to the facts. And yes, that's exactly the kind of story that this documentary tells. And I think that for that reason it breaks the pattern of storytelling in a way that might be hard for some people.

RL: Hard? In what ways?

L: It's hard to follow. I've received this criticism from some people who think that some of the facts I have put in the film are not related and have nothing to do with the ultimate outcome of who killed my uncle and how he died.

RL: What other techniques did you consciously break with?

L: The other one is visual. Initially when I was thinking about the film I thought, "Well, what I want to do is a little re-creation or reenactment." And that never works. Re-creation is so unsatisfying in documentary— it's like, what are you doing with this film? You lose track and you think, "Well, is this really a dramatic film or is this a documentary?" So I said, "We need to develop a very, very specific visual technique." So my cinematographer and I decided that we were going to use different strategies for reenactment. For example, one of the subthemes of the film is reflection, how people are reflected. So we used mirrors. Thus there are a lot of mirrors used visually in the film. There are no re-creations, no reenactments. So that you can make a kind of mental-spiritual link between what you are hearing on the soundtrack and what you are looking at visually. And that's how we approached making this film. There's a kind of collage feeling to the film. And I also decided that my style would be one that incorporated a lot of different styles, and not simply a Eurocentric style of making a film.

RL: Yes, I just realized that there is a gap between what you hear and what you see in the film. You mentioned that the film is a collage. What are the other components of this collage?

L: Well, in the editing there was a great deal of freedom. A lot of intuitive freedom in the shooting. If we had a sense of the place and we wanted to give a feeling of dryness, then we would try to capture those images. It wasn't a literal kind of shooting. It wasn't like you see on PBS: "And the lady took off her hat," and then you see the image of a lady taking off her hat. It was a collage of not only images but also of images and sounds, impressions. And I hate to use the word, because it's overused, but also a metaphorical kind of imagery.

RL: Can you mention any of your influences — other filmmakers, other films that you saw that influenced this work?

L: I have been influenced by many, many filmmakers. There isn't any one filmmaker that I think is the end-all or be-all, but I particularly like the young videomakers, and I think that they influence me. And more specifically, one film called the *Island of Flowers,* which was a film made in Brazil. It's a short film that is fantastic in the way it uses its imagery and the way it tells its story — in a nonlinear fashion, but it tells a very poignant and wonderful story. It's by Jorg Fortado.

RL: You are certainly known for making films that are not straightforward. For example, *La Ofrenda* at one level is about the Day of the Dead celebration, but at a deeper level the film is about Chicana identity, and about how one negotiates that identity when crossing the border back and forth and coming into contact with traditions that cross back and forth. By the same token, *The Devil Never Sleeps* is a film that is about something bigger than Tío Oscar's murder or suicide or people's perceptions of Tío Oscar.

L: Definitely. The film goes way beyond a specific incident in my family. And I intended for the film to have impact and meaning. What I feel the film tells is the story of Mexico. It tells the story of deception. It tells the story of pretense and of family ties — the strength of family ties, the strength of family love, the blindness of family love. It tells the folly of the filmmaker. It tells innumerable stories in my mind about what the film is really about besides what you see and what you hear. And I think when I showed the film in Mexico, the Mexicans agreed. They looked at the film and said, "I can't believe this film. This film is not about your uncle Oscar. This film is about Mexico right now, about the political situation, about deception, heroizing people."

RL: I just thought of something, Lourdes. Your film is a ranchera because that's what rancheras are all about—about deception, betrayal, the family, about love, about the heroic, about men who die for the sake of honor. The songs of Vicente Fernández, José Alfredo Jiménez, Lucha Villa . . .

L: And it ends with a ranchera . . .

RL: You are also presenting us with a culturally distinct notion of truth in the film. Could you elaborate on that?

L: It's very difficult to explain, the whole notion of what is truth. Like in this culture [U.S.], truth is what—or it is kind of like what—is collectively believed: that this fact is true—truth is related to facts. Whereas in Mexico, truth is really a very subjective feeling. What is true is what you feel is true. So that's your truth, which is different from everyone agreeing on what the truth is. So there are partial truths, and everyone has their own point of view. And that point of view, their own genuine experience as the truth—you have to honor that. So there are partial truths, in a way, if you look at this from this cultural perspective. So I'm presenting the audience with this panorama of the Mexican truth: each person had their own genuine experience and they've experienced the truth. I'm sharing this in a way that might be confusing to an American audience, which might feel like, "Well, they're all lying, and they're all negating what the other one is saying." And the American audience will get confused if they don't understand that each experience is just as much the truth.

RL: How is *The Devil* different from most Chicano documentaries?

L: First of all it doesn't address the heroics of the Chicano people, like *Requiem 29* or *Agueda Martinez,* where Agueda is mostly a saint, or the heroic in films like *Yo Soy Chicano* or *Chicana.* This really pokes fun at the frailties in human character and human life. It dares to criticize where we come from and not say that we all come from a specific kind of family. I'm sure that there are more honorable families. But that is a part of our realities: that that is Mexico. Mexico is that and more, and even more sordid stories.

RL: It does treat the subject of la familia and, by extension, the community, because the Chicano community is based on the model of the family, and it's supposed to be a positive model.

L: Yeah, but the family of not only Chicanos, because we're like a remnant of Mexican culture. In Mexico, the family is sacred. You never say things outside the family. All the dirt stays in the family. Imagine the good stories people have. You don't talk about those things. And in turn, the political structure of Mexico in the last sixty or seventy years has been constructed in just the same way that a family functions. The PRI is a family, and you don't know to this day what happens: the mechanisms at work in the PRI, the perversity of it, the corruption, the benevolence. You don't know any of it.

RL: You have thus broken a taboo. So how has your family responded to this film when they see it?

L: I have to say that the first people to respond were my parents. And my parents are very loving people to me and in general. And my mother is a very appreciative mother, so she loved the film. She loves it and she watches it every week. She used to watch every day, but now she's watching it every week—and she even broke the cassette, so now I have to send her another one. She loves to watch her brother, because she adores him. And my father loves the film, so my parents have been an incredible strength for me. They have validated my work and me and they have protected me a lot. A cousin of mine saw the film either in Chicago or San Antonio, I don't know where. Some of my relatives saw the film before I showed it to them and they went crazy. My aunt and uncle, they just thought it was horrifying that I dared say the things that are not said outside of the family and put it in a cinema and show it to strangers. [*Laughter*] So they went wild. And just recently an aunt and a niece saw it and they loved it, they really, really loved it. So they called my mom and dad and told them that they loved it. I've had mixed responses. I have yet to take it to Chihuahua and show it to Ofelia. [*Laughter*]

RL: Tell me about general audiences' and, in particular, critics' responses to your film.

L: Very few people have gotten it. I feel that it's very hard for people to get this film. I've made it in some way . . . maybe my approach to it was too complicated, maybe it was too much at one time. It's shown in really good places like New Directors, Sundance, Toronto. But the critics—for example, an Israeli named Emmanuel Levi from *Variety,* he absolutely did not get it. He was in another world, he came from the Moon. I don't know why he wanted to review it, because he really just did not get it. *The New York Times,* they kind of got it. But I think that the driving force in the critics' mind is always "Who did it?" They miss the point that this film is not about who did it. It's about this whole panorama of Mexican life. And maybe people don't find it as interesting as I found it. But there's a critic, someone who I admire quite a bit, a French critic, who really got it. So I think that it takes a sophisticated person. Maybe I made something too highbrow.

RL: But the Mexicans got it.

L: Exactly, the Mexicans get it. Maybe people are just not interested in Mexicans.

Interview with Lourdes Portillo
by Kathleen Newman and B. Ruby Rich

TIJUANA, BAJA CALIFORNIA, 1990

The following is an informal video interview which took place in Tijuana, Baja California, during "Cruzando Fronteras: Encuentro de Mujeres Cineastas y Videoastas Latinas, Mexico–Estados Unidos" (Crossing Borders: A Conference of Latina Film- and Videomakers from Mexico and the United States). The interview focuses on Portillo's career as a filmmaker, beginning in the early 1970s.

Kathleen: Why don't we start, Lourdes, by asking you to tell us how you became involved in organizing this conference?

Lourdes: I was invited to take part in a celebration of women's films here in Tijuana, with El Colegio de la Frontera Norte (COLEF), because they had done celebrations for women writers and we were invited to show our films, which we did. There were three of us, Rosa Marta Fernández, Nancy de los Santos, and myself. And there was also at the same time a male filmmaker who came from San Diego, a Chicano who showed his film. And there was a big to-do about his film—Carlos Monsiváis came and the press came to his screening, and it was very elaborate. And when it came time to show our films, we didn't have a projectionist. We were in a room that had a skylight as big as this room—and it was still daylight! It was very problematic and very few people came of course, so it didn't get . . . I mean, the whole sense of this kind of screening is about the woman's look, but the screening wasn't that way. So we complained to Jorge Bustamante, the director of COLEF, and he took it very seriously and immediately offered something better, which was an encuentro, or meeting or conference of sixteen women, eight from each side of the border, to meet here in Tijuana and to show our films. And as we structured the film festival or film seminar, Norma Iglesias and I started thinking that it would be really good if we expanded it to more than eight people, because there were more than eight filmmakers, more than eight people, trying to make, produce films and videos. We also thought of having this element of criticism and scholarship enter into this field, which had never happened before—it was the first time, here in Tijuana.

K: And when you asked for a better response on COLEF's part what happened with your organizing and Norma's organizing that sixteen suddenly turned out to be sixty? [*All laugh*]

L: Yeah, we were about sixty something, yes. I think we became very ambitious, and knowing that this wasn't going to happen in the near future, that we were going to make every effort to make it as comprehensive as possible, we started to look for funds. Norma did it here through the Colegio de la Frontera, and we did it on the other side of the border by going to Rockefeller and trying to get money from them.

K: Who were the other two people on the committee?

L: Nancy de los Santos and Rosa Marta Fernández, from UNAM.

K: Could you talk for a little bit about what it is to be a Chicana filmmaker in San Francisco? Who are the filmmakers you are bringing to the conference? I know you have Xochitl Films, which is your company, but you seem to be very involved with other people's filmmaking as well as with promoting the study of Chicano film. Also, what is the relation between Chicano filmmakers in San Francisco, Los Angeles, and Mexico?

L: Ok. First of all, the center for Chicano filmmaking has been Los Angeles. And I've always been outside of that center, because most of the independent Chicano filmmakers were coming out of UCLA, for example. They have a program there that Sylvia Morales came out of, Jesús Treviño, Moctezuma Esparza, etc. And I lived in San Francisco where there were no Chicano filmmakers. At one point there was an attempt to gather every Chicano filmmaker in the late 1970s, through the efforts of the Galería de la Raza and Ralph Maradiaga, Ray Telles, and Luis Pérez. And we looked everywhere for a filmmaker to form Cine Acción. I mean, I lived in that era, you know, when we were trying to do that. But before that time, I wasn't aware that there were any Chicanos in San Francisco making film. I belonged to a collective called Cine Manifest. It was a Marxist collective that was beginning to make feature-length films, and in the past they had done documentaries. Of course, they dealt . . . I mean thematically, from the title, you can tell what types of films we made. [*Lourdes laughs while saying this*] And then after Cine Manifest, I decided that I didn't know very much about film and that I wanted to know a lot. A lot of things that I had learned in Cine Manifest, I already knew, but there was a whole other field that I knew nothing about. And that was art film. So I went to the San Francisco Art Institute to get my master's.

K: What years would that have been?

L: It was very dispersed, because at the same time I had three children. I went off and on until I graduated, and during those years I was involved in Cine Acción, the organization and all the aspects of Cine Acción. Also,

I think I have tried to be very active in different organizations that promote the type of filmmaking I believe in. Like I belong to the board of the Film Arts Foundation and AIVF (Association of Independent Video and Film). Also, I was doing a lot of what I think are important community service things like being on panels and evaluating people's work and trying to encourage Third World filmmakers.

K: During the years when you were going on and off to the Art Institute, what surprised you? What were you learning that you hadn't learned working with the people in Cine Manifest?

L: Well, in Cine Manifest of course, we had a very strict way of looking at film. First of all, there was an ideology behind why we did everything that we did, the way that we did it. I saw that there was a lot of room for experimentation. For me it was enlightening to be able to work with George Kushar or Tony Sinden. And all the professors that I had at the Art Institute, I think, turned me on to be freer in my thinking in terms of film.

K: Was *Después del terremoto* [*After the Earthquake*] a film produced after your Art Institute study, or was it a part of your work there?

L: It was a part of my studies. Yes. It's interesting. I went to the Art Institute and I started with vanguard filmmaking and experimental filmmaking, and I ended up making *After the Earthquake,* which was a narrative film. In retrospect, I think of the valor—that I did *After the Earthquake.* That I just said I can do it, I can write a script, so I wrote a script. I was still working with my friends at Cine Manifest and they were very encouraging. That was a wonderful part of working with them. They read the script and said, "Wonderful, just go make it now. Apply to the American Film Institute. Do this and do that." And I did it. And it was a departure from the type of filmmaking that I was learning at the same time.

K: *Después del terremoto* was released in 1979?

L: Yes.

K: When did you begin filming it? In 1978, did you do the script?

L: No, we did it all in one year.

Ruby: How did you come to that subject? Because, not only were you making a film that was a dramatic film in a period when people hadn't yet switched from documentary to dramatic form—the way they would within the next five years—but this was also one of the first films about Nicaragua when a lot of people in the U.S. didn't yet know who the Sandinistas were.

L: I think that it was also a part of the influence of the Art Institute. Maybe it was in reaction to many things, not only to the Art Institute but also to Cine Manifest and the approach they had to every subject. I was also involved in the Sandinista movement in the United States in the late seven-tics, in solidarity with them, Nina Serrano and I, who was also the co-director of the film. We decided to make a film that would inform the people about the struggle, and I was concerned about the struggle and the conflicts that immigrants and Nicaraguans were going through at that point. I think I didn't want to make a film that was a documentary—a straight, hard-hitting factual documentary. And I saw the richness of their life and I wanted to capture it. At the same time, when I did that, it was a struggle against them [Sandinista movement in the United States] and they disowned us in the process. Because within the community, when we were elaborating the film and we decided that we were going to do a script and were going to do a narrative film, there was a break with them because they wanted us to do a documentary that they had been used to seeing—very factual, very political, very one-sided. Since we got an AFI grant, I figured in a certain way it was my film, so that I had control and could do what I wanted. So we broke with them and did the narrative film.

K: Did this create problems for you in getting actors too, or were the people who appeared in the film required to make a commitment that would have gotten them in trouble with people in the community as well?

L: Well, the interesting aspect of the Mission is that it is composed of Latin Americans from every conceivable Latin American country, so that there was no way that I could get all Nicaraguan actors. That, I realized the first day of casting. First there were people who had absolutely no experience. But I had no experience, so what the heck! Right? [*All laugh*] The actors came from everywhere. You know, the lead was Mexican, the other lead was Nicaraguan, and the other was Salvadoran. And some were from Uruguay, the people that played the music. So they didn't have the same commitment that I had. It wasn't very fashionable. I mean, it became very fashionable to be supportive of the Sandinistas. When I was involved with them, it was actually very marginal.

R: What period was this in Nicaragua? Was this when they were still in the mountains?

L: In 1978. Yes, they were still fighting. Yes.

R: Right before the insurrection?

L: Yes.

K: I also wanted to ask about the process of filmmaking for some of your other films. When you did a casting call, did you have an open call, or did you call up people that you knew and ask them to come and be considered for the film?

L: We did everything. Nina, who was in theater at the time—and who had been for years—had many friends in different theaters. We called people, we put ads on the radio, we walked down Mission Street and looked for people.

R: For people off the streets? [*All laugh*]

K: Nina is a Chicana?

L: Nina Serrano is not a Chicana. She is half-Colombian.

K: But she lived in the barrio?

L: Oh yes! Nina is very active.

K: And how did she come to film? Was she in the theater, or was she with you at the Film Institute?

L: She was in the theater, she had mostly been in the theater. She worked with her ex-husband, Saul Landau, in making a film called *¿Qué hacer?* She then worked with me in making this small film.

K: Small film? What kind of decisions did you find yourself making, when so much of the film takes place inside the house, upstairs, downstairs, in the small bedroom? Was it your plan? This enclosed world, the internal, domestic world of the principal female character?

L: I was close to many different types of Latin American immigrants and I had spent many hours in their houses. This was a house of friends, you see, and they had an extended family—they had aunts and everything [in the film] was reflective of the life I was living at that point. I saw them spending a lot of time indoors for many different reasons. It isn't the out-door life, the life of an unprotected immigrant. Exactly what are you looking for?

K: There is either careful planning or incredible intuition about how to frame each character in that film. Each character is shot in a way that brings out his or her personality. I was wondering if you got into that space and worked with it or you planned the shots ahead of time?

L: As a filmmaker, there are times when you make decisions that are so in-tuitive that you're not even aware of them. The film was totally story-boarded. Every minute movement was storyboarded.

K: Do you usually do that?

L: Yes, I do it. I'm not an artist, but I do it in a very kind of primitive way. But I have the ability to be able see in my head what I want. I think that is probably a gift, for a filmmaker to be able to do that. So I have to replay it, but I have a very bad memory, so I have to write it down in this prim-itive way—which is how I always refer to my storyboard. I am very con-cerned about space and how people move within the space and that sort of thing.

K: Do you recall anything about any decisions you made about that partic-ular film regarding the lighting, particularly? The way in which you filmed the kitchen and the bedroom? The use of black and white?

R: The whole question of black and white?

L: The lighting was very good, I loved the lighting. We worked very hard to make it that way. I still work with the person that did the lighting. I mean, she has been my cinematographer, just recently—Emiko Omori.

K: The cinematographer for *La Ofrenda*?

L: *La Ofrenda,* yes. And she lit the scenes and we were together thinking, you know . . . I don't remember the exact decisions and how they were made, but it was very conscious, everything was very conscious, nothing was left to chance. Things usually happened for the best in that film, which was incredible. When we had accidents it was better.

K: Tell us an accident, I always like to know what these accidents are. [*The interviewers laugh*]

L: Let's see. Let me think of an accident. Well, there were many. For example, we weren't going to shoot down the hall. When she walks down the hall. It was very difficult because we were in two different places. One bedroom was in one place, the hallway was in another place, and she couldn't open the door because we would then be in the other place. But it all worked out because when we went to the other place, for example, it had this incredible glass door, like French doors. And when she walks down the hall it is really beautiful. Because you see these squares, these panes that fall onto the hallway.

K: The panes of glass created a particular sensation that you wanted?

L: When you work with black and white, one of the most important things is designs. Color only works in color. So the more designs you can get in black-and-white film, the more interesting it becomes. In costumes or in lighting, texture is very important. When you get the gradations, that gives it more solidity.

K: There were some of the textures you conceived around Irene that made her seem trapped in a certain way. Do you have the same sensation about this film?

L: No, I never felt there were. Maybe it happened.

K: How did you preview the film, distribute the film?

R: To add one other element to that: Now, in retrospect, I think that people really see *Después del terremoto* as a classic, but what kind of response did you get back at that time, and what kind of response had you hoped for while you were making the film?

L: That's a really interesting question, because I think that with every one of my films. No, that's not true—*Madres* has its own particular history and problems—but some of the films I have made have not been received well. Initially, people see them as very problematic because I'm introducing something that is unexpected and they see me as a stereotype.

Portillo's finger pointing at
one scene in the storyboard
for *Después del Terremoto*
(photo by Ken Pate). Courtesy
of Lourdes Portillo.

Codirectors Portillo (left) and
Nina Serrano (right) (photo
by Ken Pate). Courtesy of
Lourdes Portillo.

Portillo (left) and Serrano (right) discussing a scene with lead actor Vilma Coronado (center) (photo by Ken Pate). Courtesy of Lourdes Portillo.

Taken during the shooting of the second scene in *Después del Terremoto* (photo by Ken Pate). Courtesy of Lourdes Portillo.

Cinematographer Stephen Lighthill, of Cine Manifest collective, during the shooting of *Después del Terremoto* (photo by Ken Pate). Courtesy of Lourdes Portillo.

Portillo (right) clowning around while editor Lynn Hamrick looks on (photo by Ken Pate). Courtesy of Lourdes Portillo.

Portillo (left) and sound recordist Chris Samuelson, both eight months pregnant. Courtesy of Lourdes Portillo.

They expect a certain type of film from me every time, and every time what I deliver is a different package, so with *Después del terremoto* again they expected the film that I consciously tried not to make.

K: The documentary . . . ?

L: Right.

K: Highly political . . . ?

L: Right. Of course people are saying, "Well this is fine, this is nice, nice texture, but here we're dealing with a revolution. Look at what you are doing." [*Lourdes laughs and shrugs it off*]

K: Did you have a screening for the Mission District? How did it go into distribution?

L: It had a fatal life, it was terrible! I showed it, and I was so proud of it because I thought I was so brave, I had never directed a narrative film. And I showed it to my Chicano counterparts in Los Angeles—they went ho-hum. And there was one person . . . I went to the San Antonio film festival and they showed the film, and there I got a wonderful review of the film that I still have. I don't remember it verbatim, but it was very encouraging that somebody saw it with fresh eyes, without all the preconceived notions of what I should be doing.

K: Who was the person who wrote the review?

L: Jason Johanson.

K: Did the film have any kind of national release?

L: No, the film was actually recognized in other places. I was invited to go to different film festivals in Europe—in Eastern Europe, in Poland—and it got a prize in Poland and Spain. Even in South America, but never in the United States. I gave it to a distributor that never rented it once or sold it once, for years.

K: Has it come back into you hands?

L: Yes.

K: So now you distribute it out of Xochitl Films?

L: Yes, and with other people as well, with Women Make Movies and Third World Newsreel.

K: Is it common that an independent filmmaker will place a film with two distribution companies?

L: No, it's not common. Generally they have exclusive rights, but in this case it's so old. I think sometimes people approach me more than they would the companies. So we just kind of did the deal, all of us.

K: This was all a little over a decade ago.

R: What would you say was your first involvement in film, even before Cine Manifest?

L: I've never been involved with anything but film since I was twenty years old. And I'm forty-six. So I worked in film in Los Angeles. I had a friend whose father was a screenwriter, and she made independent films for Britannica Films and I would help her. She would teach me how to write screenplays, and teach me everything. She lived in Hollywood all her life, so I learned from her.

K: Who was she?

L: Her name is Sally Loeb.

K: And do you still see her?

L: No, she lives in Mexico now.

R: But how old—approximately how old—were you at that time?

L: Twenty years old.

K: So you were learning how to write scripts by helping somebody in Los Angeles write scripts?

L: For educational films, yes.

K: And this was while you were in college?

L: Yes, yes.

K: You went to which college?

L: I went to different colleges, many different colleges. [*All laugh*]

K: When did you move to San Francisco?

L: I moved to San Francisco, let's see, twenty years ago, in 1970.

K: And how many children did you have by 1970?

L: Well that's when I was pregnant with my first son, when we moved to San Francisco. And since then, I've had three sons—I mean a total of three.

K: So by the time 1979 comes around, you're putting out your first narrative film, you have three sons, and you are now identified as a filmmaker.

L: Yes.

K: What kind of changes did that bring you in your life—to become a filmmaker, facing a new decade and . . . the triumph of the Sandinista revolution? [*All laugh*]

L: More importantly, divorce! [*All laugh*] I mean, it brought about these enormous changes in my life. I wanted to define myself as a filmmaker. My husband wanted to define me as his wife and the mother of these boys. Which I am still, that's my first title—the mother of the three boys. I can't even start . . . I mean, it's like my life radically changed—everything. I mean, the basis on which I engage myself with a man—to have a marriage and to have children—suddenly disintegrated. And then this other need surfaced, where it . . . I don't even have words for . . . it's very difficult. It was gradual and it was tumultuous and it was painful.

K: As you went through this process, when did the idea for your next film come and where did you go with it? What was the next step in your career then?

L: *After the earthquake.* [*Lourdes laughs*]

R: After, *After the Earthquake*?

L: After *After the Earthquake,* I was studying at the San Francisco Art Institute. There were other students from Latin America there—Susana Blaustein [Muñoz] was also a student there, and we became friends, we used to talk about film. And in the Art Institute, I mean there was not so much a dissatisfaction on my part about the type of filmmaking that I was learning, but I also had these other interests, which you can tell from *After the Earthquake*—political concerns. And she also had those political concerns, coming from Argentina, so we engaged in that kind of dialogue that Latin American exiles and immigrants engage in. And since we were filmmakers, we started pursuing the idea of making a film about something. We had the opportunity at one time to meet René Epelbaum, one of the mothers of Plaza de Mayo, in Washington, D.C.

K: How did you happen to be in Washington, D.C.?

L: We were visiting a friend, and we saw that there was going to be a luncheon for Mother's Day for all the mothers of the disappeared, and having in common like this interest in Latin American politics . . .

R: So you're saying that *Las Madres* came about originally by chance?

L: *Las Madres* came about . . . well, not by exactly by chance . . . yes, yeah kind of . . . Yes.

K: René Epelbaum was the mother you worked with then to begin to design the film?

L: No, we didn't design the film with her. We designed the film ourselves, but she was our contact with the group of mothers in Buenos Aires.

K: What year did you start designing the film?

L: In 1982 or 1983.

K: Could you talk about the process of getting the funding, scripting, collaboration, storyboard, flying to Argentina, living in Buenos Aires?

L: We started fund-raising with a very vague knowledge about what we were going to do. We had some concepts, we got a lot of literature, we did a lot of research. One of the things that we did with *Las Madres* was do a lot of research on many different agencies, governmental agencies—books, you name it, we had like a whole big library. After doing that we composed a proposal. A very simple proposal, in fact, because the struggle of the mothers was so incredibly dramatic that just putting it down on paper was sufficient to make anyone cry, right?

K: Yes.

L: So we did a lot of fund-raising. Of course, we both did not have experience in political filmmaking. I mean, Susana had made a film about her experience as a lesbian and in an Argentine family, and I had made *After the Earthquake.*

K: Had she made her film in Argentina?

L: No. She made it in San Francisco.

K: As a student at the Art Institute?

L: Yes. At the same time that I made *After the Earthquake.* We had the same interest, but we didn't have the same experience, so fund-raising was very, very difficult. We really nickel-and-dimed the film. It was like sometimes, when we were really broke, like another filmmaker would give us a hundred dollars. It was pathetic.

K: Where would a filmmaker in the early 1980s in San Francisco go to ask for money?

L: There are several foundations that one can go to, you know, where they will give you money. There are people that will support you when you are making a political film. The churches will give you money, the churches will help. We did fund-raisers. The thing is that the funding world changes so radically from one year to another—they lose interest in political film. Like someone that supported us at one point, a woman in Nevada who was very interested in the mothers of the Plaza de Mayo, and she was very, very supportive and gave us what we thought was a fortune, which was twenty thousand dollars—and two years later she was interested in saving trees. So it's whimsical. My experience in going from one foundation to another is not necessarily helpful to anyone at this point in time.

K: Did you raise some money and do some part of the film, or did you raise it all and then do the film?

L: No. If we had tried to raise it all, we would have never, never made the film. We raised six thousand dollars, which again we were always thinking things like, "Wow, six thousand dollars! This is great! We're going to go to Argentina with six thousand dollars—we're going to buy all the film stock, we'll buy the tickets, we'll get a cheap place in Buenos Aires, and we'll do the film." And we did!

R: [*Laughing in shock*] In what year were you living in Buenos Aires in a cheap place doing a film?

L: Alfonsín had been one hundred days in power [1984].

K: I assume since Susana is Argentine that she knew the city and knew the ins and outs of filmmaking in Argentina. What kind of on-location problems did you confront?

L: First of all, being in Argentina, we benefited only in a certain way from Susana's knowledge of Buenos Aires. In another way, she was also filled with fear. I mean, it was very curious because, you know, it wasn't all that helpful to be Argentine at that point.

R: Could you talk about the decision you made regarding the cameraman?

L: When you make crew decisions, the more deliberate the decision, the better off you'll be at the end, right? In terms of crew as well. We thought, "We are going to Argentina. It's a very machista place. What are we going to do?" I love Emiko Emori because I think she is a wonderful camerawoman. But she's Japanese—how are the Argentines going to look at that? In a racist country, that's not going to fly, this woman carrying the camera. So we thought, "We're going to get a big, tall American." [*Laughter*]

K: Who was your big, tall American?

L: Michael Anderson. We told him we were going to hire him just on his looks alone, and he was willing to go.

K: How long did the film take, when you were actually there?

L: We were there for four weeks, and the filming probably total took us about a week and a half. Of course, at another point we had to send Michael back for pickups. We couldn't afford either one of us to go, so he went on his own with a very detailed storyboard of what he was supposed to get, because we were in the editing stage at that point.

R: I would imagine that many of the mothers were eager to talk to you. How did you decide which of the mothers to interview? What did you have to do to get interviews with people who were not the mothers, who might have had reasons not to talk to you?

L: First of all, we structured the film on paper. We said we want to tell the story of the mothers. We have forty mothers right? So we wanted to ask, "How did the kids disappear? When were you aware that they were involved in anything political or, at that time, considered subversive?" Every element was structured. So then we figured we needed a mother who is going to tell us about her daughter. We needed a mother whose three children disappeared. It was like a puzzle, you know—we just constructed it on paper.

K: Before you went down?

L: When we were on the plane, when we were in the hotel. We were always playing with paper, trying to figure out how we were going to tell this story. We wanted to tell it as the chronicle of the mothers' struggle. So, with that in mind, we just had to fill in the gaps. For example, we wanted to talk to Troccoli, so how do we get to Troccoli? Maybe one of the mothers—I mean, some of these women are upper-middle-class women with a lot of connections. Eventually, so-and-so will get us there. The mothers themselves, you know, gave us the entrée to a lot of these people.

K: I take it there were the three of you . . .

L: Four or five. We also had an assistant, an Argentine assistant.

K: In the work with the crew, was there any difference in the preparation of a documentary interview because it was about such a painful subject? How did you go about planning the actual interviews on film, preparing to do these interviews and executing them?

L: Well, we knew the story beforehand, because there was a lot of research done beforehand. We learned about the different mothers, we had their case histories—not only case histories like in a documented sense, but in the kind of gossipy sense of "This happened to her," et cetera. We would already know this was the house where the son was taken from, that this is the corner he last met his mom. We were all very well prepared for those interviews—as well prepared as one can be for such painful interviews. So incredibly painful. We had to be very delicate with all of them, but at the same time we realized that they were not all as delicate as we thought. The pain always comes back very pointedly, but they were also tough—they were also very tough and they had said this many, many times.

K: Because this was a part of their struggle?

L: Right. To repeat this constantly.

K: You had never been to Argentina before?

L: No.

K: But you know a lot about Argentina, you knew the political history, you knew the history of the dictatorship, you knew what the disappearances were and what happened to the people who disappeared. I take it that they hadn't yet begun the report *Nunca más.* So the information you had was from the Amnesty International reports?

L: Yes.

K: Being there, in that nation during the return to civilian rule, is there anything that you didn't expect? Was there anything that surprised you as a Chicana, a Mexicana, about Argentina?

L: There are always stereotypes. The Argentines themselves like to promote the nation, their civilization and their . . . I don't know, their education and whatever it is that they like to lord over the rest of Latin America. That's one of the reasons people really don't like them very much. Most of the Southern Cone and the Northern Cone. [*Laughter*] If you want to call it that. What struck me the most was the fascism so inherent in every aspect of Argentine life. Unlike Mexico, which is a very anarchic place. And Mexico lives in me. [*Lourdes laughs*] Going to Argentina and seeing how everyone relates in that hierarchical way, how they are so intolerant, and also having the knowledge of the repression, I think I rejected many things that were Argentine. I was very unhappy there, extremely unhappy. Plus I had to deal with the racism. There is a deep hatred for their Indians and I'm Mexican, so I'm part Indian. And they saw me the way they see an Indian from Salta, and they treated me that way. So I was very impatient, very intolerant. I became like them.

K: Let me go in a different direction and then come back to the question of what it was like to be a Chicana in Argentina. Did being in Argentina have an impact on you as a feminist? Did it change you as a feminist in any way, or did it change your ideas of the feminist struggle?

L: It's hard for me to say. I've never considered myself a feminist.

K: Oh! Why not?

L: I don't know . . . Because I've never . . . it's been hard for me to . . . I mean, I think I am, but I've never studied anything or read anything. I feel like I believe in women's struggle, but I relate to the world in a different way, not in an elitist way but more as a mother. That's how I relate to the world, and I think that that's how I went to Argentina. I bonded with the mothers because they had children and I have children. That was the one way, in terms of women being together, that I felt a deep strength from them. They changed me. I still think about them. Not . . . not just the ones that I'm still friends with, but all of them. My heart gets all mushy and tender when I think of them.

R: Given what you were saying about the differences between Mexico and Argentina, do you think that the position of the mother or the figure of the mother was, in fact, a bridge? Was that what was in common culturally? Is that what you are saying?

L: Yes, yes, yes. Well, that was the only thing really that was very much in common with me and Argentina: the mothers.

K: Let's talk about the release and distribution of the film. What was the postproduction process? How was the film distributed?

L: The postproduction process was a very painful process. This was a process where both of the directors realized that they couldn't work together. [*All laugh*] It became a power struggle. This is common in filmmaking, this is nothing new. You always think that two people making a film just think differently. But it wasn't so much that we thought differently—in fact, we thought very, very much alike. But it went further than that: it had to do with power.

K: Were there struggles over editing?

L: No. No. It was over who would be the editor and who wouldn't be the editor. [*All laugh*] We had agreed about how it should be done. We were in complete agreement. Anyway, it was a very hard struggle. So the editing was mostly done by Susana and Irving Seraf. I would come in, see the work that had been done, and we would talk about it, and then basically I wouldn't spend a lot of time in the editing room because of this incredible conflict. I participated in a lot of the decision making, but I couldn't be there making the minute little cuts and just the everyday editing.

R: So you were more like the supervising editor than like the advising editor? [*All laugh*]

K: Did you know that you had made a film that was going to have a tremendous impact?

L: We knew. I mean, I was very well aware that this film was going to be like a bomb.

K: You mean a political bomb?

L: Yeah. I mean, the power of the film—the power of what we had—was so incredible. I was very much aware of that.

K: What preparation did you make for the film's release? How did you handle the distribution?

L: I think one of the things we did was travel with the film. We were committed to the mothers enough to know that we had to go to every event that we were invited to, and we had to follow through. It's interesting— I think maybe we got asked four questions about the technique or about the sound or about the picture in all those years. What we had to do was like political support. Basically, every time we showed the film we had to tell them what was happening in Argentina. How it came to be that it was this way in Argentina. It was an education for people, to bring us, so we were not seen as—I mean, we were filmmakers, but we were responding to the world as political activists. Consequently, that's the kind of release the film got: it got a lot of attention from political groups, it got a lot of attention from human rights groups. We would do screenings for universities. And ultimately, of course, we tried to get on PBS, and PBS rejected it—I mean, typically.

K: What were the reasons PBS gave you?

L: Because the film was one-sided, right?

R: So then, how did it come about that you ended up getting an Academy Award nomination?

L: I mean, the power of the film is so immense and it was at that point that anyone you would show the film to was just very touched, because the mothers are so powerful. I felt like we couldn't go wrong with that film. Whatever we did, it was right, because the mothers just carried it.

R: To go back to an earlier point: When you were talking about making *Después del terremoto,* you talked about the decision not to make a political documentary, and now you're talking about the effects of making a political documentary. How did you feel about that? How did you feel about the response to *Las Madres* and about your decision to go ahead and make that kind of film this time around?

L: Well, I think I was thinking, first of all, when you make a political film sometimes you feel things inside of you. With the story of *Las Madres,* it was like there was no other way to film that story. Let's put it that way—this was the only way to do it. We tried to figure it out, but this is the only avenue you can take with *Las Madres.* In terms of *Después del terremoto,* it would be more contrived. The drama inherent in *Las Madres* only allowed us to do it in that way. If I had made the choice in the other case, it would have been too contrived, too manipulative, and too obvious. That's something I don't believe in, in the obvious. So it just—the subject—lent itself to that.

K: What, in your own mind, became the time in which you were done with *Las Madres* and were moving on to a new project?

L: *Las Madres* was a very . . . how can I say it, I don't know how to say it. It . . . it really . . . it really punctuated my life with a lot of stuff, with a lot of attention. It drew a lot of attention to us. We could have become overly inflated with all the attention and the prizes that we got, and it had to end—like, all things end, right? And you can't live with that glory forever, I mean. So we had to embark on something else, because this is not a way to live, you know. So we decided thematically to make a film about death again. But *Las Madres* was filled with such negativity—the whole Argentinean situation was so negative in many ways. It was so positive in terms of the reaction that we got, but the energy of the film and what it took from us was like a negativity. So we wanted to make a film that was more positive. Almost in the same vein as in *Las Madres,* looking at death. I mean, kind of comparing, like that's how I felt. I felt like, you know, that *Las Madres* made me feel so bad that I wanted to feel good. And in order for me to feel good, I wanted to think about death the way my people think of death, not the way your people think about death. That was the reaction to *Las Madres: La Ofrenda.*

K: When did you begin working on *La Ofrenda* and what year?

L: I . . . you know dates for me. They are so hard for me, I'm terrible . . . Maybe two years earlier? Yeah.

R: In 1986. You began writing proposals for it in '86?

L: Yes.

R: And you got the first money for it in early 1987?

L: Yes, something like that.

K: If you related to *Las Madres* as a mother, was *La Ofrenda* made for your sons? If that's not too personal.

L: No, no, no. *La Ofrenda* was made for myself, you know? I feel that it was for myself. I feel like it was coming back, a coming back to my culture. In a way, I've never come back to my culture. I've always felt Mexican, because I am Mexican. I was born in Mexico, but I came to the United States when I was very young, and I had to assimilate in order to survive, because I lived in a very racist place. And I felt like I had been trying to assimilate for so many years and to incorporate this culture into me—so that I could survive and I could thrive—that I had forgotten . . . I didn't really forget who I was, but I had forgotten my culture. And I wanted to come back and I wanted to recapture even what I didn't have.

K: How long had the art altar tradition that you documented in *La Ofrenda*, in the Mission, been going on? While you were filming *Las Madres*, was Día de los Muertos the kind of festive event it is now in the Mission?

L: Yes it was. Yes. I think Ralph Maradiaga started in the late 1970s to celebrate the Day of the Dead at the Galería de la Raza.

K: Well, you said earlier in the interview that you supported community activities and things. While you were doing *La Ofrenda*, were you doing Chicana, Chicano, Latina, and Latino activism in the Mission at the same time you were doing *Las Madres*? Was it parallel, or did it come after?

L: No, no, no. I was always involved in some element of community life.

K: What is the Galería and what was your involvement with Galería?

L: I became very close to La Galería de la Raza in the late seventies, and I've been close since. Galería is a community-based exhibit space and also, in a sense a center for an artist, you know. We all meet there, we see each other, and at the same time exhibit our work there. It's a very warm and open place for us, kind of a home.

R: You know, I wanted to ask something else about *La Ofrenda*. When you were talking about *Después del terremoto*, you talked about the immigrant experience and having many friends who were immigrants. Now you've talked about yourself as an immigrant coming from Mexico as a child, and yet you identify very strongly as a Chicana. And talking about this encuentro that you helped organize, I just wonder: In what way did *La Ofrenda* play into both of those identities for you, and to what extent had you thought about that before starting to make *La Ofrenda*?

L: I was always conflicted. I'd never fully incorporated . . . I mean, now I feel like I can say safely that I'm a Chicana and I feel very good about saying that I'm a Chicana. But I can also say that I'm a Mexican, and I also feel very good about that—but not necessarily in a conflictual way, you know. And it came about by making *La Ofrenda*. I don't come from the type of class that would celebrate the Day of the Dead and . . . but then . . .

K: What class do you come from? [*All laugh*]

L: Well, I come from like a lower-middle-class family in Mexico, and traditionally the middle classes in Mexico reject anything to do with indigenous culture. But in becoming a Chicana, I incorporated all the things that had enriched me—like indigenous culture—and also accepted the fact that that's a very Chicano way of viewing my world. So *La Ofrenda* was instrumental in making me feel comfortable about my triple identity. [*All laugh*]

K: You decided to continue to collaborate with Susana [Blaustein] Muñoz, even though you fought over editing the previous film?

L: Well, let's see. [*All laugh*] When we were at the end of our partnership, we mistakenly put in an application to CPB, the Corporation for Public Broadcasting, to make *La Ofrenda*. And unfortunately it was funded! So we had to kind of commit to making this film together, and we embarked on making a film again, which we did. But immediately after we shot it we knew we couldn't work together, so we separated. And I was left with a film to finish, while she went off to Argentina.

K: She has returned to Argentina permanently?

L: No. Now she's in the United States once again.

K: So the editing—all, all the postproduction work on *La Ofrenda,* you did yourself?

L: Yes, yes, yes.

K: Could you tell us about going to Oaxaca and doing the film? And particularly, given that you are a careful storyboarder, how did you storyboard *La Ofrenda*?

L: Well, this was the one time that we didn't storyboard. [*All laugh*] We had vague ideas, we had many vague ideas. We had no one way of doing it. We knew we were going to shoot this, this, this, and this, and we hoped that it would all go together, basically.

R: Did you have simultaneous crews? Did you shoot sequentially? How did you handle that?

L: The Day of the Dead is celebrated, of course, in a couple of days, two to three days. So it necessitated different crews. In San Francisco, we had a crew filming all the Chicana/o celebrations. At the same time, there was another crew—which included both Susana and me—in Oaxaca together. Then, after being together for some time, I left and went to Mexico City to film some other stuff while Chris Samuelson was shooting in San Francisco.

K: It's clear that people who see *La Ofrenda* are fascinated with the images you put together in that film. In all of your films, the composition of the images and the editing sequences of the images are very powerful. My eyes don't ever leave the screen because of your talent for putting them together. So you are in Oaxaca—how did you find your images in Oaxaca?

L: I always think that there are too many images and not enough time in the film to use them, you know? In Oaxaca, in Mexico, again, I always feel like I can't go wrong. [*Lourdes laughs*] Mexico is like ravishingly beautiful. I mean, as a Mexican I see it. If I look here it's great and if I look there it's great—anywhere you look it's wonderful. Trying to stick to our outline was the key there. The celebration, the preparations, the dancing, the grandmother—that's how we did it. We said, "Oh, we have to shoot the grandmother. Oh, we have to go shoot the dancing," and then we just shot it.

K: When did you make the decision to use the fictional voice of the Chicana, the narrator?

L: Oh, that was so painful, it was so hard. The film was hard. I wish I had planned it better, you know? Once we were in the editing room, it was like a nightmare. Like a nightmare of all these things that didn't seem to be able to go together. But I was working with Vivien Hillgrove, an editor, a very talented and sensitive editor that was very patient and loved everything she saw on the screen. Working with her, we were able to find something. The voice was very hard. How to say it, you know who is going to say what. And I always do a lot of research on the different films that I make. So I had done a lot of research. There was a lot of literature that had some wonderful poetic-like passages that could be used and applied to the film. Some, which we used, included Octavio Paz and Carlos Fuentes—other stuff was written by writers like Fenton Johnson, Ruby Rich, and myself. Trying to find the voice there was . . . it was hard, it was a very hard film to put together. But then, once we got into this kind of "OK, this is associative thinking. Let's just, let's go for visual metaphors, let's just go for any kind of connection, let's just start doing that," then it started working, finally started working. And the voice was always very hard, but I felt that there were two voices talking at the same time. There was the voice of the historical that I feel is so important when you are making a film about another culture in the United States. You have a certain obligation, a kind of didactic obligation to your audience, to explain some of the things that they don't understand. And then there was the personal voice of remembrance and nostalgia and poetry that I thought was important for me to include. So that's how it all came about.

R: Given that double attention, how would you see your audience when you were sitting in the editing room? What sorts of audiences were you foreseeing as you were trying to make those decisions?

L: Well, in my snobbishness, I thought I was actually just making the film for the Chicana/o community. I wanted them to see themselves. I wanted them to feel that their culture is very important, that I agree with them. It was my agreement that our culture is terribly important and that it speaks to everyone and that it's important to treasure it and to make it like a jewel and to retain it.

K: The film was first released in the Mission District?

L: Yes. At the Day of the Dead.

K: The next Day of the Dead?

L: Yeah, yeah. And they loved it, of course.

K: Let me go back to something: the images of the children's faces. At the conference today, both Lillian Jiménez and I brought up the children's faces when we were talking about the film. What were the choices in your editing process, to put in those particular images of the young boy laughing and of the girl's face next to the *matachines* [dancers]?

L: Yes. The boy laughing was like, I felt a stroke of genius between Vivien and I. We, I would collect books, Vivien would collect books. She would go to the Santa Rosa library and she would come back with this book of the little faces that, I think, are at the Peabody Museum at Yale. And she said, "Look at these little faces, aren't they cute?" [*All laugh*] And I said, "Wow, they're wonderful!" And as we were editing I said, "Oh, Vivien, that boy—I love that boy when he giggles and has no teeth!" It was just like a wonderful thing, you know. Emiko did that. I mean I can't take credit for all of this, you know. They all, everybody, just did their own thing and put their heart into it and came out with this. Emiko loved this little boy and then Vivien found the book and then I had the idea. And we put them together and it was sublime. [*All laugh*]

K: Would you agree with what the New Wave Chicana/o film historians are saying regarding the importance of passing information on to the next generation?

L: Oh, is that true?

K: Well, we said it this morning! [*All laugh*] When you made this film, did you think that you were making a film for the children that will come after? Was that in your mind?

L: I think that I don't think about that too much. Film lasts for as long as film lasts, which is a very short time. The only things that really last are those big rock sculptures that the Aztecs made. [*All laugh*] I think about children. I think it's important to make films that speak to children, and I think about them and I think about leaving something for them.

K: Is that why you chose to end the film in the classroom? There is a scene where the teacher is . . .

L: Yes. I think the transmission of culture is very important.

K: Let me backtrack just a little bit. Since the time of the festivals in the 1980s—we've mentioned them at this conference of course: Cine de las Mujeres, which I believe was Cocina de Imágenes. . . .

L: In 1987.

R: Festival of the Americas . . .

K: In San Francisco in 1989. Since the 1980s, this is the third time Latin American and U.S. Latina filmmakers have gathered together. Prior to that, I think you and Sylvia Morales in the mid-1980s were coming to be considered the principal Chicana filmmakers. You were part of the CARA Exhibit [Chicano Art: Resistance and Affirmation in UCLA], on the board that planned the retrospective. What was your involvement in the exhibit?

L: I was an advisor.

K: And what kind of advice did you give them?

L: I said I'm not the only Chicana filmmaker. [*All laugh*] That was my advice to the curator. I felt that there had been a view of Chicano film mainly that there are these Chicano filmmakers who make 35mm films or big documentary films that deal with the Chicano movement. These are all the misconceptions that keep us in power. I . . . you know, they are flattering and stuff but they are very unreal. This is not the world, the world is not like that. There are young filmmakers who are making attempts to address different things about our lives, and perhaps they haven't made as much because they don't have the money or the access, but I think that they exist. And I think part of this encuentro here—my task, that I took very seriously—was to find *every* woman—Chicana, Latina—who was trying to make a film or had made a tape or a film and *drag* them here and *make* them show their stuff. [*All laugh*] Only to prove that we're not the only people trying to do this. And if we don't give them the space and give them the recognition that they deserve for their efforts, then of course Sylvia and I could always be called the Chicana filmmakers. We could be happy forever, but that doesn't make me happy. It would make me happy to see thirty Chicanas making films.

R: If we could just go back to *La Ofrenda* for a minute. You talked about the very different receptions to *Después del terremoto* and *Las Madres*. What happened with the reception to *La Ofrenda*?

L: Because I was talking about the kind of reception I get for these films. OK, the Chicana/o community, of course, loved the film. They felt reflected, they felt apoyados [supported], and they felt that this was for them and it was. I showed it at the Flaherty Film Festival in New York and it was one of the most . . . it wasn't traumatic, it was a combative encounter that I had with those filmmakers. Because of their rejection of the film, their out-and-out rejection of the film.

K: What did they say that was their basis of their rejection?

L: Well, that it was, let's see, that it exoticized the Mexican — this is from someone that works with Eskimos. And that . . .

R: That it wasn't nomadic?

L: That it wasn't nomadic. There was this incredible criticism. And of course the people that are very verbal are able to, you know, kind of construct a whole argument as to why it doesn't work for them, or that it wasn't experimental enough, that it was too pedestrian. I was flabbergasted, but I didn't take it lying down. I just felt like fighting back and I was appalled. I couldn't believe that all these filmmakers — some of them, as we say now, people of color (or colored people, for me) — were attacking me with this film. And I mean filmmakers who have made very didactic films. I thought I was actually stepping out and trying to do something a little new. Later, as I went around showing the film to American audiences, they were commonly offended by the film. I think the film is so *not* offensive. I didn't know what was wrong, and I wanted to find out. What was it about this film that makes people feel so terrible? Why, why do you . . . why don't they like it, you know? Then I found out that it has to do with bringing up death — in the most, you know, innocuous beautiful way. That this is something that the American public refuses to face in any way.

R: Meantime, when the film went to Havana or went to Puerto Rico, what was the response of Latin American filmmakers to the film?

L: That's another interesting aspect to the film. What happens when I show the film to Latin Americans, they adore the part on Mexico, they think that Mexico is so wonderful and beautiful. This is their notion of Mexico. And then they see San Francisco, and then they say, "Well that's false. That's . . . that's like . . . that's so contrived. We would have given the first prize at this film festival if you had cut off the San Francisco section." So that has happened from many Latin Americans, because there is no value to the Latin Americans of the continuation of culture. This is a specific immigrant kind of concern.

R: So with all the currently fashionable talk about the multiplicity of audiences, what do you think of *Lu Ofrenda* from the point of the filmmaker? How has this left you feeling?

L: Well, I mean, I feel like, first of all you cannot make a film thinking you are going to appeal to many different audiences. I knew that already. I mean, you can't even pretend to make it for two audiences. So then it leaves you with "Well, why don't you just make a film that you think you like . . . a lot?"

K: I think there are people who like this film a lot. But, it has to be read from both sides. It doesn't make sense if you can't see what's important about the altars in San Francisco.

L: Right, exactly. [*Lourdes laughs*]

R: Having just now talked about the whole development in your body of work, what has been most important for you in terms of your filmmaking?

L: The essence, the essential.

R: How do you see yourself as a filmmaker?

L: I see myself, as a filmmaker, as one who would like to be able to touch people. What seems the most important . . . it's not so much reflection, it's not so much technique or spectator—but emotion, you know. How I can get . . . I can get the essence of a human being on the screen—and how is that human being going to be able to relate to the audience? How can I connect the screen to the human and the human to the human through a machine, right? That's the dilemma. It's not a dilemma—it's a game, you know. And it's an aim. It's what I value in film, what touches me in film. Those are the films I really love a lot, and that's what I always go for.

R: And humor?

L: I love humor. Of course I love humor. But that's so spontaneous and so hard to come by. I think you can manipulate emotion much more easily than you can manipulate humor. Humor is very, very complicated and very different and difficult, but I think people should be entertained, and a part of entertainment is being able to laugh.

K: So this is the "twenty years later" of your politics? [*All laugh*]

L: You've got it! No, politics is about your heart, it's about charity, it's about love. That's what politics should be. It shouldn't be anything else, don't you think?

K: Yes. Thank you for this interview.

L: You're welcome, you're welcome, you're welcome.

PART TWO

CRITICAL PERSPECTIVES

This section brings together a range of academic writings on issues of cultural politics, racial, class, and sexual differences, and
identity and representation in the cinema of Lourdes Portillo.
The writers collected here represent a diverse cross-section of
scholars informed by multicultural feminist practices. Since the
1980s, critical interest in multicultural media has grown, due in
large part to the proliferation of independent works by women
of color and the sheer volume of works by Third World and di-
asporic women. So far, the demand for multicultural perspectives promises to continue well into the twenty-first century,
particularly in light of the expansion of international festival cir-
cuits and alternative venues for distributing and exhibiting independent works, which have in turn created new avenues for cultural workers to form alliances across racial, class, cultural, and
national boundaries, through transnational networks of communication and culture. Along with a greater demand for complex,
challenging, and innovative films and videos by feminists of

color, the growing importance of critical feminist race theory and queer theory within the academy has kindled an interest in visual media that deals with the interlocking issues of social marginality. Lourdes Portillo is among the many independent filmmakers currently making the rounds on college campuses and screening their films in university venues like film festivals on campus, film studies, and Latina/o and Chicano/a studies and women's studies departments. One important result of this growing link between independent filmmakers and the academic community is that more than ever scholars are conducting research on the cinema of independents.

Las Madres: The Mothers of the Plaza de Mayo received twenty international awards, including Prix du Public and Prix du Presse at the Women's Film Festival at Creteil, France; Premio Coral, Feature Documentary, Festival Internacional de Cine Latinoamericano, Havana; Special Jury Prize, Documentary, Sundance Film Festival, Salt Lake City; and Emmy Nomination, News and Documentary, National Academy of Television, Arts and Sciences. Above, codirectors Susana Blaustein Muñoz (left) and Lourdes Portillo (right). Courtesy of Lourdes Portillo.

René Epelbaum, one of the leaders of the Mothers of the Plaza de Mayo. She died in February 1998. Courtesy of Lourdes Portillo.

Scenes from *Las Madres: The Mothers of the Plaza de Mayo*. Courtesy of Lourdes
Portillo.

Scene from *Las Madres: The Mothers of the Plaza de Mayo*. Courtesy of Lourdes Portillo.

One of the mothers wearing a placard of her disappeared daughter, Nidia Beatriz Sans. Courtesy of Lourdes Portillo.

Rosa Linda Fregoso

Devils and Ghosts, Mothers and Immigrants

A CRITICAL RETROSPECTIVE OF THE WORKS OF LOURDES PORTILLO

Lourdes Portillo's films and videos are emblematic of the broad spectrum of social, cultural, and political concerns of Chicana and Latina image-makers. In writing this essay I am taking my cue from Alexandra Juhasz, who notes: "In our present climate, when women are reinventing the feminist wheel to fight yet again for our rights to health care and repro-ductive freedom, it is critical for feminist educators in film and other fields to see and show realist accounts of how women approached similar political work less than a generation before."[1] I was inspired by Juhasz's poignant reaffirmation of the theoretical import of realist political docu-mentaries (and, I would add, political narrative films), by her insightful recognition of the fundamental ways that they contribute to the project of social transformation. As Juhasz indicates, our present historical con-text demands that feminist educators, like myself, retrace and reevaluate the theoretical legacy of feminist political works.

The films of Lourdes Portillo raise a series of pertinent issues for fem-inists in the late twentieth century. Residing in northern California, Por-tillo is an internationally acclaimed documentary filmmaker who works on the borders between two or more cultures and cinematic traditions. In the late 1970s, Portillo made her first film, *After the Earthquake/Después del terremoto,* codirected by Nina Serrano. A delicate and earnest portrait of a domestic worker who migrated from Nicaragua to California, *Después del terremoto* was awarded the Diploma of Honor at the Cracow Shorts Film Festival. A few years later, Portillo traveled to Argentina and, along with Susana Blaustein Muñoz, focused on the mothers of the disappeared (*los desaparecidos*) who defied the military regime. Portillo and Muñoz's film, *Las Madres: The Mothers of the Plaza de Mayo,* played a major role in publicizing internationally the plight of the mothers and *los desaparecidos.* With the documentary *La Ofrenda: Days of the Dead* (1988), Portillo turned her focus to the realm of cultural practices, documenting the Day of the Dead celebration in Mexico and its revival and recovery by Chi-canas and Chicanos in the United States. In 1992, Portillo collaborated with the comedy trio Culture Clash to produce the experimental video *Columbus on Trial* for the international commemoration of Columbus' voyage to the Americas. Joining indigenous groups in their protest of the quincentennial celebration and the notion of Columbus as the discoverer, Portillo's video rewrites the discovery as conquest, and humorously puts Columbus on trial in a modern-day courtroom. Later, in *The Devil Never Sleeps/El diablo nunca duerme* (1994) Portillo turned her concern to the domestic sphere. An investigation into the death of her uncle, Tío Oscar, serves as the backdrop for the filmmaker's exploration into Mexican family dynamics. More recently, Portillo has extended her interrogation of the family by focusing on the death and legacy of pop Tejana singer Selena, and in the film *Corpus: A Home Movie for Selena* (1999) weaves the story of her significance around fans, the body, and patriarchy. While her films remain grounded in Chicano/a and Latina/o concerns, Portillo embraces a broader, transnational vision that positions women at the center of her stories and documents the effects of global economic and political processes, as well as intersecting structures of domination, on the everyday lives of women.

Immigrant Racialized Labor and Latino Patriarchy

A short, black-and-white fictional film, *Después del terremoto* deals with the conflicts a Latina immigrant worker faces as she struggles to define her own autonomy and independence within Latino patriarchy. The film documents the "identity in process" of the main character, Irene—her coming into gender-consciousness. Working in a plush San Francisco residence as a live-in domestic worker, Irene anticipates, with some ambivalence, a reunion with Roberto, her boyfriend from Nicaragua who has just been released from prison, after the earthquake of 1976, for political activism against the U.S.-financed military dictatorship of Anastasio Somoza. While Roberto is a leftist revolutionary, he is also portrayed as a traditional Latino male, threatened by Irene's growing economic and social independence in the United States. Portillo's first film thus explores Latina subjectivity and identity in the interstices of immigration, racialized labor, and Latino patriarchy.

Codirected by Nina Serrano, Portillo's *Después del terremoto* is made within the general context of Third World anti-imperialist politics and the specific struggles for emancipation waged by members of the Nicaraguan diaspora and the solidarity movement during the seventies. Portillo and Serrano, however, refused to construct a single narrative of emancipation centered exclusively around a political identity which did not acknowledge multiple forms of domination within the social structure. To the consternation of Nicaraguan exiles living in San Francisco, Portillo and Serrano wrote a story focusing on the impact of processes of patriarchal gender relations, migration, labor, and cultural dislocation on the identity and subjectivity of a Latina immigrant worker. As Portillo explains in an interview with Kathleen Newman and B. Ruby Rich:

> I was also involved in the Sandinista movement in the United States in the late seventies, in solidarity with them, Nina Serrano and I, who was also the codirector of the film. We decided to make a film that would inform the people about the struggle, and I was concerned about the struggles and the conflicts that immigrants and Nicaraguans were going through at that point. I think I didn't want to make a film that was a documentary—a straight, hard-hitting factual documentary. And I saw the richness of their life and I wanted to capture it. At the same time when I did that, it was a struggle against them [U.S. Sandinista movement] and they disowned us in the process. Because . . . they wanted us to do a documentary that they had been used to seeing—very factual, very political, very one-sided. Since we got an AFI grant, I figured in a certain way it was my film, so that I had control and could do what I wanted. So we broke with them and did the narrative film.[2]

In *Después del terremoto,* the narrative of radical oppositional and anti-imperialist politics of the Nicaraguan solidarity movement is woven in as a subplot to the main plotline, which locates a Latina immigrant in between languages and cultures and in relationship to the intersecting dominations of patriarchy, capitalism, and imperialism.

As I have written elsewhere, Portillo and Serrano choreograph the main character's desire for liberation within the tension between internal and external spaces, the domestic sphere of traditional Latino/a culture and the public sphere of production that paid domestic labor represents.[3] In many ways, *Después del terremoto*'s focus on a female domestic worker who migrates from Nicaragua thematizes both the racial composition of labor in the private domestic sphere and the feminization of transnational labor migrations. By portraying the ordinary life of an immigrant domestic worker, the film anticipates the groundbreaking research of feminists of color, as is evident below.

Feminist researchers have long contended that industrial capital creates a structural division between the profit-oriented economy of capitalism and domestic home life. This division between production and consumption, commonly referred to as the public-private split, gave birth to the category of housewife and to a redefinition of women as "guardians of domestic homelife." However, as feminists of color have argued, domesticity is not a universal condition for all women, but is instead rooted in the social conditions of the middle and upper classes in the nineteenth and twentieth centuries. As the experiences of former slaves and other racialized and immigrant women make evident, they were wageworkers first and housewives second. It is in this more general social arena that *Después del terremoto* captures the racialized division between unpaid domestic labor and paid domestic labor.[4]

Irene is a woman who works outside the home, a Latina who moves between cultures, languages, and the public and private spheres, possessing the ability to act on multiple levels. Like many other Latina immigrants living in the United States, Irene operates in the public sphere, working as a paid domestic laborer within an advanced capitalist economy. She is engaged in income-producing activities outside of her own home but within the private domestic sphere of another home. And while in U.S. society, at least at the ideological level, there is a separation of work and family into separate spheres, according to Mary Romero, given the nature of the work involved, Chicana domestics (and, I would add, Latina immigrants) reject the separation between work and family and see less of a distinction between the spheres of homemaking and paid domestic labor.[5]

Thus, ideologically at least, the home for domestic workers operates less as a site of homemaking than as an extension of the division of labor under capitalism. Which is precisely why Irene, in *Después del terremoto*, confronts Roberto with so much ambivalence. The film establishes Irene's financial independence at the beginning, when it shows her purchasing a television set with her own earnings. With this act, the main character enters into the sphere of consumer capitalism, for the television set also embodies the illusion of freedom through consumption. By the end of the film, viewers are well aware that a marriage with Roberto would curtail this type of freedom since, within traditional Latina/o culture, the man controls a woman's finances. Moreover, Irene's subordination through marriage would encompass other dimensions of her life as well, particularly in terms of domestic home life. Not only do Latina domestic workers experience housework as a second shift—the same as working mothers and female spouses—they are burdened by having a double shift of the same kind of work. One shift is paid, the other unpaid, but both are housework. In many respects, Irene's ambivalence toward marriage interrogates precisely the myth of domesticity and the role of women as guardians of domestic homelife.

However uncomfortable for viewers, the filmmakers thus raise the question of gender politics from a Latina immigrant's position in the dynamics between two cultural systems, visualizing the implicit discourse of a counterpoised consciousness resulting from a woman's daily lived experience of oppression. Through a realistic narrative, the filmmakers contest women's oppression, exploring the shifts in a Latina immigrant's identity and the meanings that womanhood has for a working-class Latina. *Después del terremoto* visualizes a woman who is aware of the sexual, gender, and cultural structures that formed her and who has made a decisive and deliberate break with those structures by changing her consciousness and interrogating her destiny as Roberto's wife.

In her essay about the cinema of Latinas and Latin American women, Liz Kotz writes: "Intersecting class, national and ethnic identities, complicated by personal experience, reflect a contemporary history of Latin America (and the U.S.) in which exile, rupture, transnational migration and bicultural identity have become relatively common."[6] Paralleling the insights of early feminists of color during the seventies, this short film portrays these common features of the human condition in the late twentieth century, that is, the intersectionality of social identities and the variable social conditions which affect subject formation. The filmmakers refigure Latina subjectivity by reclaiming, reinventing, and resisting individual and collective identities through cinema. In more ways than one, *Después del terremoto* reveals "how all so-called members of so-called communities live that membership in complex, contradictory, and radically different ways."[7] And while the film's main focus is on gender politics—conflicts and differences within the Nicaraguan immigrant community—the filmmakers portray many of the social processes to which Kotz makes reference, including the conditions of exile, rupture, transnational migration, and bicultural identity. In addition, the film renders the phenomenon known as the feminization of labor migration, or the rise in the number of women workers migrating in search of work.

According to UN reports, long distance migration movements in the past were comprised mostly of men. However, beginning in the 1970s and intensifying during the eighties as a result of the economic recession in Latin America, more women began to leave their homes and form a significant part of transnational labor flows. This rise in the migration of female workers was also due in large measure to the growing importance of gender in the new international division of labor, which, as I noted earlier, is a result of the demand for what is known as "women's work," especially domestic service but also in the garment and assembly industries.[8] The shift in migratory patterns from Latin America into the United States has altered the demographic composition of the Mexican and Latino/a communities of the Southwest. During this period, Central Americans, like the Nicaraguans in the film, joined the ranks of Mexican immigrants working in the low-wage service sector. And this rise in Latin American immigration was due as much to economic factors as it was to political ones for, as *Después del terremoto* makes evident, many of the Central American immigrants were also political refugees and displaced persons, fleeing repressive (U.S.-financed) military regimes.

Reinventing Motherhood

As in *Después del terremoto,* Portillo's internationalism is filtered through the lenses of gender politics in *Las Madres: The Mothers of the Plaza de Mayo* (codirected by Susana Blaustein Muñoz), a film about the mothers of the disappeared in Argentina. While Portillo and Muñoz started working on the film during the final years of the military dictatorship, they shot the film in the first hundred days of the country's return to democracy. In contrast to *Después del terremoto,* Portillo opted for the genre of political documentary to tell the story of women's oppositional struggles:

> I was thinking first of all when you make a political film, sometimes you feel things inside you. With the story of *Las Madres* . . . there was no other way to film that story. . . . We tried to figure it out, but this was the only avenue you can take with *Las Madres.* In terms of Nicaragua, [the story] would be more contrived. The drama inherent in *Las Madres* only allowed us to do it in that way.[9]

And it was a powerful drama indeed, one depicting the toll of the military regime's "dirty war" on the nation's inhabitants: a drama showing a military junta that ruled Argentina from 1976 to 1983 and that was responsible for the disappearance of eleven thousand Argentineans; a drama focusing on a group of mothers who defied a brutal military junta by staging illegal demonstrations in the "best guarded public place" in Argentina, the Plaza de Mayo, directly challenging the authority of the state.[10] The film reconstructs the drama of their ordeal with cinematic intensity. Blending the realist strategy of interviews with news footage and voice-over narration, *Las Madres* tells the riveting tale of women's struggle against a violent, repressive regime and gives voice to a female mode of resistance which emerges out of the social role historically assigned to women: motherhood.

As we know, motherhood is the traditional form through which the modern state produces women as subjects of the nation, by reinscribing women's role in reproduction and confining them to the private, domestic sphere of child-rearing. Yet it is from their social location as mothers that the women of Argentina staged their bold defiance, acting in the public sphere at a time when most people, including the media, remained indifferent to or ignored the military's dirty war. Even though the military regime retaliated against these mostly middle-aged mothers, arresting them repeatedly and even disappearing one of their founders—Azucena De Vicenti, the originator of the idea to demonstrate in the Plaza—along with two French nuns and an artist, the mothers continued their public acts of defiance and resumed their demonstrations "wearing their flat shoes and white headscarves." [11]

The filmmakers meticulously show how women, like the mothers of the disappeared, can redefine and reappropriate motherhood as a model of resistance for unifying women across various social backgrounds in their opposition to repressive patriarchal nationalism. *Las Madres*'s narrative emphasis on the process of radicalization, rather than victimization, has proved inspirational for viewers around the world, effectively thematizing how middle-aged women cultivated political consciousness and collectivity and channeled their own personal pain as mothers into radical action. By claiming the streets of Argentina, these women transformed their previously private, gendered identities as mothers and reinvented motherhood as a political identity for operating in the public sphere of the nation. As the vice president of the Plaza de Mayo mothers, Adela Antokaletz, puts it: "We decided to take to the streets, and it was the streets that taught us. . . . That was what gave us our political strength." [12]

Las Madres ends its painstaking drama of women's opposition and resistance with a collage of images of mothers who wage similar struggles on behalf of their disappeared children throughout the world. Theirs is a struggle to "make visible the unseen" or to make us see, as Avery Gordon writes in a different context, "what is usually neglected or thought by most to be dead and gone." [13] In the case of Argentina, *Las Madres* recovers "the evidence of the things not seen," or the things Argentineans were unwilling to see and to recognize. With the end of the military dictatorship, the mothers continued their campaign for "the punishment of the people who carried out the torture and disappearance of their children." [14]

In the early years of the democratic transition, the new government capitulated to the former military rulers, neglecting the concerns of the mothers. To the mothers' shocked dismay and disappointment, in 1990, President Carlos Menem pardoned the members of the military junta, including its head, General Jorge Videla. While the amnesty was couched as a gesture of national reconciliation (a "decision to pardon dictators in the interest of peace"), it was designed to appease the right-wing forces of the nation as much as to serve as a mechanism that would allow Argentineans to forget, to ignore, or otherwise refuse the haunting presence of the disappeared. But ghosts have a way of coming back to haunt the living. While the Argentinean government pardoned crimes against the dead or disappeared, crimes against the children of the disappeared were not covered by the amnesty. Thus in July of 1998, retired general Jorge Videla was charged with stealing the babies of the disappeared that were born in prison and giving them to officers and friends of the military to adopt.[15] It is as if the ghosts of the disappeared came back to vindicate the mothers' allegations about kidnapping—testimonies eloquently articulated in Portillo and Muñoz's stunning documentary *Las Madres: The Mothers of the Plaza de Mayo*.

Global migrations and cultural continuity/discontinuity

Portillo collaborated with Argentinean-born Susana Muñoz on one other project, once again charting the complex and variable points of contact among the various communities in the Americas. Turning to Portillo's own culture, the filmmakers decided on a topic that would provide them with much-needed "healing." As Portillo recalls: "*Las Madres* made me feel so bad that I wanted to feel good. And in order for me to feel good, I wanted to think about death the way my people think of death, not the way your people think about death. That was the reaction to *Las Madres: La Ofrenda*."[16]

The film *La Ofrenda* traces the continuities, as well as the discontinuities, in cultural practices that cross the U.S.-Mexico border. The film begins in Mexico, recounting the history, cultural practices, and rituals associated with the Day of the Dead celebration, which takes place each year on November 1 and 2. A festivity dating to pre-Conquest Mexico, the Day of the Dead continues as a vital cultural tradition, despite centuries of effort by colonial authorities to eradicate the practice. The second half of the film takes place in San Francisco, where in the seventies the Chicana/o cultural arts movement revived the festivity, organizing exhibitions and planning an annual parade through the streets of the Mission District.

While the Day of the Dead celebration unifies the documentary's narrative, the meanings and rituals associated with the celebration differ in each context. In Oaxaca, the Day of the Dead is portrayed as linked organically to a way of life and to a community mobilized for the festivity: from cooking the traditional foods to selling and buying the necessary items on the marketplace; from artisans making the *calaveras* (skulls) to devout praying before home altars; from visits to the grave sites to the cleaning of gravestones and dining in honor of the dead. In this manner, for the indigenous people of Oaxaca, the Day of the Dead forms an integral part of a community's traditions, its daily spiritual, cultural, and material practices.

In California, the celebration of the Day of the Dead resonates with nostalgia. *La Ofrenda* renders the cultural memory of the festivity as decontextualized, located less in everyday life than in objects like home altars and photographs, or in displays in parades and institutional sites such as museums, classrooms, universities, and cultural centers. In visualizing the contextual contrast between Oaxaca and California, however, the filmmakers offer students of culture important insights about the process of cultural transformation. For example, the film renders culture in its dynamic form, particularly evident in the filmmakers' refusal to fetishize culture, to treat it as a static object meant to be handed down unchanged from one generation to the next or across geopolitical space. Rather, culture and cultural traditions in this film are active and dynamic, lived practices. As immigrants leave their homeland, they take their cultural traditions with them. However, the cultures of transnational immigrants do not remain intact but are affected by processes of rupture and dislocation, which in turn impact the modification, transformation, and even the reinvention of cultural traditions. The film takes us into this universe of cultural change, visualizing a Mexican-origin community of Chicanos/as who creatively respond to environmental and other social pressures by reenvisioning and re-creating cultural traditions in a new context.

In mapping the continuities and discontinuities in cultural practices that cross the Mexico-U.S. border, *La Ofrenda* additionally makes evident how these processes intensify when immigrant communities (or for that matter, native racialized groups) must adapt to different circumstances in host countries that are hostile to cultural differences. And it is in this context that the revival of the Day of the Dead in the United States by Chicanas/os is a response to needs different from those in Mexico. In the face of the state's erasure of and hostility to alternative cultural and social identities in the United States, the Day of the Dead celebration performs an oppositional, political function of affirming Latina/o cultural identity and multicultural differences.

La Ofrenda has also served the Latino gay community in its efforts to confront the AIDS epidemic, particularly because the film opens up a space for understanding culturally specific modes of confronting death through ritual. For just as *La Ofrenda* was a healing film for Portillo, so have the film and the Day of the Dead celebration been appropriated by the Latino gay community for spiritual healing after the loss of many of its members. In fact, the film's submerged engagement with the problem of AIDS is part of a broader current in Latina/o film- and videomaking. According to Latina filmmaker Frances Negrón-Muntaner, the end of the 1980s witnessed a "sharp increase in gay and lesbian work" as a response to "transformations brought about by the AIDS epidemic." She further observed that "the AIDS crisis created a political and discursive need to address heterosexism and promote safer sex practices in Latino communities across the country (including those that did not self-identify as 'gay' or 'lesbian')." [17] It is in this context that Portillo made *Vida*. Framed by the melodramatic conventions of Latin America's telenovela (soap opera), *Vida* is a short didactic film designed to raise the Latina/o community's awareness about AIDS and to promote safer sex practices, particularly among young people.

The "realm of the imaginative"

Portillo's documentary forays across the border take a new turn in *The Devil Never Sleeps* by entering the realm of the imaginative. A film that tells the story of the filmmaker's investigation into the death of her beloved Tío Oscar, who died under mysterious circumstances in Mexico, *The Devil Never Sleeps* also sketches the permeable borders between nations, genres, and political/familial identities. Portillo crosses the border to lead a probe into the unresolved death of her uncle, Oscar Ruíz Almeida, utilizing his life to weave the strands of her inquiry. Official accounts rule his death a suicide, whereas some family members and friends suspect murder. In the process of her investigation, Portillo pierces the veneer of her family's secrets, disclosing conflicting testimony by family members and surprising contradictions in the life of her favorite uncle. In this manner, the murder-mystery-detective theme of the film serves as a ruse for a probing glimpse into the politics and secrets, not just of a typical private family (represented by Portillo's family), but also of the public national family, embodied in Mexico's ruling party, the PRI. Starring as niece-detective-documentarist, Portillo narrates the story in terms of intrigue, deception, hypocrisy, as well as the cultural values of honor, loyalty, and familism, foregrounding complex issues about *la familia* for Chicanos/as and Mexicans on both sides of the border.

As I have written in a longer essay, Portillo is a Chicana Catholic who transgresses the artificial boundary between the public and the private — a boundary reinforced by capitalism and Catholicism — by making available for public scrutiny the truths and falsities hidden behind her family's veil of secrecy and privacy.[18] The filmmaker violates a cultural taboo forbidding public disclosure of family matters, a taboo so sacred and powerful that even Mexican politicos are bound by its strictures; in the political arena this taboo is known as *la mordaza* (the muzzle). It is a gag order that requires even former presidents to remain silent on political matters pertaining to their *familia,* the PRI. To the extent that the political apparatus of the PRI is based on the model of *la familia,* Portillo's foray into the intimate realm of family affairs undermines the very foundation of Mexican patriarchy.

By transgressing the sacred covenant regarding public discussions of private family matters, *The Devil Never Sleeps* blurs the distinction between the private and the public, thus linking it to feminist concerns about *la familia* as both an element in power relations and a form of domination in the microstructures of everyday life. Given its centrality in the sphere of domesticity, *la familia* plays a fundamental role in upholding the law of the father and the subjugation of women. Feminist critics of U.S. Third World nationalism have argued that male privilege and hegemony derive their force from a reluctance to contest the "idealized notion" of a monolithic community and, by extension, "the family romance upon which this notion of community relies."[19] In order to weigh the significance of Portillo's submerged engagement with Chicana feminist discourse, one must first understand the centrality of family values in Chicana/o nationalist politics.

Portillo breaks the silence around family unity and the family myth-making enterprise so central to Mexican and Chicano/a nationalism and deconstructs the values associated with Chicana/o (and Mexican) families, "including familism (beliefs and behavior associated with family solidarity), *compadrazgo* (extended family via godparents), *confianza* (a system of trust and intimacy)."[20] Since the Chicano/a movement of the sixties, Chicana/o nationalists have conjured up *la familia* as the foundation of oppositional politics, insisting on a single, coherent representation of *la familia* — namely, the heterosexual, nuclear family. Traced to the master narrative of Mexican nationalism,[21] *la familia* figures as the basis for a protonationalist discourse on community loyalty. To speak out against the sexism and abuse perpetrated by Chicano males was tantamount to violating the *confianza* of the community which, because it was invested with all the emotional trappings of familism, meant one was also betraying *la familia*. The mechanisms for reproducing this nationalist discourse on community loyalty are located in the strict division between the private and public spheres that undergird the nationalist fantasy about *la familia* as an internal sanctuary against external threats.

Single-handedly targeting the normativity of the attributes of familism and *confianza*, *The Devil Never Sleeps* serves as an instrument for criticizing Chicana/o and Mexican nationalism, for these very principles also operate as twin pillars for endowing family mythologies, effacing their contradictions, and naturalizing male privilege. By taking her favorite uncle as subject matter, Portillo breaks the investment of Chicanas and Chicanos in the intertwined notions of family and community, in the artificial division between the public and private spheres, in *la familia* as a sacred institution. Positioned simultaneously as insider and outsider, Portillo removes from the family its shroud of secrecy, publicly unveiling its private face and exposing, not the blessed, untouchable Holy Family (derived from Catholicism), but *la familia,* a site of conflict and contestation.

Yet the importance of Portillo's intervention goes beyond the narrative or thematic aspects of film. Earlier I noted that this film enters the "realm of the imaginative" because I wanted to extend bell hooks' insights about *Daughters of the Dust* and argue that, like Julie Dash, Portillo insists "on a movement away from accuracy, reality and authenticity" for its narrative truth.[22] The formal structure of *The Devil Never Sleeps* simultaneously acknowledges and critiques the conventions of documentary film, for Portillo uses realist strategies in quite self-critical and self-conscious ways.

Portillo interrogates the criteria for truth and accuracy in a documentary, as well as its reliance on visual evidence, by making truth plural and drawing attention to the partial and constructed nature of images. The filmmaker resorts to well-established techniques for communicating documentary truth—i.e., interviews, actuality footage, home movies, narrator's voice—but does not ground truth in the metadiscursive, nor does she privilege one version of Tío Oscar's death over another. Each interviewee's account, each of the narrator's digressions, each actuality footage, each clip of a home movie has as much validity as the others.

Portillo thus refuses to constitute a realistic discourse based on a singular interpretation but instead formulates a plurality of versions. The strategic overlap of multiple modes of representation derived from distinct genres makes visible this refusal to privilege the documentary as the singular mode for apprehending and interpreting reality. And while the film reconstructs its plurality from a montage of modern techniques for gathering and classifying knowledge in the documentary—the interview,

footage from home movies, photo stills, actuality footage, narration—
the documentarist complicates the status of official documentary discourse within the film by drawing from other culturally specific forms of
knowledge more properly associated with the space of the popular.
Specifically, Portillo pursues clues and facts from popular forms of
knowledge and experience—that is to say, those disqualified or inade-
quate sources of knowledge passed on in the form of legends, gossip, telenovelas, canciones rancheras (folk songs), myth, proverbial wisdom; in
sum, forms which for Foucault represent "a particular, local, regional
knowledge, a differential knowledge incapable of unanimity."[23] These
sources of knowledge are at odds with the modernist project of certainty,
uniformity, absolute truth, associated with official documentary discourse, for popular forms of knowledge are often partial, contradictory,
ambivalent, and in a conflictual relation with one dominant, singular interpretation of social reality. Portillo pursues the task of producing the
truth concerning Tío Oscar's death by juxtaposing popular with official
forms of knowledge, refusing to privilege one form over the other.

This strategy is evident in the scene in which Portillo interviews Tía
Luz about Tío Oscar's conjugal relations. Pursuing a lead which implicates Ofelia (Tío Oscar's widow) in the murder/suicide, the filmmaker
begins her inquiry with a question regarding the sexual affairs of the
couple. The scene opens with a shot of Tía Luz expressing her visible reluctance to entertain such an intimate question. Yet with further probing
she is quick to confess the truth about the intimacies of the couple, including a conversation she had with Ofelia after her honeymoon with Tío
Oscar in which Ofelia reveals the proof of her virginity: bloody panties
saved from her wedding night. What is striking about this scene is the
manner in which Tía Luz's official testimony (the interview) is struc-
turally reconstructed by the filmmaker as thematically suspended and
visually framed within two other popular modes of representation: the
telenovela and the legend. Tía Luz's off-screen voice accompanies a sequence of shots depicting a mannequin dressed in a wedding dress—shot
through a bridal store's showcase while public spectators look up ador-
ingly at the mannequin—and culminates in an over-the-shoulder pin-
hole shot of Tía Luz watching the Brazilian telenovela *Roque Santeiro*.
From her confession about Ofelia's indiscretions, Tía Luz turns with ease
to a frivolous interpretation of plot details from the telenovela, thus sup-
planting the narrative value of the former, since for Tía Luz one account
has the same relevance as the other. As the camera zooms in to the television set, visual and narrative focus shifts away from the interview to
the telenovela, affecting a slippage between two forms of discourse, the

official interview and the more properly popular discourse, the telenovela. In this instance, as well as in other places throughout the film, the
strategic use of the telenovela blurs the distinction between reality and
telereality. Yet closure is not anchored on the telenovela, but rather is
achieved through a distinct popular discourse, the legend, thereby further complicating the status of truth in this film.

The narrative shifts once again by crosscutting to a close-up of the
bridal mannequin's face. Portillo's narrator-voice interjects:

> There's a legend that the owner of a Chihuahua bridal shop had a
> daughter she dearly loved. On the day of her wedding, the daughter
> died in an accident. The bereaved mother had her embalmed,
> dressed up as a bride and displayed in her store window. A tribute
> to virginal love.

Carefully crafted shots of people looking up intently at the bridal mannequin suggest that the legend of the embalmed virgin captivates these
spectators, just as it secures their alignment with those of us outside the
screen who have been nurtured on Mexican fantasy stories of family
ghosts and spirits, on the macabre flavor in legends of enchanted statues
and embalmed saints, as we too wonder about the legend's uncanny
truth. The final shot of this scene depicts store attendants raising the man-
nequin/embalmed virgin's bridal gown, allowing us to glimpse beneath
her dress as if to prove the truth of the legend and further cementing my
eerie bewilderment ("this really must be the embalmed virgin; her face
looks so real"). At this precise moment, the film resuscitates a distant
glimmering from the past. I travel to the "marvelous real" of my childhood memories—a visit to Guadalajara's majestic cathedral, where I
stand before the statue of the child-saint encased within a glass vitrine. My
wide-eyed gaze rests on the delicate, statuesque feminine figure, with its
long eyelashes and seemingly porous texture, as my Tía Fina whispers that
we are witnessing a miracle incarnate: "This is not really a statue, it's the
actual body of a young girl." I nod, fixated on those realistic features of
the immobile girl who refused to decompose and as a result was bestowed
the gift of everlasting embodiment and canonization. Curiously, until this
cinematic moment with the legend of the embalmed virgin, my childhood
encounter with the magical remained submerged in my psyche, unscruti-
nized by the laws of reason and rational discourse. Yet it undoubtedly
structures my beliefs and relation to the "real." Thus, depending on one's
belief system, the truth of the legend of the embalmed virgin seems just
as plausible as the truth in Tía Luz's testimony about Ofelia's account of
her virginity.

In some respects, the legend's location in this scene has less to do with the process of gathering empirical evidence or knowledge for documentary truth than with underscoring the veracity of popular forms of knowledge for making sense of one's reality. Reading the scene against the grain, the legend appears in conflictual relation to the interview, mapping the centrality of the cult of virginity in Mexican society. Insofar as Tía Luz's interpretation of Ofelia's virginity gains significance within the ideological framework of patriarchy, the scene highlights how we are all subjected to and interpellated by familial and political apparatuses. The legend of the embalmed virgin gives meaning to this process, revealing how women in Mexico are both victims and agents, targets and vehicles of patriarchal discourse's sublimation of female sexuality in the figure of the Virgin.

In a style that quotes, parodies, and deconstructs PBS style, *The Devil Never Sleeps* "argues against the givenness of documentary reality,"[24] rejecting as well a sense of closure and completeness. In so doing, the film

In the late 1980s, AIDS Films, a nonprofit company founded in 1985, commissioned Portillo to make an AIDS prevention film for Latinas. *Vida* is one in a series written, directed, and aimed at Latina/o and African American audiences by AIDS Films. Below: Lucy (Sandra Paulino, right) shows Olga (Teresa Yenque, left) a picture of Elsie's (Jeanette Toro, center) new boyfriend (photo by Prashant Gupta). Courtesy of Lourdes Portillo.

Portillo collaborated with the comedy trio Culture Clash (Herbert Siguenza, Richard Montoya, and Ric Salinas) in writing the script for *Columbus on Trial*. Broadcast nationally in 1992, the video was funded by the National Endowment for the Arts. Above: Cinematographer Kyle Kibbe (upper left) filming Stormcloud (Richard Montoya, right), while Lourdes Portillo (lower left) and Emiko Omori (lower right) observe. Courtesy of Lourdes Portillo.

Ishmael Saabedra, production assistant, cuing the next scene with Columbus (Herbert Siguenza). Courtesy of Lourdes Portillo.

Rehearsing during the shooting of *Columbus on Trial*. Stormcloud (left, standing), Mr. X (right, standing). Siguenza, Portillo, and Ric Salinas (left to right, sitting). Courtesy of Lourdes Portillo.

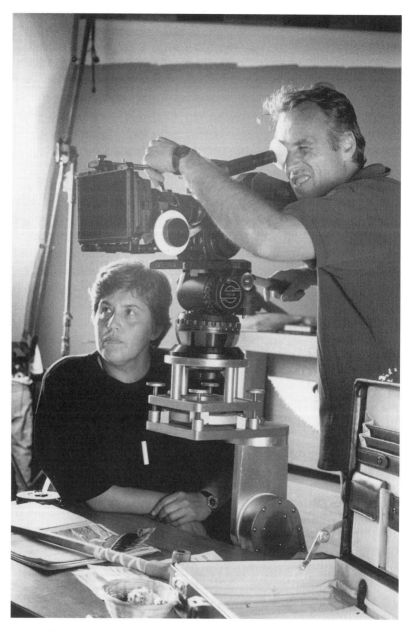

Portillo observes while Kibbe focuses on the next scene. Courtesy of Lourdes Portillo.

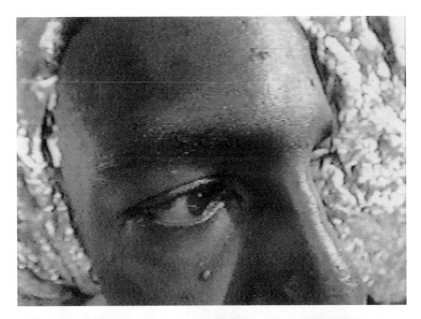

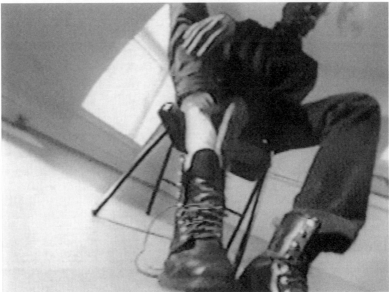

Portillo produced and directed this short experimental video, *Sometimes My Feet Go Numb,* based on the performance piece by Wayne Corbitt. Above: Scene with Wayne Corbitt. Courtesy of Lourdes Portillo.

makes viewers aware of the manipulative nature of film—in particular, of realist documentary—especially when the filmmaker inserts an oversized tomato during a segment about Tío Oscar's agricultural enterprise, or provides evidence through gossip, legends, proverbs, or parables of snakes and saints, or creates reenactments with toys. With these examples, *The Devil Never Sleeps* points to or makes "audiences aware of the process of production as a limitation of the film's neutral stance, its ability to document objectively."[25] While the film relies in part on realist strategies, it also contributes to what Juhasz terms "a critical vocabulary which has pushed many makers and viewers of realist documentaries in the nineties towards a more noticeably self-aware theoretical/political practice."[26] In this manner, by pushing the boundaries of documentary realism, Portillo has contributed to the evolution of the genre.

In Closing . . .

My aim throughout this critical essay has been to assess Lourdes Portillo's contributions to feminist, oppositional visual media in this era of global capitalism. An overview of her films and videos confirms the extent to which Portillo's signature as a filmmaker is solidly anchored in the imaginative realm, in a poetic, meditative style that is contemplative rather than simply informative. As *Las Madres: The Mothers of the Plaza de Mayo, La Ofrenda: The Days of the Dead,* and *The Devil Never Sleeps/El diablo nunca duerme* make evident, Portillo seasons realist strategies with the imaginative flavors typical of fictional narrative films. Her documentaries are narrated by a lyrical, personal, and intimate female voice rather than the distanced, authoritative "voice of God" typical in documentaries. Hers is a female voice that, as Judith Mayne observes, "destabilizes conventional symmetry whereby the register of vocal authority is presumed to be male, the realm of the visible, female."[27]

While her work conforms to the realist aesthetics of cinema, Portillo has created a genuinely hybrid style of filmmaking insofar as she crosses the border of multiple styles and playfully blends aesthetic traditions. As in *The Devil Never Sleeps,* the tension between fiction and documentary in *Después del terremoto* is due in large part to the influence of Latin America's telenovelas, neorealism, and Cuban cinema. A seasoned filmmaker, Portillo is not averse to crafting her films with novel and experimental techniques. In *Columbus on Trial,* Portillo makes extensive use of the blue screen technique commonly employed in TV newscasts and weather reports for layering images. While the blue screen is widely used today in

Independent documentaries, Portillo was one of the first to use this technique in a political, aesthetic context.

In many respects, Portillo's films and videos reflect the growing diversity of Chicana/o and Latino/a experiences in this country. No longer segregated geographically—i.e., Mexicans in the Southwest, Cubans in Florida, Puerto Ricans in New York—but living in close proximity to each other and to other ethnic groups, Latinas and Latinos are creating new and dynamic forms of culture, language, politics, and traditions. And it is precisely this Latina/o hybridity, its bicultural, multilingual, and multicultural perspectives, that are visibly crafted in films like *Columbus on Trial, Vida, La Ofrenda, Después del terremoto, The Devil Never Sleeps,* and *Corpus: A Home Movie for Selena.*

Despite her international recognition, Portillo passionately guards her independence, remaining on the fringes of the commercial dominion of Hollywood. And it is perhaps her freedom from the constraints of the Studio marketplace that accounts for the subversive and transgressive qualities in her work. A trailblazer in the Chicana and Chicano film movement, Portillo's defiant irreverence serves as a model of inspiration for the younger generation of aspiring, independent film- and videomakers. Her work reflects the broad range of concerns and the growing diversity among Chicana/o and Latino/a alternative imagemakers. And, like so many feminist artists, Portillo's work destabilizes cinematic regimes and introduces different ways of seeing.

Yvonne Yarbro-Bejarano

Ironic Framings: A Queer Reading of the Family (Melo)drama in Lourdes Portillo's *The Devil Never Sleeps/El diablo nunca duerme*

The Devil Never Sleeps/El diablo nunca duerme (1996) responds to a unique event in San Francisco-based Lourdes Portillo's life: news of her favorite uncle Oscar's death in Chihuahua, Mexico. The multiple layering and ironic framings of this film create a house of mirrors that allows for queer identifications and semirevelations. Through these identifications and by foregrounding her authority as filmmaker to investigate rumors that her uncle was a homosexual, Portillo's film constructs an ambivalent space into which she insinuates her own queerness. My queer reading of *Diablo* is not put forward as excluding or superior to postcolonial, postmodern, or feminist readings of the film, but, as Sylvia Molloy suggests, to provide one of a number of possible slanted readings, "tentative and provisional, but no less pertinent."[1] A queer reading of *Diablo,* especially the narrator's resolution to solve the mystery of Oscar's death, puts pieces of the film's detective puzzle together in a different though too familiar narrative: the reference to family secrets, which Portillo as narrator (LP) says the family clung to as tightly at the end as at the beginning, or to suicide, as decoded by many to signify a queer form of death, at least in the United States.

In her decision to return to her childhood home in northern Mexico to make the film, Portillo confronts a number of elements that disempower her vis-à-vis her family and provincial norms. In this transnational situation, Portillo is subject to culturally specific discriminatory attitudes and practices against women and lesbians. Her racialized identification as a Chicana, popularized during the sixties out of people of color's lived experience of U.S. racism, becomes less salient than one defined in terms of place, borders and land: she is *pocha,* one who left to live in the United States, often considered a cultural (and economic) traitor. Linguistic markers—such as when Portillo's cousin uses a proverb and remarks, "como decimos aquí en México" ("as we say here in Mexico")—function to exclude the U.S. filmmaker from a Mexican "we," as if the native Spanish speaker would have forgotten common phrases, culturally alienated *en el otro lado* (on the other side).

Both of there and of here (through family, cultural ties, and places of birth and residence), Portillo focuses on family and Mexico as her childhood home. In the process of framing this subjectivity, the film negotiates differentials of power: the social and familial devaluation she experiences in Mexico as a *pocha,* woman, and lesbian, but also her status as a professional U.S. filmmaker. In this capacity, Portillo uses the film apparatus to establish power over her family, especially in the areas of authority and sexuality. Filmic techniques of empowerment in the film's particular aesthetic languages include the representation of the adult director and voice-over narrator within the film. Using original music and rancheras, family photos, LP's voice-over narrations, and old home movies, *Diablo* juxtaposes LP's cherished childhood memories of Oscar with footage and documentary-style interviews about him in the present, which are manipulated and ironized by Portillo.

Portillo and her film operate from what cultural anthropologist José Limón terms "consciousness of critical difference." In his book *Dancing*

Portillo talking to her crew during the shooting of *The Devil Never Sleeps.* Courtesy of Lourdes Portillo.

with the Devil, Limón employs this concept to describe his working-class subjects' cultural response to dominant society(ies) as well as his awareness of his own positioning as postmodern native ethnographer vis-à-vis these social groups.[2] Neither totally "inside" nor "outside," both Portillo and Limón practice "participant-observation" in the respective cultural milieus treated in *Diablo* and *Dancing with the Devil.* Playing the role of Devil through this ambivalent position, LP identifies with its power, but also suffers the cultural legacy of Christian sin and guilt.

In Portillo's case, her subjective stakes in taking this power to make the film heighten the consciousness of critical difference with respect not only to the social and political realities of Mexican provincial conservatism. Underlying her obvious motivation to investigate her favorite uncle's mysterious death, the desire to uncover other mysteries compels her. In the opening close-up of gently rippling water, evocative, poignant music accompanies LP's voice-over narration: "When I dream of home, something always slips away from me, just below the surface. Faces of my family, old stories, the land, and mysteries about to be revealed." This first shot already implies that the central concern in the film is not to discover the truth of Oscar's death but the desire of memory itself, of that which "slips away just below the surface." Viewers familiar with Portillo's work will recognize this subjective framing from *La Ofrenda: The Days of the Dead* (1988), a film on the Days of the Dead in Greater Mexico. The nature of that "I" marked a shift toward a more subjective exploration from the collectively oriented perspectives of such prior films as *Yo soy Joaquín/I Am Joaquín* (1969) or *Chicana!* (1979).[3] In *La Ofrenda* the narrating "I" wants to understand her relationship to Mexico's multileveled history. Similarly, yet to a much expanded degree, LP's subjective investment in returning to Chihuahua to make *Diablo* is her desire to know, to reveal mysteries and bring to light family "secrets," connoting among other things transgressive sexuality.

As Rosa Linda Fregoso has pointed out, LP's subjective narrative functions in a metonymic modality.[4] In particular, by specifying *dreams* of home rather than waking or analytical consciousness, the voice-over narration suggests that the viewer must search for meaning in the realm of metaphor and metonymy (if, indeed, the unconscious is structured like language). LP's elusive memories of home are figured through the metaphor of water, associating her metonymically with Oscar, whose fortune was based on ill-gotten water for his desert farming. While water connects LP with this taint of exploiter (she deploys her memories and brings family secrets to light for her own gain, both personally and professionally), it also foreshadows their linkage under the sign of queerness, submerged in the old stories and veiled in the open secrets.

As filmmaker, Portillo is authorized to return to Mexico; however, this professional role also mediates her emotional points of reference to Mexico and the power relations within her family that make her vulnerable: as niece, a disempowered child's identity not privy to family secrets; as woman and as queer, an adult identity rumored but never acknowledged (always known and not known) in the family culture of secrets. One way she deflects hierarchical kinship relationships from herself through her filmmaker persona is by consistently defining her relatives in exclusive relationship to Oscar in titles on the screen ("his brother-in-law," "his sister," "his other sister," etc.); names known by viewers are given only in dialogue.

A juxtaposition of sequences at the beginning of *Diablo* represents the two worlds that formed her subjectivity, capturing the tension between LP's relationship to Mexico as a child and her adult persona as filmmaker there: the family home and the local movie theater. Cinematically, this tension translates into the devalued nonpresence or valued presence of LP's body. Immediately after the shot representing LP's landing in Chihuahua, viewers see only a hand push open the door to the decrepit family home. LP reveals, "I'm reluctant, maybe a bit fearful to return to my childhood home. Everything we left behind is now gone, except my memories." In this scenario, there is no body to represent: LP's fear and vulnerability in returning home finds its metaphor in the absence of the body, erased along with all that was left behind (in migrating north, in becoming an adult). The adult body is also invisible in this childhood and familial context on both sexual and professional grounds.

Against a background shot of the movie house, LP's face enters the frame for the first time, as she points toward the building and says to the camera: "Cine Azteca, the first place I saw film." LP implies that film is her legacy from Chihuahua—"I'm happy to see that some places haven't changed"—by placing the Cine Azteca sequence after the scene about her grandmother's legacy to her eight children of three pairs of orthopedic shoes. Facilitating identification between LP and viewers, the camera's angle first looks at her (night shots of LP in a car) and then at what she sees, aligning viewers with her in surveying the theater. The voice-over narration adds the subjective impact of memory: "All those years I would immerse myself in melodrama. In that magical darkness I found what would obsess me for the rest of my life. The movies." In contrast to the absent body in the context of the family home, in the context of consuming or making films LP's body can be represented, as filmmaking is what entitles her as an adult and a professional beyond traditionally gendered roles. In turn, as filmmaker she will make a space for her sexual body as well.

In the rest of *Diablo* LP is seen mainly with her crew and in the process of making the film, as in the scenes of Ofelia's phone conversations. This play with LP's visibility and invisibility on-screen suggests that only through the film apparatus can she vest herself with the creative authority needed to confront the mysteries and secrets of her family. The words "magical darkness" quoted above serve to link her with the queer Oscar in this (creative) process. The home movies included in the film record his talent for delighting children with magic tricks. *Diablo* represents these two childhood memories, Oscar's magic and the magic of the movies, as spaces of desire, sensuality, and imagination. Besides this identification with Oscar, LP's magical "immersion in melodrama" gives her the intimate knowledge of a genre recognized for its pervasiveness in Mexican culture, which she uses as a tool to distance herself ironically from the material she is filming.

In capturing this tension between her control as filmmaker and the cultural and familial relations that marginalize her, the film explores the authoring of LP's own empowered subjectivity vis-à-vis her family as she approaches the secret of Oscar's sexuality. For this subversive project, LP marshals a repertory of techniques that foreground her critical difference, couched in an aesthetic of playful resistance and ironic critique.

Ironic Framings

Ironic quoting of noir detective and melodrama conventions in *Diablo* undermine the singular notion of truth as well as the authority of LP's family. As "filmmaker sleuth," dedicated to finding out "what really happened," LP shines flashlights on maps to chart her journey back to Mexico and her sunglasses reflect and distort the image of interviewees, establishing her critical distance. Dark lighting characterizes all her interactions with Oscar's widow Ofelia, whom LP suspects was involved in Oscar's death. In this same line of ironic quotation from other genres, a thunderstorm illuminates the cemetery and the scene of the crime. In pursuit of the truth, LP circles and crosses out relatives' faces on photographs as they enter and exit the film's voice-over narration. She inscribes questions upon these family photos ("Who killed you?") and examines Oscar and Ofelia's wedding picture through a magnifying glass, as if through sheer augmentation of the material evidence of their lives the truth could be found.

While such tongue-in-cheek detective framings ironize the filmmaker's search for the truth (someone to "frame"), the highly charged, extreme aesthetic of melodrama frames her subjects' *own* versions of the truth in the interviews, as well as provincial understandings of history. In *Diablo*, melodrama recurs in the form of a Mexican telenovela, or soap opera, featuring a scheming, overly possessive mother and her attempts to control her son's life and turn him against his wife. In the Cine Azteca sequence, LP watches a telenovela on a maquette of the stage. When emotions reach fever pitch between mother and son, LP turns to the camera, calling upon viewers for recognition and analysis of the role of melodrama in Greater Mexican culture. LP's gaze seeks confirmation of a shared perception of this prevalent overdramatization of family affairs.[5] By blending film and

Cinematographer Kyle Kibbe shooting in El Panteón de Dolores, Portillo's ancestral burial grounds in Chihuahua. Courtesy of Lourdes Portillo.

telenovela on the Cine Azteca maquette, *Diablo* blurs the distinction among the media that produce and reproduce a pleasurable aesthetic and cultural practice, as well as conservative cultural beliefs and attitudes about family, kinship, and sexuality.

The telenovela prefigures or follows the increasingly charged family "drama," as the various versions of Oscar's life and death unfold. LP ironizes her parents' narrative, relatively authorized in *Diablo,* by literally framing their story in the same maquette of the Cine Azteca: according to them, Ofelia accused Oscar's son of coming on to her so Oscar would pay him to go away. As in the earlier scene, LP turns away from the maquette to the camera with that "Can you believe this?" look. Fregoso notes that "throughout the film, the strategic use of the telenovela blurs the distinction between 'reality' and 'telereality'";[6] at this meshing of media and life, perhaps the implied question in her gaze is, which drama is more melodramatic? LP extends this ironic framing to all attempts to fix the meaning of Oscar's death, including her own. In one scene, for instance, she turns the TV on and articulates her suspicion that Ofelia murdered Oscar against the background of the telenovela mother ranting against her *sucia* (dirty) daughter-in-law.[7]

According to Chencho, Oscar's brother and Portillo's father, there are "muchas versiones" ("many versions") of Oscar's death. LP records all these versions and plays them against themselves and against one another. Though some narratives of Oscar's death are more compelling than others, none is allowed to represent the one true version, anticipating the film's narrative closure on precisely this impossibility.[8] By the end, the viewer has already been prepared to accept LP's concluding narration through the ironic framing of her aesthetic throughout:

> I came back to Mexico with the naive idea that if I pursued all the clues and found out all the facts, I'd uncover the truth, just like in the movies. Did Oscar commit suicide or was he killed by a hired assassin? Maybe I'll never know. The only thing I'm sure of is that by his own choices he contributed to his destiny. The family still holds to its secrets, and once again I realize there are no clear answers, no simple solutions to life's mysteries, just half-glimpsed truths and tantalizing questions.

On-screen, footage from Oscar's Christmas home movie provides an almost magically invested countermemory to the more recent, uglier images and sadder narratives. On the sound track Lola Beltrán sings a ranchera about the diabolical yet alluring passion of romantic love as the toy trains rush off in different circles. The film ends with a close-up of a little car tumbling front over end, an image of life's elusiveness and an adult aesthetic tribute to the whimsical playfulness of the childhood Oscar. This cluster of identifications and dis-identifications and the interweaving of meanings through the juxtaposition of sounds, voice-over narration and images call upon viewers to participate in the making of narrative while acknowledging its inability to speak any one/single life.

LP recasts her personal and professional relationship to her childhood home in these framings. Melodrama provides the metaphorical transition from family drama to the social and historical fabric of provincial life. Moving from the Cine Azteca to the cathedral, LP's voice-over narration comments, "History is followed like melodrama here. The passion for the great heroic legends is what people hold on to"—against photos of Pancho Villa and an energetic Villa corrido. Over shots of the cathedral, LP implicates the Catholic Church in her critique of the hypocritical social relations and betrayals in her hometown: "The provinces have long been the stronghold of conservative values. In Chihuahua, as I soon found out, these values were a thin veneer of respectability which obscured the sordid details of my uncle Oscar's death." A photo of the corpse of Villa, assassinated by fellow revolutionaries, introduces the notion of betrayal inherent in such coercive social hypocrisy. *Diablo* and its aesthetic choices make a forceful indictment of family betrayal and community hypocrisy that goes beyond the framing of Ofelia's guilt.

The opening scenes of the film reveal the subjective spectrum that guides the choices in making the narrative of the film (as distinguished from the narratives *in* the film). Viewers are positioned and aligned with LP's ambivalent perspective in relation to family and Chihuahua through ironic framings, the direct address in the voice-over narration ("You see, a lot of intrigue . . .") and the gazes that seek to establish LP and viewer in a complicit reading of the provincial Mexican (and family) melodrama. The response to that invitation will vary drastically according to the social and cultural positioning of the viewer.

A Queer Reading

Through the identifications traced above and by refusing to authorize one version about Oscar's death as true, offering instead a multiplicity of readings, LP opens up a space for a queer reading of the film. Together, secrets and suicide send multiple messages, including the repression of queer desire. Suicidality could be read in the film's visual aesthetic of representing the body in fragments rather than in its entirety, a technique which applies equally to Oscar and LP. Such a reading also dislodges the family's censuring narrative about Oscar marrying a young and working-class woman to permit queer resonances in this relationship based on age and class difference or even of the way Ofelia "dominated" Oscar. The discourses on illness link cancer or incurable disease to gayness and AIDS in the person of Oscar, as does his sister Luz's reference to his thinness.[9] Chencho's exaggerated account evokes *el chisme,* gossip, with close-ups of moving lips embellishing and elaborating on Oscar's supposed illness, "todo invadido de cáncer, la cara, los ojos" ("completely invaded by cancer, his face, the eyes"). These narratives "summon" the viewer to a queer reading, citing from the repertory of AIDS discourses.

In these queer quotes or traces, LP opens up a potential space for her own queer identification and that of viewers. Toward the beginning of the film, the camera floats over the harbor, then zeros in on a ship and a group of men moving a mast. Against Lola Beltrán singing the ranchera "La barca de Guaymas" on the soundtrack, a single young man catches and holds the camera's gaze with his blatantly erotic one. His (homo)erotic body precedes any verbal mention of Oscar's possible homosexuality. In the next scene, piloting Catalina and LP in the passenger boat to Oscar's house, he lolls in the prow, caressing the camera (and vice versa), while Catalina speaks of Oscar's penchant for expensive colognes.

An explicitly queer narrative supports these citations and visual traces, thanks to LP's explicit choice to ask the people she interviewed what they thought of the rumor that Oscar was homosexual, *in spite of* the opposition of certain relatives to this line of questioning. The queer sequence of questioning is placed near the end of the film, creating an effective counterpoint to the various official stories of Oscar's death. The film apparatus obliges that the "secret"—often spoken, witnessed, and obsessively and reiteratively rumored—be addressed in the openly documentary interview format, the same potentially public arena (the interviewees think) that authorizes their version of Oscar as true. LP's power as director extends to the interviews (the question asked or not asked), and to directorial oversight of the editing of footage and the ordering of the interview segments.[10]

A queer reading (of Oscar by LP and of *Diablo* and LP by viewers) calls out the desire of the text: to air the "sordid details" of provincial Mexican conservative values and to out herself while not actually having to out herself ("lesbian is said but not pronounced," as Molloy phrases it). Only the word "homosexual" is *pronounced* in the interviews, but the nature of LP's inquest says the word "lesbian" for certain audiences. The interview with Luz stages this veiled self-outing through the outing of Oscar. Since for

Luz, Portillo's sexuality was an open secret, her aunt's adamant denial that Oscar was homosexual, or indignation that anyone could dare insinuate that he was, functions as a condemnation of LP, providing a glimpse of the wounding exclusions Portillo experiences on the personal familial level.

This interview segment is characterized by a disproportion that calls attention to the social and cultural regulation of sexuality. The charged vocabulary Luz employs ("infames" ["infamous ones"], "mentirosos" ["liars"], "qué barbaridad" ["what an outrage"]) is out of proportion to her subdued demeanor, contrasting with another scene in which Luz throws herself into her histrionic impersonation of Ofelia's behavior at the funeral. Luz's virulent condemnation of Ofelia risks alienating the viewer, who is left feeling that the close-up of swarming ants at the cemetery refers, not only to Ofelia, but to Luz's venomous tongue as well. Even if her intention is to denounce LP by saying it, Luz's palpable discomfort may stem from having to openly communicate her belief to the niece she knows to be queer that it is an abomination even to *say* Oscar was homosexual. At any rate, Luz's incommensurate no in response to LP's question is more important than the content of what she is denying. The result is a performance emphasizing the punitive aspect of the regulatory norm as well as the highly scripted nature of social interactions for both Oscar and LP.

A queer reading links the violent images of Pancho Villa in the film to this context of familial and social coercion. As an alternative to the police, press, and lawyers, the authorities discredited as corrupt by her father, LP seeks out the alternative space of the séance, reminiscent of the nonanalytical consciousness of her "dreams of home." In this similarly nonauthoritative space, she succeeds in communicating with her uncle. LP voices the anxiety and fear concerning her film project at this juncture between the ghostly queer uncle and queer niece/sleuthing filmmaker: over images of Villa, LP recounts how her mother warned her that some relatives wouldn't like what LP is doing and wouldn't help her. The violence of this second Villa sequence—combining close-ups of bullet holes in Villa's car with gunshots on the sound track and archival photos of the corpse—seems out of proportion to the formulation of the mother's concerns. As in the queer scene with Luz, excess guides viewers to look for meanings associated with sexuality, "queering" the revelation as a reference to her desire to pursue the fraught question of homosexuality. These images represent violent betrayal by one's own, as in Villa's case, whether Oscar's betrayal of his family by marrying Ofelia, or the betrayal perpetrated on him—and by extension on LP—by secrets and silences enforced by regulatory social norms of sexuality and gender.[11]

Portillo's grandmother, Francisca Ruiz Almeida, on her trip to Mexico City from Chihuahua in *The Devil Never Sleeps*. Courtesy of Lourdes Portillo.

What identifies LP and Oscar most, however, is the potential for the "many versions" others create about them. What versions circulate about LP in this provincial milieu concerning her sexuality and her status in this community? Faced with the vehement official affirmation of Oscar's normative heterosexuality, she decides to trouble this lie. The decision not to back off from the queer question in her interviews empowers her, from her own and sympathetic viewers' positions, to approach the family's regulatory role, and gives her some degree of power over relatives by obliging them to confront queer sexuality (Oscar's, her own) within the context of the family and in the interview format.

A queer reading, with the social locations it implies, organizes a strong social critique in the film addressing inequities and contradictions in the sex/gender system that benefit or punish Oscar. Justifying Oscar's affair with Ofelia, the "other brother-in-law" (married to Luz), and "Oscar's friend," Manuelita, agree that it is acceptable, natural, and a bodily necessity for married men to have lovers on the side. For Manuelita, there is no betrayal unless the man flaunts it, because "women want men to lie to them." Gender is also deployed to shift part of the blame for his unhappiness onto Oscar himself, implying that he "was not man enough," i.e., did not fulfill the masculine ideal: he "wasn't a man suspicious enough to defend himself" from his debtors and he was unable to father children (his good friend Josefina Fierro even refuses to believe his third and fourth children were the results of artificial insemination).

A queer reading implicates other gender discourses surrounding Oscar, for example, his penchant for cosmetic surgery and injections of bovine embryo to look younger. The two brothers-in-law explicitly unman Oscar in their narratives that criticize Oscar for allowing Ofelia to dominate him. But the film eludes presenting Oscar as the victim of these attitudes and beliefs by "framing" his own behavior (the affair with Ofelia) and his own participation in and enforcement of these gender roles. Although he hated guns, according to Manuelita, her own enthusiasm for firearms prompted him to enforce their gender coding at the same time: "Es deporte de hombres" (It's a man's sport").

By far the most damning informant, in terms of the family's and provincial society's stock in keeping secrets, is the "other brother-in-law," who, not coincidentally, is also the most patriarchal interviewee in the film. With a conservative belief system and condescending attitude toward LP, he attempts to position her once again as a devalued niece through frequent imperatives, patronizing tone, and use of her childhood nickname, Luli. LP resists this positioning by exposing it through (comically) low-angle shots that accentuate his self-importance and looming, threatening appearance, while humorously subverting it. He is the one who admits that Oscar's homosexuality was rumored in Chihuahua (but not that he had AIDS) and actually talks about a man Oscar went around with, whom he treated with "excessive affection."

The male responses to LP's broaching the subject of homosexuality in her interviews with them are telling for their homophobia as well as for their evocation of silence. The other brother-in-law says that one must not speak of such delicate things, especially when they concern the honor of a man, yet it is he who violates the code of silence by confirming the family secret of Oscar's homosexuality. The local historian privileges silence around Oscar's sexuality as the utmost gift of generosity one can give the dead. The film's critique of the sex/gender system goes directly to this homophobic affront that it is more troubling to say it than to know it, especially if it is a woman who says it, as LP does in *Diablo.*

Characteristically, the film extends this critique of gender and sexual enforcement through the subjective image of the water, where things slip away, such as LP's memories of home, the photo of Oscar's first wife after she dies, and Oscar's first tractor. The only thing that is represented visually as coming *out* of the water again is Oscar's tractor, but only after he has collected the insurance on it and bought another one. *Diablo* stages this by filming a toy tractor disappearing into and then reemerging from the water, in the playful aesthetic that connects Portillo to Oscar's magical Christmas persona. Just as she insists on dredging up the unsavory side of his rise to riches and power, she will also dredge up the rumors of his ho-

Scene from *The Devil Never Sleeps:* Portillo at the acupuncturist. Courtesy of Lourdes Portillo.

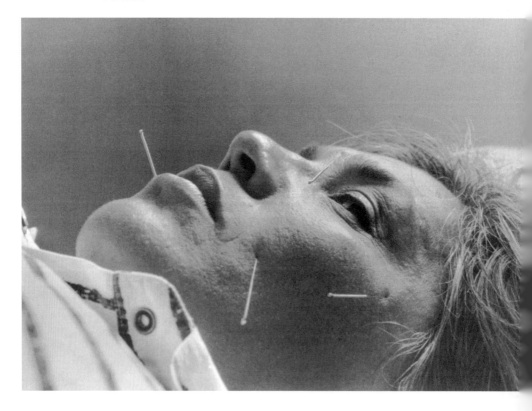

mosexuality to the light and, even more important, the lengths to which Oscar's family and friends will go to repress this intimation.

Will the Real Devil . . .

From beginning to end the film is saturated with a devilish atmosphere, a certain smell evocative of sulfur and mystery. By the end of the film it is difficult to separate cultural links between evil and queerness. The lyrics of the two rancheras send up romantic passion in terms of evil's seductive power ("carried away by evil's dark spell . . . work your evil on me, make me happy"). The ironic ending scene plays the ranchera over footage from the childhood Christmas movie, hinting that the devil of queer desire may exist among them.[12]

In *Dancing with the Devil* Limón intones the refrain that the "Devil takes many forms," and the same is true of *Diablo*. The film plays with (at least) two satanic traditions, one of them being the Mexican Catholic or Christian Devil, the personification of evil. Deciding who the Devil is in the film depends in part on one's definition of evil; either the rich or the U.S. late-capitalist exploitation of Mexico could fill the role. In terms of the characters in the film, the two who best fit the bill are Ofelia and LP.

Ofelia is consistently demonized by the others; she made life hell for Oscar; and she quotes the proverb that serves as the film's title. In contrast to LP's citational strategies that ironically frame what she presents to viewers, Ofelia invokes oral tradition in attempt to reinforce her position of innocence and others' unfair suspicions: "El diablo nunca duerme." Folk wisdom is summoned in an absurd context: Ofelia cites the proverb after she claims that Luz stole a tool from her (the camera underlines this absurdity in a close-up and slow pan of a wrench). From the family's perspective, in which class is the most significant social norm, Ofelia is the Devil in their midst, the working-class mistress that got lucky and became a wife, the person enveloped in sin and sexuality, driven by greed for riches and social status to invade their territory (it's one thing to tacitly accept the existence of mistresses . . .).

Most problematically, Ofelia is linked to the Devil through a representation of evil and witchcraft as blackness. Shortly after Oscar died, LP's mother, who lives in Los Angeles, told her how a car had crashed into a tree in front of their house; at first she thought she was seeing things: "On the ground, a black man with matted dreads . . . , a large black snake slithering around his neck and live little goldfish swarming all over his blood-spattered chest. At that instant, Ofelia flashed into my mind." The snake, as a sign of *brujería* (witchcraft), is the main source of her horror, doubled since black is the color of the Devil (referred to as *el tiznado*). The man himself is multiply marked through his color, his dreads, and the bizarre juxtaposition of his bloody body, the snake around his neck, and above all, the swarming goldfish. In this representation, a man who has the misfortune to be in an accident driving home with food for his pet snake gets hyperinvested with certain cultural contents by the bicultural experience of LP's parents. All the elements of the accident are reordered, underlined by LP's father reenacting the events narrated in voice-over by her mother, to produce meanings that depend on multiply marked blackness to associate evil witchcraft with Ofelia. Chencho's reenactment occurs within a highly concentrated blue circle surrounded by black. The intensity and relatively technical complexity of the depiction of the Los Angeles incident places this scene on a par in expressive power with other framings of Ofelia in the film, particularly the shark story.[13]

In casting herself as the Devil, LP draws on both the Christian Devil and the Mephistopheles of Faustian traditions: ". . . varied as the world. . . . [Mephisto's] nature is left unclear. . . . much too complex, diverse and ambiguous to be identified with the Christian Devil . . . as part of Mephisto's function is to deny any dichotomy in nature, moral or otherwise. . . . He is an invitation to the reader to face the multiplicity of reality. . . . Mephistopheles is partly a Christian devil, partly an ironic commentator on society."[14] The framing of the film's title shot and the title itself with its twitching red tail signal a devilish playfulness on the part of the filmmaker, but also her authority to manipulate. Although her social location as queer niece makes her vulnerable in her hometown, she is also powerful like the Devil. She comes to rile things up Mephisto-style, working family secrets to expose rigid dichotomies and inviting the viewer to join in her social commentary and her ironic take on the multiplicity of reality.

In one scene in particular, the Devil converges with the filmmaker's persona in her power to bedevil Luz into talking about sexuality, for Mexican women a taboo subject associated with sin and the temptations of the Christian Devil. In lieu of answering LP's prodding to reveal the *content* of what Ofelia told her about her honeymoon, Luz offers only judgments, drawing from the same vocabulary she used to decry those who spread rumors of Oscar's homosexuality ("barbaridad y medio" ["an outrage and a half"]). This time the niece/filmmaker succeeds: Luz finally reveals that Ofelia told Luz she saved her bloody panties to prove she was a virgin on her wedding night. Intercut with this interview segment are shots of a bridal shop mannequin revered and desired by passersby. The high value invested in virginity and incumbent attitudes about normative gender and sexuality (and the ways they can be performed) contrast with LP's ability to coax Luz into talking about "barbaridad y medio." When Luz tells LP not to put *that* ("qué feo" ["how gross"]) in her film (or at least not to say Luz told her), LP responds to these dissembling disclaimers with a laugh that is equal parts irony and triumph. In this moment of highly concentrated energy in the film, LP's relation to her family is one of domination: she has the power to compel these disclosures.[15] Luz complains that LP makes her say things, through her persistent (childlike?) questions, but also because of "tanta comitiva" ("so many people"), which reminds us that the crew would have been present in the room when Luz was "speaking the unspeakable." In this sense, not only the director but also the film apparatus itself are imbued with devilish properties.

In contrast to this nexus of filmmaker as powerful Devil, in other scenes LP confronts her "sinful" film practices with guilt, a legacy of her residual relationship with the Church. The film includes two interviews with a priest, one to ask whether it is considered a sin to commit suicide, to which he answers somewhat unconventionally, excusing the suicide as the act of someone who "never matured." In the second interview LP inquires whether it is permissible to tape phone calls without the interlocutor's knowledge when you suspect someone of murder. To this the priest delivers a rotund no, based on the respect owed the individual. He lambastes the media (and by extension the film) for encouraging the invasion of privacy. This answer is unsettling, because Portillo has taped several conversations with Ofelia without her knowledge. Due to legal and possibly religious issues and/or fear of reprisals, Portillo transcribed these conversations and had them read into the film by an actress (who appears in the credits). Drawing on her experience doing voice-overs in telenovelas (and the culture of melodramatic comportment), the actress reproduced each conversation exactly, down to the "slurps and saliva."[16] But the moral dilemma, exacerbated by her interview with the priest, that LP (as opposed to Portillo) grapples with is whether she should continue the illicit taping of Ofelia's phone conversations, which are represented in the film as if they are still being taped. In this way, the ethical choices involved in filmmaking are represented as part of the film apparatus's diabolical potential to manipulate and disclose.

After the priest's censure of the invasion of privacy, LP has an acupuncture treatment, mimicking and further identifying with Oscar as part of her investigation, since he became an acupuncturist late in life. The acupuncture scene is a relatively sterile space compared to the cozy lamp-filled rooms of Luz's interviews. It is framed by medical discourse in the form of the white-coated doctor-relative, recalling the authoritative discourse of the priest. It is also one of the rare times LP's body is represented outside the context of filmmaking. LP's voice-over narration commutes the association of her body stuck with needles from a relaxing healing practice to connotations of corporal punishment and guilt related to making the film: "Sin—bad news for a Catholic, even a lapsed one. . . . I'm torn between concern and manipulation. Is it a sin to look for the truth? But I've gone too far to stop."

A queer reading of this scene recalls Oscar's response to LP in the séance on why he killed himself: "complejos de culpabilidad" ("guilt complexes"). The queer connection between LP and Oscar is thus strengthened through religious discourses of sin and guilt, including, in her case, making films. In this sense, LP's pierced body resembles more than anything an effigy of San Sebastián, the martyred saint who is portrayed tied to a tree and pierced by many arrows. *Diablo* gives the association with the image, which is something of a gay icon, an ironic twist, portraying LP as suffering guilt and fearing sin, martyred for her cause, yet determined nonetheless to continue looking for the truth, even if the ends must justify the means. This dilemma, between her desire to keep going with the film and the "sinful" use of Ofelia's taped conversations, is represented in the film and constructed in the making of it, and returns us to questions of Portillo's social location and the processes involved in projects of framing queer subjectivity. In the film, LP makes it clear that with the stakes as high as they were, the ends did justify the means: a Machiavellian—or should we say, a Mephistophelean—positionality.

While the Christian Devil adds a powerful cultural referent to the film, as well as a certain flavor of sin, guilt, and suffering, it is Mephisto who best articulates an ironic awareness of multiple, nondichotomous realities with the ambivalent filmmaker, never inside or outside one place. The wakeful and ambiguous identification with the Devil is part of an aesthetic language in *Diablo,* desirous of breaking down binaries and advocating for a multiplicitous reading of social texts. Inhabiting the ambivalent position of devilish filmmaker-ethnographer makes possible (though certainly does not guarantee) an "oppositional break" (Limón) from dominant cultures invested in *un*ambiguous dichotomies. LP's consciousness of critical difference produces a playfully ironic and subjective critique, materialized in concrete choices of what to frame and how to frame it. These choices are announced at the beginning of the film, in LP's dreams of home: "faces of my family, old stories" (social and gender inequities), the land (and the impact of U.S. capitalist agribusiness), and mysteries about to be revealed (secrets, sexuality, silence).

Sylvie Thouard

Performances of *The Devil Never Sleeps/ El diablo nunca duerme*

Returning to the memories of her childhood with *The Devil Never Sleeps/ El diablo nunca duerme,* Lourdes Portillo locates herself at the unstable intersection of various roles: niece, coming back to Chihuahua after the mysterious death of a beloved uncle, Tío Oscar; detective, trying to find out if he committed suicide or if he was murdered, as some of her relatives suggested; and documentarist, an outsider living abroad yet filming her own family. As she travels across cultures and moves the documentary toward detective movies and telenovelas, she seems to propose a broad crossover to diverse audiences. Yet it is not a harmonious one: the film playfully undermines the various cultural frameworks it enters and does not seek to ease the tensions of its audiences in the theater, the classroom, and the living room. *The Devil Never Sleeps* calls to mind feminist performance art, one that confers an active role to the spaces in which it takes place and calls upon personal appropriations to trigger collective debates.

On Performance

The interactive theatricality associated with the notion of performance was long denied to the documentary by the disembodied voice of the television narrator and the realism of reportage techniques. Still, the use of the documentary as a tool to foster debates can be considered a performance, in the broader sense feminist activists gave to the term, because it plays with specific sites and audiences. Besides theaters and television, documentaries have often been shown in union halls, classrooms, and other public places where presenters and spectators interact and the film assumes various roles in a process that does not end with the projection. Difficult to define, the documentary can be seen as a genre that was open to various performances.

In the early nineties, the theatrical connotations of the term "performance" became used to highlight documentarists' tendency to film people able to present themselves in an eloquent yet unaffected manner, non-actors with an "expressive capacity" free of self-consciousness.[1] At that time, the "social performances" of everyday life were examined in relation to gender identities, class, and culture, and some of the discourses that Anglo-Saxon standards branded "theatrical" were at times connected to film practices in terms of performance (for example, the "hyperbolic discourses" favored by lesbian, gay, and queer documentaries,[2] or the "double consciousness"—in the words of W. E. B. Dubois—of black performers and spectators[3]). Remembering in particular "the Mexican tradition of performance"[4] and the fondness for melodramas that Portillo professes early in *The Devil Never Sleeps,* we could also generalize that Latina/o culture favors theatricality, at least by comparison with Anglo culture. Indeed, Portillo does not shy away from filming dramatic or self-conscious behaviors, including her own. Wearing mirrored sunglasses that reflect interviewees ostensibly as if they were a costume, or addressing spectators with her face pierced by needles—acupuncture was one of Oscar's many interests—she explores the paradoxes of theatricality in daily life and documentary. Departing from a standard medium shot, the documentary sometimes frames interviewees through high and wide angles, and their occasional affected or theatrical statements did not always end up on the cutting room floor. This endeavor links Portillo's work to filmmakers coming from diverse backgrounds, whose hybrid influences moved the U.S. documentary away from verité realism and reached other spaces and audiences.

The Devil Never Sleeps brings to the fore the polysemy of the notion of performance. And while specific uses of the term have come into play, I have approached it broadly as the relation between spectators and film in a particular time and place. A performance is, therefore, a complex interplay whose partners must be specified.

The ideal spectator sketched by theoreticians in the seventies has been much revised. In contemporary studies of spectatorship, diverse bodies have emerged, fleshed out with gender, race, class, sexual orientation, and endowed with memories that depart from official histories and with a psyche able to defy Freudian canons.[5] Insofar as these theoretical embodiments represent an act of political resistance to powers negating cultural minorities, a similar engagement can be felt in *The Devil Never Sleeps,* which addresses distinct and culturally specific audiences while simultaneously accounting for individual heterogeneous identities (a hybridity theorized in Chicana theory as "mestizaje"[6]). Yet a theory or a film can only problematize hypothetical spectators; the actual viewer remains elusive. Even ethnographic studies, which have been major challengers of the concept of the spectator as neutral receiver, are unavoidably mediated by a researcher who is no less neutral.

In the following, I will explore the problematic encounter between actual viewers and the hypothetical spectators addressed by film and exhibitors as a social event that must be historicized and specifically located. *The Devil Never Sleeps* is a partial choice, certainly, since its journey through film genres, Mexican politics, and domestic lives crosses paths with personal memories and brings institutional and experiential spaces into the

Portillo, Kibbe, and Paul Mailman (production assistant, right) talking to one of the interviewees in *The Devil Never Sleeps. Courtesy of Lourdes Portillo.

realm of the explicit. I combined fragments of film analysis with an empirical study of reviews, critical essays, and audience discussions recorded in various contexts. Audience discussions often revolve around stumbling points encountered in the many paths opened by *The Devil Never Sleeps,* and can only provide limited insight into the film itself and into the spectators' participation, since there are those who do not speak up, and since, above all, a viewer's experience cannot be reduced to her or his remarks. Despite—and because of—these contingencies, spectators' comments point the way to how a film is remembered, understood, and used. A comparative study allows for the questioning of some of the relations between film and viewers within various spaces.

Examining the role of spaces in various performances of *The Devil Never Sleeps,* I distinguished broadly the actual spaces of exhibition, the virtual spaces called upon by cultural frameworks and the play with genres, and the places presented on-screen that are both actual (the city of Chihuahua, the land of Sonora, private homes) and imagined (the filmmaker's memories, the various stories she is told, and the ones that we, the viewers, confabulate with the film). These spaces are not neatly delineated, as spectators interweave and locate themselves in between their various dimensions, actively contributing to generate the unique space of a film performance. Insofar as a performance is a social event, audience discussions provide indications about the dialogical dimension of viewing films. Thus, I also looked at the relationships between spectators coming from different backgrounds into the cultural frameworks delineated by exhibitors. Just as the individual and the social self cannot be simply opposed, it could be argued that collective spaces and audiences are not forgotten in the privacy of a home.

Constructing Spectators, Feeling Addressed, and Talking Back

Since late 1994 *The Devil Never Sleeps* has been presented at film festivals, independent venues, museums, and universities,[7] which often explore particular themes, in this case Latino/a culture, the documentary,[8] women and film.[9] It was funded by the Independent Television Service, whose mandate is to address the "underserved audiences" of U.S. public television. A shorter version was eventually broadcast by PBS, in the fall of 1997. The two versions are distributed by Xochitl Films and Women Make Movies.[10]

Taking into account exhibitors' tendency to delineate one audience within cultural parameters, I will first consider the spaces of exhibition which locate the film in Latina/o culture. Even though Portillo's roles span the vast mediatic landscape in which films circulate, she definitely locates herself within the Latino/a community, creating an interplay between film and viewers in terms of shared culture and experiences.

By all accounts *The Devil Never Sleeps* was well received in Latina/o spaces of exhibition: it was greeted with standing ovations in New Mexico[11] and chosen Best Documentary at the San Juan and San Antonio film festivals. A poster in Spanish could be interpreted as an invitation to enter an intersubjective relation to the film and other viewers:

> Los amores, desamores y odios de una familia mexicana torturada por el misterio detrás de la muerte de uno de sus miembros. Poética, trágica, humorística y mítica: una película que trasciende fronteras culturales y personales. [The loves, aversions, and hatreds of a Mexican family tormented by the mystery surrounding the death of one of its members. Poetic, tragic, humorous, and mythic: a film that transcends cultural and personal frontiers.]

It offers to explore the intricate web of ties and tensions in a family as do melodramas and novelas, suggesting that if cultural frontiers are to be crossed it will be while traveling through Mexico. The film itself explicitly proposes a journey in its beginning: it locates Chihuahua on a map (crossing the U.S. border, it highlights roads in the northern part of Mexico) and enters the country via a cheerful musical sequence in which the camera dances around a flag. Its playfulness acts out the joyful anticipation of a traveler and the irony of a migrant aware of the stereotypical dimensions of her homeland. To put it abstractly and again using W. E. B. Dubois' words, the montage conveys a double-consciousness. A familiarity with cultural borders pervades the sequence; as a tangible frontier is crossed, a playful look at the national imagery accompanies the emotions of the return. This seems to designate Chicana/o viewers as those who would best relate to the filmmaker's journey, and it raises questions of cultural specificity within a Latino/a context. This early sequence (as well as the bilingual title) favors Chicana/o audiences. Yet most of the film takes place in Mexico: viewers' familiarity with landscapes, local history and social actors cannot be easily bypassed, particularly when documentary techniques stress the actuality of locations and people.

I briefly compared Chicana/o and Mexican audience responses within spaces whose geographical location and framework of exhibition gather Latina/o communities (using essays written by students in Chicano Studies and Portillo's recollections of screenings in Mexico and on its borders). While I do not have the insight into Latino/a culture nor the documentation to examine these performances in depth, they constitute an indispensable point of comparison to the debates recorded in spaces drawing together mixed audiences (such as the Brooklyn Museum series "Self Discoveries: A Festival of Latin American Cinema").[12] I also considered the spectators that different institutions bring together and construct. Festivals, museums, universities, and public television are all noncommercial spaces often labeled "educational"; indeed, they draw mostly middle-class, college-educated spectators who continue to find pleasure in learning.[13] However, the geographical location of a screening and its promotion at a local level can modify the statistical homogeneity of the audience. This unquantified but specific dynamic was anticipated, since *The Devil Never Sleeps* mixes documentary with entertainment genres. Also, there were some theatrical showings in addition to the film's mostly educational distribution. How did Latina/o viewers locate themselves within a culture that is both a lived experience and the object of a learning endeavor? How did they relate, if at all, to the socially coded notion of "popular audience"? I also drew straightforward behavioral distinctions between viewers watching television at home, the convivial participants in public debates, and those writing an essay.

Essays, based on a sustained interplay with the film, led to a deeper involvement with its maker. Students in Chicano Studies empathized with Portillo's critical look at Mexican culture, all the more since many had themselves accomplished or imagined a similar journey. They outlined the landmarks emerging from Portillo's trip, with Mexican culture a recurrent focus in most papers: "She, more importantly, educates her audience on Mexican culture, the institution of family and the politics of a corrupt government . . . music, religion, and novelas."[14] While pointing out the educational value of *The Devil Never Sleeps,* their writings offer insight into personal memories that might not be brought up in public discussions—for example, the mysterious death of a relative or family gossip about a rejected in-law (like Ofelia, Oscar's second wife ostracized by Portillo's family). Interestingly, when Chicana/o students commented on the shot featuring the Mexican flag, they downplayed the significance of the national icon. One essay highlights the composition and the sky in the background: "There are several 'sky' shots, in one case behind an upside-down Mexican flag."[15] In another essay, "the low-angle shot of the symbol of Mexico" is related to the low-angle shot of a man in a cemetery and to "a stone angel with womanly characteristics behind yet above him"; the flag eventually serves to comment upon "the duality between man and woman."[16] Many students saw in the film's imagery a complex network of symbols: the cross as both a reminder of the importance of religion, and an emblem of Oscar's second marriage, of which he said, "This is my cross. I have to carry it" ("Es mi cruz, tengo que cargarla"); and water as an image of womanhood and of Chicana/o culture, "a separate entity, a unique culture with perplexities of its own."[17] Drawing from their history, they focused at times on specific points such as "the impact that agriculture had on Chicano laborers"; this was suggested by the evocation of Tío Oscar's beginnings in agriculture and the close-up of a tomato sprinkled by pesticides—a shot that was read less specifically by other audiences.[18] Personal and collective memories served as points of departure for occasional discussions primarily of novelas and secondarily of documentary techniques. When Chicana/o students suggested that Portillo might "educate" viewers about Mexican culture, they clearly included themselves and seemed comfortable mingling distant observations with personal appropriations. Adopting Portillo's position of outsider/insider to Mexican culture, they confabulated freely with the film and preferred reassembling some of its images to following the investigative thread of Oscar's death (*The Devil Never Sleeps* was compared to a peeled onion that does not reveal a core[19]). As they chose to comment upon layers of the film that triggered their memories and interest, images were at once references and textual devices that engaged their fantasies. Chicana/o students strongly identified with Portillo as Chicana and as filmmaker, and indeed contradictory viewing positions were mediated by her conflicting screen roles. Embodying some of the dilemmas of their lives, she allowed them the pleasures of fantasy (not unlike popular fictions that call upon collective fantasies—which is not to say that students lost sight of the filmed subjects' realities). Rather, blurring the line between roles and real people, filmic and self-representation, the film was perceived as made by, about, and for "a Chicano audience who can empathize and sympathize with these Chicano conflicting circumstances."[20] This particular interplay, in which film, viewers, and the context of the screening played an active role, delineated the intersubjective space of the Chicana/o community. Clearly, there were distinct subjectivities within this space that other viewing contexts might have made more salient (I read, for example, several feminist confabulations, such as those linking ocean and womanhood or the Mexican flag and gender relations).[21] What is striking here, when compared as a whole with other performances, is the intimate and imaginary dimension of these dialogues with a Chicana filmmaker.

The primacy of a Chicana/o viewpoint could also be heard in public discussions, although voiced quite differently. Debates often revolved around problems spectators found in the film, such as the filmmaker's choice of portraying a middle-class family. Lourdes Portillo remarked: "People expect the film to be from the stereotypical class they believe Chicanos to be from, or any Latino. And when they see this is a middle class Mexican family, they are taken aback." When asked to whom she was referring, Portillo replied, "Some of the Chicano kids that I showed it to," and she went on to the question of self-stereotypes.[22] Thus *The Devil Never Sleeps* unveils class divisions as well as the appropriation of cultural images, and seemingly is eager to take the viewer on a journey from the idealized memories of Portillo's childhood to the realities of the present. This includes looking at and being looked at through the prism of another class, gender, or culture. Indeed, we see middle-class family members looking at the lower class (embodied by Ofelia, Oscar's second wife suspected of crime by some), women looking at men and at other women (Oscar's two wives providing two contrasting figures), men looking at women and at men (many interviewees comment on Oscar's role as a father, husband, and businessman), children looking at adults (as when Oscar's daughter and the filmmaker remember their childhood). Behind the respectable facade the family offers to a provincial town, we hear spiteful gossips around Oscar's grave; as the archetype of the closely knit Mexican family crumbles, its members are being anchored in the reality of their rural land and the wealth that some accumulated in dealing with the United States. Ultimately Oscar's life could be read as the biography of an outsider, from his youth when he used perfumes to conceal the odor of manure to his later life when he was a millionaire at odds with his family roles. From the play with Mexican archetypes and telenovelas, as well as the notion of self-stereotypes brought up by the filmmaker's roles and some of the interviewees acting out their emotions with the self-consciousness of melodrama, we see the "outsider within." And as Lourdes Portillo's mirrored sunglasses at times suggest, we also see ourselves looking at them, with an empathy that almost comes as a surprise given the criticism she offers. Outsiders are within the performing space because spectators bring to the screening the contingent experiences of their lives and because the film does not attempt to reconcile all the spaces, real and imagined, of Latina/o culture. Indeed, a spectator objected to Oscar's brother stating that many Mexicans are treacherous, commenting that "it sounds like an Anglo statement"; Portillo replied that the fact that "not only Americans but also Mexicans" make such a statement was a good reason to include it in the film.[23] Her irreverent toying with stereotypes was controversial in public debates where reactions are quick (by contrast, in his essay one student concluded that she went "beyond cultural archetypes"[24]). It takes time to process the density and rough edges of *The Devil Never Sleeps,* but this also suggests that Chicana/o viewers' interplay with the film exceeded the simple equation of shared experiences.

In the public screenings that Portillo attended in Mexico, spectators primarily discussed what was for them the most provocative aspect of the film: the revelation of disfunctionality in the family and its most hidden secrets, in particular Oscar's possible homosexuality (AIDS is mentioned as a possible cause of his death). Following a feminist tradition and a practice found today in many popular talk shows, Portillo collapses the distinction between Oscar's public and private lives. As we learn of his career, from agriculture to business and politics, we also hear of his relation to his children and of his marital and sexual life. With a provocative audacity, his niece-filmmaker reveals the intimacies that Oscar had hidden all his life from those close to him, who did not, however, fail to gossip about them: injections of cattle embryos to preserve his youth, which might have caused his cancer; the artificial insemination of Ofelia; their separate bedrooms; her telling of stained panties after their honeymoon; his extramarital affairs and possible homosexuality.

Everywhere, not just in Mexico, the filmmaker was asked, "Has your family seen the film yet?"—a question regularly accompanied by a collective laugh, as if people were willing to share the weight of the transgressive portrait they had watched and often enjoyed.[25] Insofar as question and answer sessions constitute a distancing from the viewing experience, the spectators used Portillo's presence to disengage themselves from the insights they were given into her family, and they did so in many different locations and cultural frameworks. She remarked, however, that Mexican spectators objected mostly to the suggestion of Oscar's homosexuality, as opposed to other aspects of his life or even the portrayal of private feuds within the family (which could be attributed in part to their familiarity with telenovelas; indeed, the ongoing "telenovelization" of North American news programs might have contributed to the mixed reactions the film received in the United States[26]). The same was true of Portillo's own parents, who "loved to watch the family members and loved the story" and often played *El diablo nunca duerme* on their VCR, but who objected to the speculation that Oscar was gay when "nothing else scandalized them."[27] After the television broadcast, Portillo received phone calls from Mexicans who were able to see the program on their side of the border. The revealing aspects of a film that "said it all" had disturbed quite a few of these callers, some of whom felt "almost appalled"—

in particular by Oscar's "biggest sin"—while others genuinely enjoyed a film that they found "very Mexican."[28] Set in a family context, the revelation of family secrets in *El diablo nunca duerme,* in particular the possible homosexuality of its patriarch, constituted an oblique yet provocative form of address to Mexican audiences.[29] Conversely, viewers addressed the film with their own interests and concerns (the homophobia of Mexican society took precedence, for example, over the relationships between Oscar and his children).[30] The specific context of exhibition (public place or domestic setting) played a secondary role in these dialogues, which were shaped by the viewers' different levels of adhesion to societal values and their personal affinities with the filmmaker's discourse. However Mexico—i.e., the geographical location in which *El diablo nunca duerme* was seen—brought up questions of national identity; everyone agreed that the film was "about" Mexico, but uncertainties clouded its performance "for and by" Mexicans.

I would like to suggest that the film drew its disturbing dimension from being anchored in the world of its viewers. Similar responses occurred in a variety of contexts (public and private) and with two distinct versions of the film. Although the TV version does not contain all of the film's "shocking" anecdotes, local legends, and references to Sonora, it retains the film's experiential fabric: as in the long version, its editing interweaves a whimsical imagery, and most of the interviews remain. It seems to matter, indeed, that actual spaces and Mexicans can be seen and heard in the film, and for all of *El diablo nunca duerme*'s constructed aspects, they do not infringe on the performance of the filmed subjects. To the extent that she is an immigrant, Portillo is an outsider to Mexico, and she further distances herself from her audience by exposing those family affairs which are normally discussed only in whispers or not at all. However, she is also a family member, an insider who shares with her Mexican spectators subjective affinities and a knowledge of their country; they, in turn, enjoyed drawing parallels between Oscar's life and death, national politics, and their everyday lives.[31] Portillo's kinship with her interviewees, together with her provocative questions and critique, outlined a space that most Mexican spectators agreed to call "home." This might explain why they overlooked an "educational" approach to Latino/a culture and preferred discussing some of the problems and taboos encumbering their lives, although these can also be found in other cultures.

The experiential dimension of viewing images of actual people and places seemed to matter as much as narrative or generic features (indeed, notions of closure, film genres, or "popular audience" were seldom dis-

Portillo speaking to the detective in charge of investigating Tío Oscar's death, while Kibbe is filming. Courtesy of Lourdes Portillo.

cussed, which could be attributed to the film's kinship with telenovelas as well as to people, situations, and themes that touched and concerned viewers more than metatheory). The warm reception that most Latina/o audiences gave to *El diablo nunca duerme* was indicative of the viewers' emotional involvement with the film and other spectators. That is not to say that Latino/a audiences responded homogeneously, or that critical distance and diverse interpretations were absent from these perform-ances. It is one thing to see images as denotative — evidence of shared ex-periences that allowed Latina/o spectators to engage a dialogue with the filmed subjects and the filmmaker as members of their community. Yet within this space, various degrees of identification with the filmmaker, as well as diverse interpretations of the many stories and discursive layers proposed by the film, shaped these dialogues. Even though Latinos/as were clearly its first intended audience (and within this broad community Chicanas/os and Mexicans were addressed specifically at various levels), *El diablo nunca duerme* destabilizes the very audiences that it "authenti-cates."[32] It suggests fissures along various lines rather than drawing a neat separation between Latinas/os and others. Ultimately, in a particular in-terplay with the film and its site of exhibition, the spectators themselves chose to make the film performance a dialogue amid Latinos/as.

Their partial and perhaps enjoyable forgetfulness of Anglo culture was fragile and linked to actual viewing spaces. In the United States some rejoiced to "hear the Spanish on PBS"; [33] others wondered how this film, which "does not have the *Leave It to Beaver* flavor or Anglo favor, was received in Mexico or more generally in the Latina/o community compared to the Anglo community." [34]

Appropriations and Disagreements—Dialogues across the Border

What happened, then, when mixed audiences met in a space that invited them to look at Latino/a culture? I compared several audience discussions that took place in various contexts in San Francisco and New York. [35]

For one thing, Anglo spectators' reactions ranged from the comfort of accepting their positions as tourists or ethnographers, to unease:

> I don't know much about Mexico. But what I guess my misconception is, is that everything down there is corrupt, and that they all have big families and get together. . . . I see my misconception brought to light. [36]

Latinas/os in the audience who generally agreed with the documentary aspect of the film ("It's a pretty good portrait of a family down there") were then in the odd position of invalidating the stereotypes. They entered a self-reflexive space about their relationships to telenovelas ("I don't know if we are imitating the telenovela or if the telenovela is imitating our life") and Latinos/as' "treacherous" use of lies (the film ends with the bolero line "Lie to me forever, work your evil on me, make me happy"), pointing out that some things were not discussed openly, such as homosexuality and not telling to Oscar's children that they were adopted.

I will take a chronological sequence of excerpts as an example of the relation between Latina/o and Anglo spectators. As it happened throughout the evening, the discussion drifted in and out of the cultural framework outlined by the exhibitor (Latin Americanist Electa Arenal moderated this debate in New York City):

> **Woman 1:** I might be wrong but, about the need of people trying to find the answer, the last song was "Lie to Me." I cannot deal with the truth, so lie to me.
> **Woman 2:** But I don't want to be lied to.
> **Woman 1:** You don't have to agree or not. Because it is a cultural thing. . . . Many things are never said. Like this girl [Oscar and first wife's adopted daughter] who questioned her mother on her

deathbed: "Are you my mother?" [The mother] could not say. "I
love you as my daughter, like a mother. But I don't want you to
say that I am not your mother, because I am your mother." It's a
different cultural thing, in my mind.

Man 1: She uses mirrors a lot. And sometimes we see reflections. I
see that as a distancing from that Mexican tradition. Also, the way
that she uses the soap operas. I see this film as a soap opera. I see
the film as a mockery of that life down there in Mexico. And I
can't in the world see why she makes the film. Why mock something? . . . it does not teach us. . . .

Electa Arenal: Some of the greatest baroque art deals precisely with
the question of mirroring. Almost any twentieth-century artist
in Mexico has used that, not in this way, but in some way. You can
relate it to Frida Kahlo, you can relate it to many great artists,
even now. Some use irony, critique, saying that in some way you
can create a piece of art even showing ugly aspects of things. In
the film you get something about people of a certain social class.
I think that's very important. . . . And I must say there are so
many things that ring true in this question of not being able to say
what the truth is. Maybe there is a different way among wasps.
Every culture has its ways of not being able to face the truth.

Woman 3: It's clear to me it's lies—some quote-unquote lies. It's a
certain code for how you deal with harsh reality. And at the same
time everybody has a different story and is transmitting different
codes of what it's all about. And that, I found really interesting.
About the mirrors: I did not know that there was such a long tradition, but the obvious part of it is that everything is just a reflection of people's views. Also, the use of the sunglasses to me says
that it is not only a reflection of the person who is saying what he
or she is saying, but it is a reflection of the person who listens to
what this person is saying. So that we become like the other mirror within the mirror.[37]

To be sure, the presenter and the Mexican spectators participating
in the debate highlighted aspects of the film that would otherwise have
gone unnoticed. Cast in the role of guide, they played their role willingly.
Scenes that played within the fabric of a preexisting awareness and were
only occasionally discussed amid Latino/a communities—the "corrupción en la policía," the ecological problems in Sonora, or the political situation (a Mexican spectator offered a double reading of Oscar's story,

paralleling it to the life of Salinas)—were commented upon for Anglo spectators, who then took the position of curious observers praising at times the "ethnographic" quality of the film.

For all their interest and curiosity in learning more about Mexico, most spectators refused to see *The Devil Never Sleeps* as just for Latinas/os. Although Latinos/as perceived themselves as the film's intended audience, Anglo viewers felt addressed as well. They appropriated the film by making universalist claims or delving into metatheory (looking at Latinas/os as represented in the film while bypassing the possibility of their particular responses to the film), or else choosing one theme. Woman 3 (quoted above), for example, expressed much understanding and appreciation of the baroque filmic approach, although by her own account she was unfamiliar with Mexican culture. Similarly, the many Anglo viewers who used the filmmaker as a subjective point of entry into the film often underplayed the fact that she is a Chicana in spite of the cultural framework proposed by the exhibitors. A few explanations can be offered. The narration was delivered in English. Chicana/o films are not well known as an entity. To the extent that she is an immigrant, Portillo is an outsider, which allowed for the film to be seen sometimes as "ethnographic" and for non-Mexican viewers to relate to her on a subjective level. Many Anglos considered the film "legible for everybody, not specifically for a Mexican audience." They found the critique of the family universal, and interpreted the close-up of the sprinkled tomato as a general concern for the use of pesticides, as opposed to the specific plight of Chicana/o laborers.[38]

Viewers' appropriations of Mexican imagery in *The Devil Never Sleeps* call to mind a distinction that characterizes documentary and fiction films by the degree of specificity of their references: documentaries invite one to see a reference "determinate, particular, and unique," while a fiction film "initially is merely indeterminate and nonspecific," leaving it up to the viewer to discover what the film is about.[39] *The Devil Never Sleeps* makes this distinction problematic by encouraging us to assign simultaneously various degrees of specificity and indeterminacy to its references. We are invited here to look at this question in terms of personal experience, confabulations, and address. The film enters at times a playful dialogue with its viewers by visually making general statements. The use of pesticides in the land of Sonora, for example, constitutes a specific reference. The close-up of a tomato is just that: a big red fruit with a blue sky for background. Decontextualized from the fields where it grows and disproportionately out of scale with other shots, it becomes an abstract generalization that explicitly allows viewers to reinvest it with their own concerns and memories. Similarly, the policeman in Chihuahua searching his office hopelessly for Oscar's file constitutes a specific reference, while the close-up of a newspaper headline about police corruption is a generalization; the spectator can expand it to the police of Chihuahua, of Mexico, or of other countries. In the United States, the exhibition frameworks which grounded the film in a foreign culture and the Latina/o spectators participating in the discussion reinforced the overlapping and conflicting drives non-Latino viewers experienced in assigning specific and indefinite references; they often entered the film at a personal level or via generalizations, when they had come to look at Latina/o culture in the first place.

> "Why do you make a film with so many unanswered questions? Is it peculiarly Mexican?"[40]

> "This has nothing to do with Mexican culture. This is twentieth-century postmodern theory."[41]

Just as spectators who enjoyed the film sought to appropriate it in different ways, those who rejected it advanced various motives. Although most spectators would not deny *The Devil Never Sleeps* its Mexican features, they were positioned and positioned themselves as either "Latino/a" or "non-Latino/a," a simplistic construct that was both contested and used. Many of those who strongly objected to the film's journey through Mexico and found it too stereotypical or not Mexican enough were equally concerned by the absence of closure to the investigation of Oscar's death. They often interpreted—and at times rejected—the lack of resolution to the murder mystery as a provocative form of address. Here mixed audiences' discussions must be contrasted with domestic viewings. A number of Anglo spectators, as well as newspaper reviews written in the United States, focused on the broken murder mystery narrative (for example, the critique in the *New York Times* employed the standards of film noir to conclude that *The Devil Never Sleeps* "creates more mysteries than it solves").[42] Most Latina/o spectators did not have problems with the lack of narrative closure, and the comments they made were of unique importance: after these discussions, some people indicated that second thoughts had caused them to modify their interpretation of the film. Given spectators' tendency to first use the cultural frameworks they are familiar with—and the film's irreverent ways to destabilize them—the encounter between Latino/a and Anglo viewers could be seen as one of the intended performances of *The Devil Never Sleeps/El diablo nunca duerme*. In the tradition of documentaries, the film was used as a tool for public debates. And in the public spheres temporally formed around the film, spectators voiced their arguments by combining experience and interpretation.

> **Man 1:** I think that the interpretation that you make out of the movie is also a point of reference in the background that you are coming from. Maybe it's Spanish culture. I also happen to be an Argentinian, and I can relate to some of the things that are part of the culture in South America. It could be that certain things irritate your patience; in many ways they outline things that are valid in those cultures.

> **Woman 1:** I had a long experience in Mexico because one of my daughters lived there fifteen years. So I observed the whole Salinas situation. I feel that it is a marvelous portrait of a certain level of society. We do not see the real poverty in Mexico, we do not see the revolution or any of that what's going on. But we see a social class and we see the power of money—we see the innuendos, the lies, the silences, the cover-ups, the charms. And I feel that it is an ethical statement, I am sorry. The last statement represents what she is getting at: decisions that Oscar made were part of the fabric. And I feel that this is true beyond Mexico, in life.

> **Man 2:** Perhaps the film does get to the bottom of many more questions, the first one being how her uncle died. It is fascinating to see how all these revelations spring up during the course of the film, about the family, the state of the culture, how intricately it all works. And how difficult it is just to answer a single question, because it does give birth to other questions which perhaps supersede the initial one.

> **Electa Arenal:** That's the last line. She says she is left with mysterious and tantalizing questions.

Indeed, the film's own resistance to being framed invites viewers to wander onto many roads besides the one exploring Latina/o culture. To some spectators, the uses of popular genres in *The Devil Never Sleeps,* as well as its lack of closure, implicitly represent a postmodern aesthetic. When associated with the dissolution of a sense of history and human agency, it strongly contrasts with the documentary tradition. The spectator who saw postmodern theory in the film also made this comment:

> There is an ethical hole in the film, an absence at the center of the film. I think it's quite strong. Actually it makes me very angry this film. It never seeks to find the truth . . . because to deal with it di-

rectly would undercut the primary premise of the film, which is the impossibility of creating history.[43]

It would be well beyond the scope of this study to discuss at length the controversies surrounding the notion of postmodernism.[44] However, I would argue, as did many viewers, that *The Devil Never Sleeps* does not renounce a sense of historical agency.

Cultures of Resistance

Viewers entered those imaginary and dialogical spaces sketched by personal and political affinities for—or divergences from—the filmmaker. I will briefly outline the journey of *The Devil Never Sleeps* through cultures of resistance (feminist, Chicana/o, queer), as well as its subversion of the virtual spaces offered by film and TV genres. For all their abstraction, these spaces cannot be simply opposed to concrete spaces. Notions of genres, and even of cultures of resistance (that have a long tradition of using documentaries), overlap with notions of audiences and exhibition, and cannot be dissociated from their social dimension, nor from the filmmaker and the viewers' previous experiences and memories. Furthermore, these abstract spaces are alluded to either directly or obliquely in the film and thus given a concrete dimension. For example, historical memories and politics are featured in an image of Pancho Villa and a TV clip of Colosio's assassination. Also, it is hard for feminists and Chicanas/os alike not to hear machismo and the discourses of the Mexican patriarchy in the observation of Oscar's brother-in-law that "if it is delicate to talk about the honor of a woman, it is still more delicate to talk about the honor of a man."[45] And, of course, there are many visual references, often staged and theatrical, to telenovelas, melodramas, documentaries, and detective movies. *The Devil Never Sleeps* explicitly reminds us that each performance combines concrete and abstract spaces, experience and interpretation, in ways that cannot be neatly delineated—all the more because each performance is geographically and historically grounded in the world of the viewers.

The aesthetic of subversion and interaction that characterized the feminist performances of the seventies, particularly its relational aspects, can be found at many levels, from the blurring of the distinction between individual and social actors, as well as between filmed subjects and viewers, to the play with and against its framework of exhibition and to a genuine engagement in political struggles.

At festivals specifically showing works by women, we know the film has been well received, but audience comments have not been recorded.

Viewers' reactions might have been complex as well. In Chihuahua a young student objected to the portrayal of Ofelia on gender grounds, as it relies on negative images of women. At the Sundance Film Festival, an older woman suggested that she embodied the archetype of the wicked stepmother. I found that most spectators ended up empathizing with Ofelia, at least with the filmed subject, if not with her role in the family or the film. The family gossip brought to the screen particularly revealed many intimate details of her life, and some interviewees even suggested that she might be responsible for Oscar's death (I think that this concern also highlighted the spectators' uneasy voyeurism, and their possible transgressive identification with Ofelia).[46] In proposing my own reading of *The Devil Never Sleeps* I would suggest that it fosters a feminist approach, playing with the notion of gender as cultural and social construct.

The film's central character is a man who unknowingly shares with women the burdens (and joys) of role-playing in his family and society. There is Oscar who, lacking in confidence, resorts to plastic surgery. Then there is the businessman Oscar, game for anything profitable from exporting vegetables, to construction, minting and selling numismatic coins. There is also Oscar the local politician. And Oscar the adoptive father, the homosexual, and the husband. Like many women who cannot easily juggle their inner desires and the many roles they are assigned in family and society, Oscar is seemingly unable to assume all of his roles. Victim-of-the-murder Oscar would have the innocence of he who does not have to choose. But as his niece explores his life, she adds the question of choice of existence, which he could not have made in complete innocence. "The only thing I'm sure is that by his own choices he contributed to his destiny." The filmmaker's voice-over narration, echoing the statement of a male interviewee, further departs from the "feminine" role of the unconditionally admiring niece. In the film, unlike a hostess striving to please us in her home or a tour guide devoted to the comfort of visitors, Portillo is not afraid to unsettle her viewers. And like many of her interviewees, she locates herself at the fragile juncture of intimate discourses and social role-playing. The connections are numerous between the personal and the political, sustained by a critique and a desire for change that are reminiscent of feminist activism, albeit never explicitly formulated.

Questions of gender and genres arose in unexpected ways, as I came to realize that the stronger objections to the film were voiced in the context of documentary festivals and came from men, while a great number of women expressed an affinity for Portillo's approach. If one chooses to look at the relation to genres through the spectators' practices and memories, given the context in which these discussions took place (documentary festivals in New York and France), one finds it is unlikely that these women regularly watched daytime soap operas, and even less likely telenovelas from Latin America. Rather, they might have genuinely enjoyed seeing a woman director embodying a departure from the long-standing tradition of male detectives or documentarists.[47] Conversely, some men rejected Portillo's persona and roles, such as a New Yorker who objected to "the woman herself," to "how she manage[d] to carry herself in the absence of the so-called hard facts," and to "the tomato, and the kind of cute angles and the strange sort of mini strategies." A female spectator responded:

> How are you going to deal with the fact that you are an event? That you are entering a culture, that is supposedly yours, but is not yours because you don't live there. It's your family: how do you *not* become an ethnographer? How do you deal with the fact you are documenting things? Are you really a documentarian, are you really a filmmaker, where is your presence there? All those are strategies. To me they were really satisfying.[48]

A similar exchange took place in France in a milieu that has kept the documentary on a pedestal: a male spectator was "almost disgusted by an accumulation of gossip when the film does not present itself as a work made solely about rumor" and was frustrated to find *The Devil Never Sleeps* not entirely constructed as a fiction, a metaphor, or else a home movie.[49] There again women were "not disturbed at all" by the film's mingling of gossip, small talk, local legends, dreams, and memories, with the factual explanatory systems traditionally proposed by documentaries or detective movies. Generally comfortable watching Portillo's juggling of various roles, women seemed to switch easily between the viewing positions that diverse genres propose, from detached observer to voyeur of private dramas to participant in a dialogue that encompasses politics and family life. *The Devil Never Sleeps* brought to the fore gender divisions even within the progressive audiences that documentary festivals are likely to gather. Indeed, Portillo's approach can be related to a feminist aesthetic that resists tidy definitions, the primacy of detached viewing positions, and the elitism of high culture.

It is tempting to essentialize the female (or male) psyche when the strongest disagreements with the film were voiced by men seeking to

clearly delineate cultural and social spaces as the notion of genre promises, to close the narrative line of the murder mystery, and to assume a
stable viewing position. But things being what they are when the Devil
does not sleep, most Latinos/as did not object to the lack of narrative closure or to the gossip that troubled other spectators, and they spoke of telenovelas as a Mexican reality rather than as a genre favored by a gender
or a class.

At this point I would like to stress that a number of spectators of both
sexes allied themselves with the film's rejection of fixed identities and singular viewing position, a fluidity that was contested by others and can be
related to recent queer theory. Furthermore, the film's revelations of
family secrets, together with the question of choice of existence raised by
Oscar's life, can be linked to the political choice of coming out during the
AIDS crisis. From an activist's standpoint, the questions the film raised
among Latina/o viewers constitute a successful performance. For those
familiar with Portillo's previous work this will not come as a surprise.
Speaking of La Ofrenda: The Days of the Dead, a film Portillo directed in
1988, Rosa Linda Fregoso notes that it has been used to raise awareness
about AIDS, a pressing social issue in countries "where Catholicism does
not sanction public discussion of sexuality, [and] talking about 'sex'
among U.S. Latinos is particularly difficult," which might explain Portillo's oblique mode of representation.[50] Fregoso also remarks that the
question of address was as "paramount to the cultural politics of Chicano
filmmaking once upon a time" as it was for feminist filmmakers.[51] The political legacy of Latin American cinema, in particular the one of guerrilla
filmmaking that inspired a generation of Chicana/o filmmakers,[52] can also
be felt in The Devil Never Sleeps. Although its strategies are indeed often
oblique, they seek to create strong responses in particular locations and
take into account the specificity of its historical context. Interestingly an
Argentinean student established a political connection between Portillo's
work and contemporary history, stressing the filmmaker's position "in between" cultures:

> El continente latinoamericano vive un período de agitación social y
> cultural que influye marcadamente en la expresión de la cultura au-
> diovisual. El cine nacional, realista y crítico nutre teórica e ideológi-
> camente al cine independiente. Lourdes Portillo quiere y cree ser
> parte del cine latinoamericano, aunque se le plantean inseguridades
> en cuanto a ser discriminada por estar viviendo actualmente en Los
> Estados Unidos. [The Latin American continent is living through a

Kibbe and Mailman filming the "disappearing truck" scene in *The Devil Never Sleeps*. Courtesy of Lourdes Portillo.

Portillo, Kibbe, and Mailman preparing the next scene. Courtesy of Lourdes Portillo.

period of social and cultural unrest that markedly influences expressions in audiovisual culture. The national, realistic, and critical cinema fosters independent cinema both theoretically and ideologically. Lourdes Portillo wants to be, and believes she is, part of Latin American cinema, although this is uncertain, as she is discriminated against for presently living in the United States.][53]

Ultimately *The Devil Never Sleeps*—and its viewers—cannot be reduced to one reading; the hybridity of experiences presented by the filmmaker does not allow us to label a preferred audience as "feminist", "queer," or

"Chicana/o." Rather, these are specific cultures of resistance from which Portillo seems to draw the joyful defiance of a vast system of values. Revisiting her family as the site of subject formation, she approaches identity as a becoming within social constructions and the current politics of globalization (Oscar's life and the filmmaker's journey can be seen as embodying this process).

The film opens a historical space in which viewers might connect at an intersubjective level that can be broadly interpreted as a form of political dissent from an oppression disseminated by powers that are sometimes hard to locate. This abstract—although subjective—response might constitute a link between spectators from different backgrounds, perceptible in the images some offered of the film as a whole: the Argentinean student quoted above talked of a "callejón sin salida" (dead-end street); a French woman saw the story of a "Mexican bourgeois family divided by a beauty queen (Ofelia) and a man living a life at odds with the social fabric in which he was born"; in New York someone suggested a visually and metaphorically retroactive reading of the last shot from a home movie, a tipped-over toy car that Oscar played with: "About the end of the movie, the car that tipped over: it is sort of happening all the way through." These comments have in common the reading of oppression (someone also spoke of "cultural walls") and were sometimes accompanied by visions of resistance in the filmmaker's work: "What she is doing cinematically is revealing things you are not supposed to see. She is revealing all these things that would be illusions very explicitly, in the open." "Is the playful approach immoral or a dishonest approach? I think that in a very profound, philosophical sense the play is going deeper, a philosophy of play is there, and she plays at all sorts of levels."[54]

Performative Documentary, Film as Performance

At this point the image of the "performative" documentary begins to emerge as a revealer of social and political affinities among viewers from different cultural backgrounds emerges. The concept of the performative documentary proposed by Bill Nichols was developed in the midst of the renewed interest in the notion of performance that I mentioned above.[55] Nichols comments on a number of recent films and videos produced by Third World, lesbian, gay, and queer documentarists. Nurtured by practices at times favoring the artificial and the theatrical, the overlaps between "performance" and "performative" stem from etymology.[56] To perform also means executing an action. Expanded by speech acts theories, the term "performative" was eventually employed broadly to characterize speeches, texts, or films that transform the relationship between speaker and listener. It is important, however, to note that many linguists chose to study performativity in the texts and the intentions of their producers; for reasons of obvious methodological difficulties, they often put aside the actual responses of the readers or viewers. Rather, a favorable context of reception was presupposed, unless a context inducing "infelicities" was examined. Bill Nichols outlines the postcolonial and global landscape of the nineties as a historical and experiential context in which the performative documentary flourishes and opens its viewing context to all "feminist" spectators. A community of viewers crossing the boundaries of nation, race, and gender is at the heart of this inclusive project, sharing what Nichols broadly names a "social subjectivity."[57] It calls to mind the affinity that some spectators seemed to share in speaking of *The Devil Never Sleeps*. And indeed one will find in the film a number of the formal aspects of the performative documentary: a referentiality mixed with expressiveness and reflexivity, as well as "this kind of richly and fully evoked specificity and overarching conceptual categories such as exile, racism, sexism, or homophobia . . . seldom named and never described or explained in any detail" but left to the viewers.[58] However, *The Devil Never Sleeps* also offers a practical critique of the notion of an avant-garde that sustains the concept of social subjectivity (and that Nichols himself, only at a textual level, sees as a possible limitation of the performative documentary).[59] Discerning "the politics of location and experience," along with a utopian yearning, constitutes only one of the film's possible performances. As Judith Mayne has remarked, "The possibility of spectatorship as a potential vanguard activity still haunts film studies."[60] I would add that it also haunts the documentary field (in Bourdieu's sense): a number of documentarists and their exhibitors, critics, and spectators have traditionally considered the act of making and viewing a documentary a political act. In a world permeated by audiovisual practices, and given the current commercialization of documentaries, Mayne's suggestion that "spectatorship needs to be treated as one of those ordinary activities" is especially relevant.[61] A similar approach can be found in the various performances "imagined" by *The Devil Never Sleeps*.

The Devil Never Sleeps seems to reject a favorable context in which it would play for an audience made up of spectators sharing similar views, and willingly addresses the "infelicities" of its viewing contexts as another way to trigger debates. By acknowledging some of the current media practices we all share, the film opens up its performing space to "popular audiences" and simultaneously shows how genres are competing practices at the social and personal level of viewers' experiences.

Early in *The Devil Never Sleeps,* Lourdes Portillo takes us to an old movie theater in Chihuahua, where as a child she loved to watch melodramas. She finds that it has been replaced by a parking lot and chooses to speak of her memories in front of a maquette of the movie theater interior. Telenovelas appear on TV sets in homes and offices, suggesting—as did a spectator—that they are part of daily life in Mexico. Home movies of birthdays and Christmas celebrations remind us that these gatherings are also the preferred occasions to screen home movies that celebrate the unity of the family. The educational uses of the documentary come to mind when a man interviewed about Sonora is identified with the title "local historian"; documentary ethics are addressed in a scene in which Portillo confers with the local priest. It is from a complex nexus of rejections and desires that *The Devil Never Sleeps* calls for viewers to rework their memories of genres. Documentary exhibitors of the past favored a collective and societal dimension of spectatorship that overrode the possibilities of transgressions and secret fantasies: even when short documentaries were shown before the main feature film, the lights were often left on and people felt free to move around. By contrast, in the darkness of a theater, personal and collective fantasies, transgressive identifications, can safely take place, and the films so viewed enter the specific slots of time our cultures allot to leisure, which of course includes viewing murder mysteries. As for telenovelas that display family tensions on television, they run counter to home movies that seek to reinforce emotional ties in showing idealized moments of family life via ritualized screenings.[62] By presenting itself as the site of overlapping publics within the current media landscape, *The Devil Never Sleeps* triggers memories of conflicting experiences both at the personal level of the viewing positions they foster and at a social level. Portillo reminds us that as "virtual" spaces, genres combine institutional territories delineated by packaging, narrative formulas, and audience niches, as well as experiential spaces grounded in our everyday practices. Moreover, she uses the flexible narratives of soap operas to allow the entrance of different modes of storytelling, such as legends, family stories, and gossip, all opening to the narrative spaces that lay beyond the mediatic world. In the end, the stories brought to light are problematized by their relations with each other.[63] In offering plural but specific readings inserted into stories, the film indicates clearly that what is at stake is the autonomy of the parts. That which is at stake is not just the cinema. In between film genres, legends, and stories emerges the actual world of the filmmaker, the filmed subjects, and the viewers.

Conclusions

By creating a space for the confrontation of diverse subjectivities and experiences, *The Devil Never Sleeps* reveals frictions in our historical realities. Members of specific audiences do not mingle easily. Large public spheres are just memories—that linger; political dissent on a global scale is an intersubjective dialogue that takes place in the virtual space of utopia. Small specific public spaces remain open (largely but not only in academia). Because it opened itself to the possibility of conflicting viewer responses, the film was used in subjective and pragmatic ways. Partial readings prevailed. Yet *The Devil Never Sleeps* remained a distinct participant of the performances: from Oscar's life and death in Mexico to the tomato in close-up, it was always part of the debates, often expressing viewpoints contradicting its spectators.

As an interplay between film and spectators in a particular place and time, a performance is a unique event; its social dimension invites us to consider the dynamics of diverse encounters in specific cultural spaces and historical times. The complexity of the parameters involved, especially the variety of spectators' responses, should not let us forget that the film plays an active role, nor that a large number of films and TV programs work toward easing historical tensions and silencing philosophical and political controversies. What is remarkable is not that *The Devil Never Sleeps/El diablo nunca duerme* triggers various readings—most films do—but that it brings the possibility of distinct approaches into the realm of the explicit, resists some, and becomes an active participant in a dialogical process. In the activist tradition of documentary exhibition and feminist performance art, the film acknowledges the historical and cultural specificity of diverse sites and audiences. Grounded in both the intimate and the social dimension of spectatorship, it opens all its performing spaces to contradictions, debates, and "tantalizing questions."

Norma Iglesias Prieto

Who Is the Devil, and How or Why Does He or She Sleep?*

VIEWING A CHICANA FILM IN MEXICO

From a Mexican audience's point of view, the cinematic works of Lourdes Portillo, especially her documentary *The Devil Never Sleeps,* play an important role in the deconstruction of Mexican culture. *The Devil Never Sleeps* is a film that, as much in form as in content, breaks with the established canons of its genre and reveals unspoken aspects of Mexican culture. These characteristics make Portillo's film very useful for the study of the relationship between film and audience because it brings the more private aspects of subjectivity to the fore. The film's cinematographic reflection, with suggestions of social and political criticism, and even film noir intrigue, casts a critical gaze upon an event, the death of the filmmaker's uncle in Mexico—a personal and private event which is, at the same time, public. Without a doubt, *The Devil Never Sleeps* is transgressive and innovative in many different ways, but from the point of view of Mexican audiences, one of the most transgressive aspects is that it brings into public view matters thought more properly to belong in the home (Fregoso, 1997). In other words, the film does not respect the deeply-rooted Mexican principle that "dirty linen should be washed at home" (*la ropa sucia se lava en casa*). That a Chicana filmmaker commits the transgression may be of even greater significance. Portillo's identity is important because generally in Mexico (especially in the central and southern parts of the country) the "Chicana/o" is viewed as a person who has "betrayed" Mexico simply because his or her family has left the country, living and establishing links in another economic, political, and social reality. While some Mexicans view living in the United States as treachery, those that live abroad are also secretly envied, in large measure because "the American way of life" serves as the ideal of modernity. For these reasons, *The Devil Never Sleeps'* critique of deep-rooted Mexican traditions is seen by Mexican audiences as doubly transgressive.

*See Appendix for original Spanish version of this chapter: ¿Quién es el diablo, cómo y por qué duerme?

This article will examine the following questions: What happens when an audience views a film that questions a series of conventions, customs, or certainties that are as much cinematographic as they are social and cultural? How do Mexican viewers interpret these transgressions? How does the discursive reconstruction of events in the documentary differentiate between matters that are Mexican and those that are Chicano, between the personal and the political, and between that which is "ours" and that which is "foreign"? Who, for the young Mexican public, is the devil, and just how and why does he or she sleep? The main focus of this study is the "cinematographic reception process" or viewership—that is, the viewing and assimilation process of an audience, or the relationship between a film and the spectators.

I present here my analysis of Mexican audiences' responses to *The Devil Never Sleeps*. The audiences were made up of graduate students from El Colegio de la Frontera Norte in Tijuana, Mexico. I organized three discussion groups made up of students from different disciplines (Economy, Regional Development, and Environmental Administration). The first group was made up of students from northern Mexico; the other two groups were comprised of students who had recently arrived in Tijuana from central and southern Mexico.[1]

The Discussion Groups and the Presentation of the Film

Analyzing audience perceptions of a film is a challenge for researchers because it demands that they search for a way to analyze the feelings and opinions of the audience, while, at the same time, not interfering with the natural process of viewing a film. The research for this project had to be conducted outside of commercial movie theaters, since, like the work of most Chicana filmmakers, Lourdes Portillo's films are not shown commercially in Mexico. Therefore, discussion groups offered the best way to analyze the film. Discussion groups are not exactly like traditional focus groups since no preset questions are asked of the group members. Rather, without the researcher asking any questions, the group members freely debated the merits of the movie they had watched. More importantly, discussion groups exist without the presence of a moderator; hence, the discussion takes any course the group members want it to. This adds a certain spontaneity to the proceedings.

The strongest justification for using discussion groups is that the responses they generate can be considered realistic because their opinions are based on consensus. During the discussion, individual points of view are woven into the framework of the group's discourse. The group's findings also represent social intercourse (or even ideology) since the group is a sample of society.

Discussion group members know that they have been invited to share their opinions about the film. The group's dynamic, in this sense, mirrors that of a work team. Thus, we see two forms of interaction, work-related discussions (which is the reason for the group's existence in the first place) and the pleasure of speaking with a group of one's peers about a movie. As a group, the students were able to reconstruct the film, and give their collective opinion about the movie. During orientation, the participants were told that they were going to see a film by a Chicana director, thus preparing the viewers for a discussion of the differences between Chicanos and Mexicans.

A Chicana Film

The discussion group from the border region (Discussion Group 1 [DG1]) was familiar with the term "Chicano" and its connotations, but the other two groups were from the interior of the country. Lacking concrete experience, these groups' opinions of Chicanos were shaped by media-created stereotypes. Perhaps because of these stereotypes, the groups from the interior expressed surprise that the movie "didn't seem like a Chicana movie" since, in their opinion, Chicano filmmaking was characterized by the appearance of *Cholos,* or "poor people with problems," or by excessive violence.

> In the Chicano movies I've seen, there is a lot of violence. They show people's ignorance, and the movies stress not so much the scene but the essence and the problems of poorer people, drugs etc. (DG2)

> I live in Northern Mexico, and I have the impression that to be a Chicano, and Chicanos themselves will tell you this, means to wear zoot suits, have a big mustache and drive lowriders. (DG2)

> I imagined that it would be a different kind of movie, not like this. (DG2)

> When I found out it was going to be a Chicano movie, I thought it would be about gangs, *Cholos* and that sort of thing. (DG2)

The above quotes show how Chicanos are stereotyped in interior Mexico. The discussion group made up of border residents did not make these kinds of comments, which shows they have more exposure to Chicanos. Although two-thirds of the discussion groups had a stereotyped view of Chicano movies, and Chicano culture in general, the group members were nonetheless able to avoid stereotypes when talking about what they saw as one of the main themes of the movie.

All three discussion groups perceived the movie as a unique form of documentary, not only because it discussed and questioned many norms, but also because it discussed Mexican customs from the point of view of someone who is a semi-foreigner. In other words, although Lourdes Portillo is of Mexican descent and understands the country, she is removed from the day-to-day reality of Mexico, and its norms and rules. However, she has the "cultural capability" to understand these rules and to appreciate the "Mexicanness" of the culture. The group members were strongly impressed by the fact that the movie was not just another documentary about Mexicans living in the United States but offered something new: a documentary about Mexico, from the Chicano point of view. The group members felt that Portillo's perspective made for a rich viewing experience, but at the same time, limited the movie.

In general terms, what makes *The Devil Never Sleeps* most novel, indeed revolutionary, is that it "shows—for better or worse—many elements of Mexican culture by discussing the family" (DG1), bringing into public view all the family dynamics that reflect the social relations within Mexico. The fact that Portillo is Chicana allowed for this critical reflection. The group members felt that as a "partial" Mexican, Portillo understood Mexican reality without being bound by Mexican social strictures.

> She shows Mexico in this light because she isn't in Mexican culture; that is the advantage of living abroad. (DG2)

> She has the advantage of returning, to enter (Mexico) without feeling lost, to understand our codes and rules without being influenced by Gringo stereotypes, but, by being from the United States [she can] say what she wants to without facing any consequences. (DG3)

> Since she comes from outside Mexico she has less moral baggage and commitments, and hence fewer limitations. (DG1)

> Lourdes does not want to just investigate the death of her uncle, she wants to make a documentary, and this lets her be almost a detective, because with the camera and microphone she can ask questions, and people have to answer those questions. Even without a camera and microphone, she would probably have found another way to ask the same questions. (DG1)

> Maybe if she had stayed in Chihuahua, or even gone to live in some other part of Mexico, and not seen her uncle and her family for some

time, but had not left the country, she would have tried to solve her problems in some other way, without breaking so many taboos. (DG1)

It would appear that Lourdes Portillo can be more critical, since she has the advantage of being an outsider, and a filmmaker, while still understanding Mexican mores as if she were an insider.

She is exhibiting her Mexicanness because she understands it, she has lived here (Mexico), but her experience of having lived there (United States) allows her to understand the contrasts. (DG1)

Without doubt, I'm convinced that she sees us from the point of view of an outsider, she can also say 'I don't live here, I'm going to leave.' She seems like family, but [she] is looking at us from the outside and from a different perspective.

She is from a very distinct culture, she came from abroad, she came to make her film, to ask questions.(DG2)

Again, the fact that Portillo is a Chicana—which is such an important part of why she is able to criticize, and to break taboos—was also seen by the different groups as limiting her understanding of what is Mexican.

The Mexico that many emigrants see is a romanticized Mexico, traditional, where they still sing *ranchero* songs, wear *sombreros* etc., and Mexico is not only like that. (DG3)

They (Chicanos) come back to what they think they have left behind, they see a Mexico full of things they miss, a Mexico that used to be and that they want to remember. That is why when they come here they go to traditional neighborhoods, they listen to traditional music, they idolize the classic heroes, but modern Mexico is more than that, it is visually and socially more complex, but Lourdes' images show the most traditional or even stereotypical views of Mexico. Mexico seems like a ranch, with music and pictures of Pancho Villa, mariachis, and the flag; in Mexico, there is much more than this. (DG3)

She herself shows the shock of coming face-to-face with this Mexico that is not what she remembers, in other words there is nothing left of her memories because the social and physical reality has changed. (DG3)

It is important to mention that the majority of the group members had never seen a film by Lourdes Portillo before, they had not even heard about her. Nonetheless, the viewers were able to connect with the movie and even with the filmmaker. This bond is probably attributable to Portillo's obvious feelings about her uncle's death. In spite of their previous criticisms, the viewers were able to bond with her to such an extent that they even referred to her by her first name. In addition to facilitating the analysis of the content, rhythm, format, themes, and problems which the documentary covers, this sense of identification with the absent filmmaker and her work opened a space for viewers to talk about the filmmaker herself and her intentions, questions, and point of view, as well as the moral and ethical questions she touches upon. It also led the audience to freely discuss the death of Portillo's uncle, a death that they had at first thought to be a private matter.

Two questions put forth by the group members were: Why did "Lulis" (a term of endearment for the filmmaker) want to make a documentary about the death of her uncle? What truth was she seeking? These questions demonstrate that the audience understood that this production intentionally criticizes and contravenes the traditional conventions of documentary filmmaking. The filmmaker appears in the movie, making her intentions and motives a subject of discussion—something that would not happen in a traditional documentary where the filmmaker's intentions are not usually at issue, since his or her neutrality and objectivity are assumed.

A general answer to these questions concerning Lourdes' intentions (which occupied a lot of the discussion group's time) was that through the death of her uncle, Lourdes hoped to see and understand her family and her relation to it. Understanding her family allows her to understand herself; it is like looking in a mirror. Thus, understanding her family, Lourdes begins to understand herself, and begins to understand the country from which she came.

> It can be seen as a search by Luli for herself; to find herself she has to look behind her, and to do that she has to find her origins, her roots, her family, and the pretext to find her family was the death of her uncle Oscar. (DG I)

> Luli wants to find her roots, and she does it using her uncle and the mysteries surrounding his death. (DG I)

> It seems that for her, understanding her family and Mexico is a necessity. (DG I)

In Discussion Group I, made up primarily of women from the border region, one of the first comments was about the relation between the distinct identities Lourdes Portillo had throughout her movie. She identified herself in different forms, as a Chicana, as a niece, as an investigator, as a filmmaker, as a woman, as a Catholic, etc. And thanks to the multiple personas Portillo embodies, we can understand the complexity in the lives of all women. With this explicit game of different identities, Lourdes questions not just the relations within the genre, but the documentary genre itself, and the overarching problem of objectivity.

The women of group 1 also talked about sexism in Mexican society, which *The Devil Never Sleeps* clearly shows as embedded in familial relations. The topic of sexism was completely ignored by the other two groups, which were made up primarily of men. One of the women in group 1 said:

> The movie shows many of the practices and cultural norms of Mexicans, many of the aspects of our culture, and one of these aspects is machismo. When talking about the problems of Uncle Oscar's wives, Lourdes is talking about machismo, something so obvious, and that makes us laugh when we see it in the movie, but which is something terrible [in reality]. For example, the illness of Oscar's first wife being used as an excuse for his unfaithfulness because after all, 'He is a man. He has needs.' We see how there is always justification for machismo, even by women. Sometimes it seems that the women are the most machos, or like they say, machismo exists because we women tolerate it.

> The movie reminds us of just how much machismo there is in our culture. (DG1)

The Thematic Richness in the Death of Uncle Oscar

Another question that the groups touched upon was the thematic richness and different layers of meaning in the movie. The problem of death is one such theme. Death is an important theme in Mexican traditions, as seen in the cultural significance of remembering a lost loved one. But this theme also relates to the problem of justice in Mexico. There are so many mysterious deaths that never seem to be resolved. One of the groups argued that discussion about the cultural aspects of death is something very Mexican; hence, the fact that Lourdes Portillo does this is proof that she is participating in Mexican culture, and further reinforced the audiences strong bond both to the filmmaker and to her film.

> It is very curious the way we Mexicans develop and live so many uncertainties and projects about death. (DG1)

Scene from *The Devil Never Sleeps.* Courtesy of Lourdes Portillo.

His other sister

We were an inseparable bunch, all of us.

Scene from *The Devil Never Sleeps:* Sabella Ruiz Almeida de Portillo, Tío Oscar's sister and Lourdes Portillo's mother. Courtesy of Lourdes Portillo.

Well, I believe the one who cried most was me.

Scene from *The Devil Never Sleeps:* Tío Oscar's other sister, Luz Ruiz de la Torre. Courtesy of Lourdes Portillo.

Scene from *The Devil Never Sleeps:* Tío Oscar's loyal friend, Josefina Borboa. Borboa was a pachuca involved in the *Sleepy Lagoon* case of the 1940s who later married one of the Hollywood Ten; she immigrated to Mexico more than thirty years ago. Courtesy of Lourdes Portillo.

Scene from *The Devil Never Sleeps:* Tío Oscar's widow, Ofeli Torres. Courtesy of Lourdes Portillo.

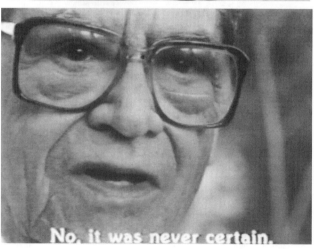

No, it was never certain.

Scene from *The Devil Never Sleeps:* Tío Oscar's brother-in-law, husband of Luz. Courtesy of Lourdes Portillo.

Scene from *The Devil Never Sleeps.* Courtesy of Lourdes Portillo.

Not in the film. Definitely not.

Scene from *The Devil Never Sleeps:* Lourdes Portillo, Tío Oscar's niece. Courtesy of Lourdes Portillo.

We are distinguished by being a death-oriented culture. (DG1)

The lack of respect given to the memory of Uncle Oscar was unusual, since in Mexico people do not speak ill of the dead. (DG1)

All the groups commented, at length, on the fact that in Mexico it is not common to speak poorly of the dead; indeed, there is a tendency to "convert them into saints" (DG2), to simplify their personality, to "forget their defects." "In the desire to pardon and forget, we sometimes lose the perspective of who they really were" (DG1). Thus, it is common to hear, "He was so good, *pobrecito*" (DG3).

However, in the case of Uncle Oscar, in order to begin to understand

who he was and how he died—to, in a sense, pressure people to talk—
Lourdes did everything backwards. As the film unfolds, we see more and
more defects and problems; the good qualities Oscar had at the beginning of the film disappear. But, at the same time, a new Uncle Oscar
emerges, more flesh and blood, more complex, and seen from different
perspectives—no longer is he the simple, happy uncle. An Uncle Oscar
emerges who embodies the multiple contradictions, conflicts, and interests not just of a single person, but of a whole country. As the different
people who appear in the film talk about Uncle Oscar, he becomes more
and more complex, and the audience is surprised at this, in the same way
that the audience assumes Portillo must have been surprised when making the film.

> How she proposed to rediscover a person seems to me very interest-
> ing, how she wants to reencounter her uncle, and, [how] in the end,
> she discovers, as do we, many distinct realities that neither she nor
> we would have imagined. (DG2)

The varied images of Oscar Ruiz Almeida show us the intrigues, gossip,
rumors, and all the construction and reconstruction that is reality.

> The documentary shows us how rumors can turn into accepted
> truth, and how these supposed truths can mark the path of a man or
> a country. (DG2)

Uncle Oscar's death, like the deaths of other public figures that appear
in the documentary (that of Colosio, for example) provide insight into the
traditions of silence, secrecy, and impunity that exist in Mexico. The second side of death discussed by the groups had to do with precisely these
aspects of Mexican society. By linking the death of her uncle with those of
other public figures, the documentary acquires a political and social tone.

> In the movie, we see a political aspect when it touches on the death
> of Pancho Villa, shows a photo of his bullet-ridden car, as when it
> mentions the assassination of Colosio. At that point (the death of
> Colosio) we see an image of a shadow that looks like the silhouette
> of Carlos Salinas.(DG3)

Through Uncle Oscar's death, the movie exposes serious vices within
Mexican society: corruption, silence, impunity, and secrets.

> This mindset explains why so many illicit acts are not denounced
> in Mexico, for example, rapes, domestic violence, child abuse, etc.

So much is not discussed, but neither is it forgotten, nor resolved. (DG2)

The Melodramatic Mexican Reality

Another aspect of the film that pleased group members was the use of soap operas (telenovelas) to describe Mexican culture.

> Another thing that struck me as very interesting, and which I really liked, was the inclusion of telenovelas because they form a part of our national culture; we are like telenovelas, very melodramatic. It is like an analogy "life is melodramatic, life is a soap opera." The plots, which we saw in the telenovelas, helped form the dialogues in the documentary. The new wife is bad, she married Oscar for his money, she has to keep up appearances, she has lovers, but they have to be discrete. The truth is that one can understand very well the way we Mexicans are by looking at our soap operas; our lives are soap operas without the famous actors. (DG1)

The subject of the telenovelas gave the groups the chance to talk about different social and cultural conventions in Mexico: for example classism, sexism, class differences, and the preoccupation among the middle and upper classes with protecting appearances, even if this requires ethical and moral dishonesty. This preoccupation is illustrated by the fact that infidelity is accepted for men but not for women, by sexual taboos, by the prominent role of religion in Mexican society, by the power of the Catholic Church, and by Malinchismo (preferring the foreign over the Mexican). This last feature is manifest in Uncle Oscar's family's insistence that his first wife was from Yugoslavia:

> I don't think that his family was mad at him for getting remarried so fast, without going through a period of mourning, but for marrying his lover, who was from a poor family and not well educated. Had he married a woman of the same social class, from the same circle of people, no one would have been upset. (DG1)

The Debate about "Washing Dirty Clothes at Home"

In each of the three groups there was a heated debate over the fact that Portillo's film drags "private" matters into public view, violating a cultural taboo. Questions included: "What was Lourdes really looking for?" "Was what she did ethically and morally correct?" "What does the documentary really show us?" "What can the audience learn from these occurrences in the movie?" The group members either liked or disliked Portillo's intentions; the documentary forced everyone to take sides; there were no neutral opinions. Hence there was a polarization, with people strongly attacking or defending the movie, and Portillo's work as a filmmaker. Thus we have, on the one hand, supporters of the movie, and on the other hand, those who were very critical of the film.

Supporters of the first position, those who defended or supported the movie, argued that Lourdes Portillo was motivated to make the movie in order to investigate and bring into the open the circumstances surrounding the death of her uncle because she was really interested in understanding what had happened. In their opinion, she used the film as an instrument to investigate the events surrounding her uncle's death. She used documentary to carry out her investigation because that is what she knows how to do; she is a filmmaker. Portillo's supporters commented that if she were an author, for example, she probably would have written a novel or an essay to try to come to grips with Oscar's death. Furthermore, Portillo's defenders argued that by making the documentary, she was better able to understand her family, and her relationship with family members. Moreover, through her work, as she helped spread understanding of Mexican culture and traditions, she was able to come to grips with her own cultural identity. She was also able to deconstruct the documentary genre by exploring new narrative ideas. This group of students summed up the many contributions of *The Devil Never Sleeps* in the following manner:

> The movie showed the foundations on which both the family as an institution, and society in general, rest. It also exposed the beliefs and prejudices which are built up around the family. (DG2)

The movie's supporters also were impressed by the number of barriers that the movie overcame. They pointed out the difficulties inherent in the creation, development, and production of such a movie, problems which were not just technical but also social. Lourdes Portillo had to create an atmosphere of trust that would encourage the different family members, friends, and other social actors to speak comfortably about the life and death of Uncle Oscar.

> It must have been hard both for her and her family to talk about these sad occurrences. She had to pressure them to talk and to confront their own secrets. She shared the romanticized view that many had of her uncle and the events of his life. It must have been like opening Pandora's box. (DG1)

I'm sure it was painful, but it must have also been an enriching and fascinating experience. (DG1)

She did not seem to worry that a lot of bad things were said about her family, she sustained herself by telling the truth, although the truth sometimes hurts. (DG1)

Another important aspect of this film, according to its defenders, is that it forces viewers to take a hard look at their own families, with their own problems and secrets. The movie touches many "sensitive points" not only in Portillo's family, but in viewers' families as well.

It is true that privacy and secrecy are strong aspects of Mexican culture, but why should we not talk about our fathers or our grandfathers, since that is who we really are? It is necessary to talk about these things in order to recognize them. (DG2)

The supporters also mentioned that while they liked the movie's social transgressions, in some ways they felt uncomfortable with so much private matter being placed in public view; yet they recognized that by doing this, the film more closely involved viewers.

We are not used to seeing in public view what goes on in the home, in the family. (DG2)

By recognizing how uncomfortable they felt about seeing Uncle Oscar's familial secrets, the viewers also recognized how difficult it must have been for Portillo to have made this movie about her own family, and they applauded her work both as a maker of documentaries and as a film producer.

We would all like to have a movie or a book about the history of our own family, but what we would not like is for this information to become public. Talking about our families and their conflicts and secrets bothers us because, although we might like to, we don't know if we would have the courage or the valor to make these conflicts and secrets public. We are limited by our own culture, our principles and prejudices, and it is very difficult to overcome them. (DG2)

Criticism of the movie was much simpler. In general, the group members who did not like the movie argued that by making *The Devil Never Sleeps,* Lourdes Portillo used the death of her uncle to create something interesting, but morbid. For some, this seemed unethical.

I think that Lourdes just used the death of her uncle as a pretext to make an interesting movie, but that she did not really care about the pain she was causing her family. She only cared about her movie and getting the information necessary to make it. (DG2)

She publicly offended both her family and the viewing public because these are things that nobody needs to know about. (DG2)

It is wrong because "dirty linen should be washed at home." (DG2)

All this movie does is reinforce the culture of gossip, in fact all it is is a bunch of gossip. (DG3)

It is like she overdid it, she included things that were not necessary; what is the point of seeing a bunch of gossip in a movie? (DG3)

In the more critical discussions of the movie, no one wanted to be specific about the parts they were criticizing; the producer is also ignored. In other words, criticism is expressed silently, demonstrating just how strong the power of silence is in Mexican culture.

Conclusions

As one of the viewers mentioned, the group discussions generated by *The Devil Never Sleeps* reproduced the forms, structures, fears, taboos, and prejudices that highlight Mexican culture.

Everyday we reproduce the theme of the movie, we have shown how Mexican culture is a function of the political, economic, and social system in which we live. As I was listening to the discussions I found myself liking the movie more because it mirrored the debates and prejudices that go on in all families and in society, prejudices that demand we protect intimacy or private life rather than help clear up a crime. We do not like for others to see us, for others to analyze us, or, more to the point, we do not like to truly see and analyze ourselves. In a sense we feel that it is better not to understand ourselves than to clear up a crime or other injustice. (DG2)

This study of *The Devil Never Sleeps* demonstrates the connections the movie forms with a group of Mexican filmgoers, especially the ways in which these viewers internalize and reconstruct the movie. In other words, this study shows what the film does to the viewers and what the viewers do to the film.

One of the main contributions of *The Devil Never Sleeps* is its capacity to show the complexity and different levels of social reality, as well as its capacity to question the dualistic logic where some are seen as the bad guys and others as the good guys—where everything is white or black. This film presents the social complexity that allows us to discover several devils and angels, and also the different faces of a person who sometimes seems to be a devil and sometimes an angel. If on occasions and for some people the devil is Ofelia—the second wife—, on other occasions the devil seems to be Portillo, or Uncle Oscar. In other moments of the film and the discussion, the devil could be the police, the relatives, the friends, or the different social groups that surrounded the life of Oscar Almeida. The relationship that the film establishes with audiences and the transgressive format and content of *The Devil Never Sleeps* produce a certain effect on the audience, making them feel that they could also be the devils. Which is why the popular phrase, "the devil never sleeps" has such a profound significance within the film.

Portillo's documentary questions not just one person and his actions, but the society as a whole. Through her criticism, the filmmaker knows that as a member of that social group, she is not exempt from responsibility. *The Devil Never Sleeps* makes audiences meditate on Chicano and Mexican societies, on the limits of the private and public, on family matters, on the dead and the pain of loss. But the film is also important because it focuses attention on the limits and possibilities of a genre and the link between a film and the filmmaker. Re-discovering the multiple and varied devils and angels that surround us may make us better able to eradicate the limits imposed upon us by society.

Barbara McBane

Pinning Down the Bad-Luck Butterfly

PHOTOGRAPHY AND IDENTITY IN THE FILMS OF LOURDES PORTILLO

> **Manuelita:** Esa es una mariposa de mala suerte.
> ¡Que no se me acerque a mí te digo!
> (That's a bad-luck butterfly. Don't let it near me!)
> *The Devil Never Sleeps*

In this paper I will examine three films directed or codirected by Lourdes Portillo that privilege the photographic image in various ways: *Las Madres: The Mothers of the Plaza de Mayo* (codirected with Susana Blaustein Muñoz, 1986); *La Ofrenda: The Days of the Dead* (also codirected with Susana Blaustein Muñoz, 1988); and *The Devil Never Sleeps/El diablo nunca duerme* (1994). In these films, questions regarding identity are staged through stories that involve the photographic image as an integral feature of the history told, as a technology within the practices documented, as a formal strategy of cinematic representation, or as all three. That the photographic image is a key thematic as well as formal concern of these projects appears to issue directly from Portillo's consistent interest in the subject of death, a subject that has frequently noted associations both with the ancient roots of Mexican culture and with photography.

By analyzing these three films, I hope to explore some questions concerning the relationship between representations of identity that utilize the still image and other representations that rely on the moving one. Do the formal differences between the two result in different constructions or representations of identity, and, if so, how do we read the difference? When they are combined, do they operate in the same way as when they are not? I will approach Portillo's films through an inquiry aimed at the intersection between the representation of identity, on one hand, and the relationship between film and photography, on the other. There are many ways identity can be read through Portillo's films. After mapping some of these out by giving each film a brief description and reading, I would like to reexamine the three films together, considered as a kind of expanded semiotic field in which each text illuminates the others. In the end, my primary interest will be focused on questions that interrogate issues of sexual and gender identity. Can a formal or representational connection be made between the introduction of still images into a moving text and the construction of political or cultural identities in film? If such a link can be established, what form(s) does it take in Portillo's three films, and what might be its bearing on the articulation of gendered or sexualized identities in particular?

Las Madres

Las Madres: The Mothers of the Plaza de Mayo (1986) is a documentary codirected by Portillo and Susana Blaustein Muñoz that reconstructs the history of a group of politically active women during a period of military terrorism in Argentina. The film maps a process by which these women constructed a public political identity as "Las Madres" and created a politicized visual language in which portraits of murdered civilians functioned as emblems or signs.

The Plaza de Mayo in Buenos Aires is a public square in front of the presidential palace, where the mothers of surreptitiously kidnapped, tortured, and executed political prisoners demonstrated for more than a decade, carrying or wearing photographs of their absent ("disappeared") children. These protests began with meetings in the privacy of homes but moved to the space of the Plaza; ultimately they sparked a general political protest that altered repressive conditions in Argentina. Portillo and Muñoz's documentary is organized basically around interviews with these mothers, with archival footage and other interviews intercut between them. It adheres to a relatively conventional documentary structure, strengthened by the force of the story, the women themselves, and the photographic visual elements that are part of the history.[1]

The photographic image was fundamental to the administration of state terrorism in Argentina. Family photographs were regularly confiscated by the military during kidnappings and used during torture as one of the mechanisms by which individuals and families were de- and reconstituted along lines consistent with the interests of the terrorist state.[2] The photographs that survived these invasions were therefore precious, and their enlistment into a counterstrategy by which family and individual identities were once again affirmed was, in its own right, an act of survival and resistance.

Before the demonstrations in the Plaza de Mayo, the women interviewed in *Las Madres* led conventional lives as mothers and housewives.

The role of middle-class women in Argentina then was traditionally defined and restrictive: they were relegated to the domestic space of the household and to the roles of nurturing wives and mothers. On the other hand, however, under the military government, women were expected, as citizens, to support the regime by informing on "subversives" (often their children) and accepting what, to mothers, was intolerable: the abduction and murder of their own family members. This contradiction between private and public roles for women produced an identity rupture, of which the mothers took effective political advantage. In this respect, they instituted a political movement against prevailing powers by availing themselves of what Chela Sandoval calls "tactical subjectivity": the "capacity to recenter depending on the kinds of oppression to be confronted."[3]

Photographs of disappeared children were removed from their usual niches in the household (walls, mantles, etc.), enlarged into placards, worn as pendants, pinned to clothes, and xeroxed and plastered on city walls; sometimes details (eyes, mouths, noses) were made into enlargements and distributed at strategic moments. These uses of the photograph are the background against which *Las Madres* takes place.[4] When we first meet the mothers, they are inside their homes, and each describes her disappeared child or children, the circumstances of abduction, and her own efforts to acquire information concerning their current condition. These interviews alternate with reconstructions of the political history leading up to the kidnappings. The move from airing griefs inside the home to protesting outside in the Plaza de Mayo marks an important structural shift in the film and in the history. The mothers are represented as almost literally getting up from their living room or kitchen chairs and marching into the streets. This move divides the film between an initial introductory segment of personal anguish, contained inside the private sphere of the home, and subsequent segments in which the mothers' losses take on an increasingly public and actively politicized aspect, and gain increasing national and international attention. This structural fulcrum occurs when the four featured interviewees (señoras Epelbaum, Suárez, Galleti, and Haschman) reach the end of their tolerance (or fear) and publicly march to the plaza, prominently displaying photos of their disappeared children. More than a formally foregrounded element, the photographs are an integral part of this history. However, there are some formal devices used by Portillo and Muñoz worth noting.

Each of the early interviews is introduced in the company of portraiture in one way or another. The first two interviews with Aída Suárez and

Elida Galleti, for example, are preceded by full-frame portraits showing disappeared children with family members. The mother's voice-over narration covers the still images and continues as a synch-sound interview. Thus, images of the dead precede and authenticate the words of the living. This strategy is echoed throughout the film, with the introduction of interviews preceded by a freeze-frame or photograph, either of a disappeared person or of the interviewee her- or himself. The repetition of the device and the alternation of images of the dead and living have the effect of permeating the otherwise ordinary structure of the film with the (random) possibility of death or disappearance: death seems to haunt the edges of the screen and constitute the enunciative frame of the subject in this menacing, unstable environment.

Finally, in the story itself, the photographic portrait takes on expanding and changing significations as it moves from private to public discursive and physical spaces. It shifts from a semiosis of the image as individual portrait to its reinscription as ideological icon, or political abstraction. The faces of the disappeared become generic representations of anybody/ everybody. Relocated from personal domestic space to the public street, they are transformed into political emblems and rallying signs: material signifiers of the personal made political.

The relationship of this language of body images to the context of torture is significant. A view of torture offered by Elaine Scarry in *The Body in Pain* is that it is a process of reconstructing the identity of the prisoner by destroying language and restoring it in the terms of the system of oppression. The mothers assumed the considerable task of creating a counterlanguage able to resist the official state language, a language of deception (lies), silence, and pain. Physical pain is an experience that stubbornly resists objectification in language: it "is not *of* or *for* anything. It is precisely because it takes no object that it, more than any other phenomenon, resists objectification in language."[5] By using the photograph to specify the identities and material evidences of "those who were here," the mothers were able to give voice to an internal reality that resisted representation. Often this "reality" was their own experience, as well as that of the disappeared. María Haschman tries to voice the virtually inexpressible experience of torture: "I didn't see the prod, but I felt it. They put it on my breast and genitals. Then I understood why young people would kill themselves before being tortured—because that pain can't be measured until you feel it—it's as if they cut off a body part without anesthesia."

Eventually, under the reformed government of civilian president Raúl

Alfonsín, a proposal was made to declare the disappeared dead to avoid further investigation into the circumstances of their disappearance. This rewritten identity was refused by the mothers. By inventing a language able to represent a counternarrative to the various self-serving official stories, as well as the almost inarticulable experience of physical torture and pain, the mothers began a process of reinscribing the value of the human body *as a body:* of reclaiming it from the degrading discourse of torture. Roland Barthes in *Camera Lucida* says that a crucial function of the photographic image is to proclaim the existence of "what-has-been."[6] Creating a visual language in which photographic elements were primary signifiers and were used to make a public statement affirming the reality of this what-has-been, as well as affirming the value of the body *before* torture, was fundamental to initiating a movement of widespread resistance to political oppression and military terrorism in Argentina: through this counterlanguage, both the rewriting of the social subject as a political subject and an "oppositional consciousness" became possible.

La Ofrenda

La Ofrenda: The Days of the Dead (1988), codirected by Portillo and Susana Muñoz, documents the activities associated with Day of the Dead (Día de los Muertos) in traditional Mexican culture and the adaptation of these in the Latino/a and Chicana/o community around the Mission District in San Francisco. Day of the Dead practices become an entry point for exploring questions of identity on both sides of the border. The film is structured in two halves, the first set in Mexico and the second in the United States.

La Ofrenda begins with a visit to a local cemetery, followed by a montage representing food and altar-building preparations. It then locates the viewer in a Mexican (Oaxacan) household, where Day of the Dead activities are underway. The first half of the film builds toward a village performance and procession, which features several cross-dressing characters and is narrated by a man clothed in the somberly sumptuous dress of a mourning widow. The second half of the film is set in San Francisco's Mission District and shows the adaptation of traditional customs and rituals to a Mexican culture outside of Mexico. We see the differences in altars and art practices (they are more high-tech, more urban, more eclectic in their influences). We see how these altars are made and the different purposes they serve: as forms of personal expression; to commemorate those dead from AIDS; as memorials to children killed in war; as monuments to cultural attainment and visibility (for example, the Rita Moreno

Scene from *La Ofrenda: The Days of the Dead*. Courtesy of Lourdes Portillo.

Four young girls at the cemetery in Oaxaca, Mexico, on the Day of the Dead celebration during shooting of *La Ofrenda: The Days of the Dead*. Courtesy of Lourdes Portillo.

altar); and more. The film concludes with an epilogue from Octavio Paz, followed by a montage intercutting shots from both sides of the border. We come to rest finally back in the graveyard in Mexico, where a bent old man with his back to the camera sweeps the dust off a family plot.

The first half of the film does two things: it describes Day of the Dead remembrances and celebrations in Mexico, and it constructs a history that traces the origins and importance of these rituals. In general, organization in terms of several sets of binaries or paired terms and the boundary or borderland between them is the principal structural trope of *La Ofrenda*. For example, the documentary history or "literal discourse" of the film begins as two alternating voice-overs: an official or "public" history narrated by a male voice; and a mythical, personal, or "private" history with a female narrator.[7] As I will show below, the narrational space claimed by this second female voice contains points of analogy with the space of the still or photographic image. The alternating narrations proceed in a rhetoric of paired terms: life/death, light/dark, night/day, Spanish/Indigenous, Mexico/Mexican America. The second half of the film is primarily narrated by two women (a psychologist, Concha Saucedo, and an artist, Amalia Mesa-Bains), from whom we learn about the importance of Day of the Dead in sustaining a sense of cultural continuity, healing, and wholeness, even under conditions of dispersal and diaspora.

In *The Bronze Screen*, Fregoso devotes several paragraphs to the film's voice-overs.[8] Her reading aligns the male and female voice-overs with temporality and spatiality, respectively. The interplay between the two produces a processual present-time, the time of the filmmaker's "work on the text": this "work" is the production of identity politics as an ongoing project as opposed to a "fixed meaning." Some other features of this voice-over narration are also worth mentioning. In the first half of the film, voice-over narration is constructed along essentialist male and female lines, with the male voice, as already mentioned, entrusted with the imparting of public or official history, and the female narrator giving voice to a personal, intimate, or domestic history. This division adheres to the formula of classical Hollywood cinema, where the female voice is the voice of interiority and is contained within the diegesis.[9] In *La Ofrenda*, however, the female narrator speaks both a personal and a cultural interiority; the male/female division of narration breaks down across the geopolitical divide of the international border and the structural divide of the cut from Old Mexico to new, urban Mexico-America. The movement across the border occurs as a series of vocal shifts, first to the "third sex" voice of a cross-dressing actor in the Mexican Day of the Dead

A home altar honoring the dead. Courtesy of Lourdes Portillo.

An art installation for the Day of the Dead. Courtesy of Lourdes Portillo.

Relatives taking flowers to the tombs of their dead during the shooting of *La Ofrenda: The Days of the Dead.* Courtesy of Lourdes Portillo.

Sarah Chin (sound recordist, left) during an interview at the graveyard in Oaxaca for *La Ofrenda: The Days of the Dead.* Courtesy of Lourdes Portillo.

Sarah Chin (left) and Portillo (center) interviewing a man at the graveyard for *La Ofrenda: The Days of the Dead.* Courtesy of Lourdes Portillo.

Codirectors Portillo and Blaustein Muñoz in Mexico during the filming. Courtesy of Lourdes Portillo.

pageant; then, in San Francisco, to the voices of the two principal narrating women, whose voice-over commentaries are supplemented by other on-camera narrators, including a man inventorying the photos on his AIDS altar. The essentialized male and female voices are thus replaced by a more fluidly and unspecifically embodied auditory space, and the altars represented in the montages of the second half of the film reflect a corresponding fluidity, playfulness, and distance from tradition.

The two opening narrations of La Ofrenda also introduce the film's concern with memory, ethics, and temporalities. The female narrator says, "What seemed unimportant then has now possessed my memory. How we treated one another, how we lived, takes on great significance." A man's voice follows, "In its celebrations a culture steps outside time to acknowledge enduring truths. Time is no longer a succession, but becomes what it originally was: the present, in which past and future are reconciled. In celebrating death, we step outside time." Besides introducing the public and personal temporalities already mentioned, these voices introduce the thematic of festivals and rituals as "heterotopic" sites, and the "heterochronies" or alternate temporalities associated with them.

Michel Foucault, in his article "Of Other Spaces," offers a definition of the concept "heterotopia" as a "space-off" from, or a countersite to, ordinary social life.[10] Jennifer Gonzalez and Michelle Habell-Pallan summarize the main points of Foucault's definition as follows:

> Heterotopias are mutable (the counter-site can change with historical and social change); they are multiple (several incompatible spaces can be juxtaposed in a single space); they are a-temporal (linked to different slices of time); they have an ambiguous threshold (both open and restricted).[11]

According to Foucault, the graveyard, the church, the carnival, the festival, the museum, the library, and the movie theater all constitute heterotopias. The heterotopic space, claims Foucault, opens onto a "hetero chronie": a "time-off" or alternate temporality that constitutes an "absolute break with traditional time."[12] Gonzalez uses Foucault's model to describe the space created by Chicana artist Amalia Mesa-Bains in her altar installation art. The same concept could be used to describe not only the spaces of the altar and the cemetery in La Ofrenda, but the micro-heterotopic space of the photographic portrait as well. The concept of heterochronie can be imagined as an analogue to the "spatialization" Fregoso identifies with the second (female) narrating voice: a form of temporality that is nonlinear and tied up with personal memory as represented in the photograph. Such a heterochronie or time-off introduces a rupture into cinematic time: the same rupture that occurs with the introduction of the still image into a medium of moving pictures.

The photograph makes only a few appearances in *La Ofrenda,* but it appears at important moments and in strategic ways. Near the beginning of the film, a family in Mexico prepares and sits down to a meal on the evening of Day of the Dead. A voice-over explains, "The dead return on this night to become, once again, part of the family, sharing in the everyday life of those who remember them. The family lives, not in anticipation, but memory." When the meal is over, a woman removes a framed photograph from the wall and places it on the family altar, "inaugurating" the altar for use. The link between photograph, death, altar, extrapublic space, and memory is explicitly made. The woman speaks aloud to the image on the altar: "Dear Heliodoro, please ask God on my behalf that I live a bit longer, so I can be here with our children." The photograph shares the ontological space of the dead: it is situated somewhere between the living and the "Divine." It posits a space of intercession and translation, where the desires of the living are made intelligible to what is "beyond": a spatialized medium of memory, communication, and exchange, marked off from the time and space of the "ordinary" by proximity to the altar and to death. In "How Things Mean: Objects and Identity," Jennifer González discusses the similarities of the personal altar to what Pierre Nora calls "lieux de memoires" or "memory-places": "Memory takes root in the concrete, in spaces, gesture, images, and objects; history binds itself strictly to temporal continuities, to progressions and to relations between things."[13] The tension between memory and history produces these "lieux de memoires." The photographic portrait, as it functions in *La Ofrenda,* constitutes such a memory-place: the representational space of a physical enclosure, comparable to the altar or cemetery itself, within which the personal past can be invoked, a time-and-space removed from the ordinary. Moreover, an analogy might be proposed between González' description of memory and history, on the one hand, and the photographic (still) and cinematic (moving) image on the other. She says:

> In the activity of contemporary Western cultures, history proclaims its authority. The sites of memory can be seen as a resistance to this totalizing tendency—they undermine a seamless narrative by providing the material traces of a symbolic and sacred relationship to things. More importantly, memory implies, as against history, that there are multiple stories to be told in an overlapping layer of signification that does not take place in a linear, linguistic, or necessarily coherent manner.[14]

The two different conceptions of time (the time of memory implied by the "objectness" and spatiality of the photograph, and the time of history implied by the forward-moving linear narrativity of cinema) are posed as differentials within a single identity in *La Ofrenda* and aligned with the distinct cultural components of that identity. The female narrator says, "To my ancient Indian ancestors, life and death were cycles of nature, and duality the essence of life. Life is destroyed to be reborn." Then she wonders, "What is there in me of my Indian past? What is there in me of that conqueror of yesterday?" Here, identity is hybrid and contains elements of at least two sets of temporalities, spatialities, "genders" (insofar as the spatiotemporal constructions are vocally "gendered"), and cultures.

The association of the Day of the Dead, as a heterotopia, with gender ambivalence is taken up in the prominent role assigned to another narrator, a cross-dressing man, as Rosa Linda Fregoso points out in *The Bronze Screen* in her discussion of gender in *La Ofrenda*.[15] She glosses these cross-dressing Day of the Dead activities in the following way:

> In a culture strictly driven by Catholicism with its deeply embedded religious and social prescription of strict gender roles, the public domain of the streets and special festive occasions figure as the few socially sanctioned spaces where a clearly identifiable cross-dresser may operate. On the Day of the Dead, a cross-dresser assumes a subject position by subjecting himself to public acknowledgment and ridicule.[16]

Like the photograph, the body of the cross-dresser constitutes a heterotopic, threshold, or border space: a fluid position that allows a single image to embody multiple levels of public/private, interior/exterior, private fantasy/public enactment, United States/Mexico. The figure of the cross-dresser bridges the transition to the U.S. (second) half of the film, where the subject of homosexuality and, in particular, AIDS, is more explicitly introduced. The Día de los Muertos ritual environment can, in one sense, be regarded as a heterotopic site for stretching and reworking constraining notions of gender; and in Fregoso's reading, *La Ofrenda* becomes a cautionary tale about the underdiscussed effects of AIDS in the Latina/o community.

With the shift to a U.S. location, attention is directed toward the ways the Day of the Dead rituals have been adapted to produce and affirm Chicana/o identity. The photographic image is strategically reintroduced, functioning as a flux-field or space within which difference and distance are momentarily resolved. A narrator says, "Chicanos have revived and adapted Día de los Muertos. To us, the past is a never-ending source of active nostalgia. Here, our celebrations may be different than in Mexico, but the spirit of tradition lives on." This narration occurs over a slow zoom out from an altar to a photograph of a man stooping in front of a fountain. The conjunction of image and narration posits the still image as a site joining "there" (Mexico) to "here" (the United States), and past to present: this shift is the geographic cultural and structural pivot of the film, and its various vectors of time, space, culture, and identity converge within and through it. The photograph, here, comprises a "trans-space," across and through which the consolidation of identity is facilitated and affirmed.

The Day of the Dead in Mexico, then, is mapped out as a heterotopic space where rigidities of sex and gender identification are momentarily suspended. In traditional Mexican society, formed, as *La Ofrenda* stresses, from an overlay of European-Spanish Catholicism onto ancient indigenous practices and beliefs, the enactment of gender fluidity is reserved for the heterotopic, carnivalesque space of these Day of the Dead activities. The men who cross-dress do more than cross-dress; they flirt provocatively with the men cast in straight roles in the village performance. In the United States (at least in San Francisco), strict sex and gender demarcations are represented as more generally open to suspension and contestation. A narrator can present himself in a queer-marked context and openly introduce the photographs of his many friends who have died of AIDS. The photos of these (presumably gay) friends are mixed in with other (presumably straight) childhood friends. Thus, the relative openness surrounding sexual identity (at least for men) in this instance of San Francisco Latina/o and Chicano/a culture is represented as extending as much to the daily life of this narrator as the cross-dressing performance in Mexico is represented as reserved to the set-apart time of the Day of the Dead. The film depicts a social environment in the United States with a relative tolerance of everyday sex and gender mobility that is absent in Old Mexico. In *La Ofrenda,* the U.S. Latino/a and Chicana/o photograph (as we see it on the AIDS altar as well as the Rita Moreno altar) functions to allow us to foreground, at least momentarily, those who are "gender deviant" (gay men and women who occupy a "masculine" position in that they command a high degree of public visibility) and to pay them respect.

The Devil Never Sleeps

The Devil Never Sleeps/El diablo nunca duerme (1994), an experimental documentary directed by Portillo, sets out to examine the circumstances surrounding the mysterious death of Portillo's favorite uncle, Tío Oscar, and in the process becomes a many layered meditation on the complexities of modern (or postmodern) identity and the elusive nature of truth. It is constructed out of many accounts of and rumors about Oscar's life. These accounts mostly take the form of interviews with family, friends, and business associates, but also include newspaper stories, police reports, opinions of doctors, lawyers, and historians, and, importantly, phone conversations with Oscar's second wife, Ofelia. Amassed from frequently inconsistent details, it is a long and winding tale.

Portillo herself is the narrator. The beginning of the film locates the tale as a transborder story and introduces important characters (like Ofelia), motifs (like the telenovela), and visual devices (the uses of photography and "miniature" images). It then moves forward through interviews with family members and others. From the start, we are offered many speculations about the circumstances of or motives behind Oscar's death: heart attack, suicide, murder. Family and friends dispute over these conflicting speculations. Lies and secrets are revealed and silences remain unbroken. The interviews abound in small revelations of family dysfunction and downright random strangeness.

We learn that Oscar was born into a middle-class Mexican family of eight children, one of whom (Chencho) is Portillo's father. The principal interviewees in the film are Chencho; Sabella (Portillo's mother; Chencho's wife); Luz (Oscar and Chencho's sister); Jesús (Luz's husband); Manuelita (Oscar's friend); Josefina (Oscar's friend); Catalina (Oscar's daughter from his first marriage); and Ofelia (Oscar's second wife; through simulated interviews, based on the form and content of actual interviews conducted with Ofelia and rerecorded using the voice of an actress).

The telling of Oscar's tale relies heavily on the ingenious use of family photographs. Portillo develops an enlarged repertoire of devices for incorporating the photographic image into her film, and in *The Devil,* formal or aesthetic photographic strategies are more complex, various, and technically refined than in either *Las Madres* or *La Ofrenda.* The same can be said of the development of the photograph as a trope. For example, in *The Devil* the photograph is frequently animated, placed in natural surroundings, and treated as if it were a puppet or stand-in for characters in Portillo's family story. So a photo of Oscar and Catalina in bathing suits is stuck in the sand as if on a beach outing; and when Catalina dies, her photograph sinks down into water, reenacting the death of its subject. The animation of these photographs is not created by single-frame filming but is real-time animation. The photographs, whose motion is imparted within the same temporal structure as narrative motion, often seem to move beyond their constitutional flatness and assume a three-dimensionality that makes them seem graspable and possessable, like things that could be held and hoarded as "hard facts" or "solid truths." Re-animation literalizes the function of the photograph as a resurrrector of the dead that was foregrounded so prominently in *Las Madres*. In *The Devil*, however, the photograph promises to resolve the ambiguities of the living into a single sliced moment of time.

When placed in natural surroundings, the photograph produces an acute awareness in the viewer of the split levels of representation that constitute Portillo's cinematic images: of a prior text inscribed within the present one, of the pro-filmic level, and of the pro-pro-filmic. The viewer is made distinctly conscious, in other words, of confronting a representation alongside a representation of a representation. Examples of such images abound in *The Devil*. The photograph is placed in front of cloud-filled skies, sunsets, landscapes, or it floats in water. It is placed in settings at once natural and contrived: it lies on top of a mirror while rose petals, or perhaps sand, blow over it. These contrived contexts are sometimes quite complicated. Deeply reflected in the mirror, we see a distant blue sky. Affixed to the surface of the mirror is a photograph of Grandfather Ruiz (the photograph is thus framed by the reflections in the mirror). A pair of cowboy-booted feet walks by, between the mirror and the camera, so the reflection of these feet as we see them appears to move behind Grandfather Ruiz' photo (but in front of the distant sky). An image is thus yielded containing at least five separate and simultaneous layers of surface/image/movement in a single (fleeting) shot: the supporting wall; the passing feet; the reflection of the feet in the mirror; the sky reflected in the mirror; and the photograph attached to the surface of the mirror. Yet another layer (the time/surface of the optical printing process) is added by fading the reflected sky to black as the narrator references Grandfather Ruiz' death. Through the use of such multilayered visual constructions, the photograph is invested with a complex weight of connotation and "ways of meaning" in *The Devil*. It is also given a strategic structural position in this eminently nonlinear story, which unfolds by contradictory accretions, twistings, and turnings, and often discrepant private and public accounts of Tío Oscar's life, activities, and death. The photographic image often functions formally as an articulation, or joint, between differently flexing narrational "limbs" or versions of Oscar's story: it becomes a moving zone of reinterpretation that recurs in the text, able to accommodate all, even conflicting, accounts of the meaning of the visible image.

In many cases, recontextualized family photos are black-and-white images rephotographed on color film stock (hence with natural color backgrounds). Portillo's combining of visual styles in this way has many effects; among them is the production of a heightened awareness of the artificial and socially constructed status of the subjects of photographic representation (usually Portillo's family members). There are several images of Portillo visually examining family photographs, sometimes through optical devices like film viewers or magnifying glasses, sometimes with her naked eye. If, with Althusser, we view the family as an Ideological State Apparatus, and if an important aspect of that apparatus is the surveillance it encourages us to internalize, then we can regard Portillo in these sequences as inverting this ideologically generated self-surveillance and conducting a campaign of counterespionage. She spies back on the family as both a source of personal history and an institution.

The results of this investigatory effort are indeterminate, as there is no "outside" to the interlocked society/family/self formation from which to claim a separate vantage point. Such scrutinizing of the image is, in any case, frustrated by the material reality of the photograph-as-object. Looking at Ofelia's newspaper image in extreme close-up, for example, only reveals the half-tone particles of which it is composed through greater and greater degrees of magnification. Such disintegrating images can be read ambiguously as a trope that might apply to the physical identities, or to the social or moral natures of the subjects of these photographic representations, or else to the investigatory gaze itself, which seems to "decompose" the closer it gets to its subject. Under close examination, the photograph (though not the filmic representation of the photograph) is only particles of ink on paper.

We are reminded of the flat materiality of the photograph when Portillo's writing hand enters the frame and marks the photograph's surface in various acts of reconstructed semiosis, commentary, or censorship. The dialogue she conducts with the photograph in these moments is not unlike the spoken dialogue conducted with the dead and mediated through the photograph in *La Ofrenda*. Portillo's practice of recontextualizing the photograph and of always reminding us of its separate materiality "denaturalizes" the photograph in other ways as well. The photographic frame, contained inside the cinematic one, is established as marked-off narrative or diegetic space that is anterior to, and separate from, the narrative space of Portillo's documentary. The two planes of narration can be placed side by side but cannot be forced to interpenetrate, as the hand marking on the photograph reminds us. This interior, and separated, framing of visual images is a repeated trope of the film and assumes many forms: TV screens (from normal sized to diminutive ones, these latter either physically minuscule or perspectivally shrunk); mirror images (of all types, including reflections of photographs); images reflected in the lenses of sunglasses; etc. These miniaturizations or constructions of set-apart interior spaces might be regarded as visual formal analogues to the eruptions into the narrative of seemingly random "syncretic" or "magical realist" moments. Such narrational detours occur periodically and seem unmotivated, non sequitur, and inexplicable. The following anecdotes are examples: the story of a black man in dreadlocks whose car crashes into a tree and whose head is covered with goldfish and a large snake; the tale of a mother who turns her embalmed daughter into a mannequin for the display window of her bridal shop; the family séance. These moments appear in the narrative with little or no context. They have the effect of being strangely "deterritorialized" cultural moments whose sources have been lost or erased. They are detached from the conventions of narrative progression and appear to float through the narrative groundlessly, somewhat in the way that Portillo's family photographs float through air or water, inexplicably cut off from their context and thus unanchored physically, narratively, and culturally.

Used in this way, miniaturized images and photographs have the effect of constructing multiple visual registers by interpolating separate, interior visual spaces within a single frame. These interior visual spaces represent each in turn a separate temporality as well: the stopped time of the *stationary* photograph; the time created by moving the *camera* in rephotography (which is different from projection time); the time created by moving the *photograph* in Portillo's real-time animation technique; the internal diegetic time of the telenovela or video interview reflected in the sunglasses (for example).

In an analysis of a Portillo film not discussed in this essay (*After the Earthquake / Después del terremoto*), Rosa Linda Fregoso points out that Portillo's construction of multiple discursive layers is a way of giving narrative voice to a "contradictory Latina subject." Portillo's simultaneous internal framings might be understood as a formal device and a visual trope for expressing this kind of contradictory subjectivity along with the "flexible politics of identity" described by Fregoso and others.[17] Such "enframings" as the "miniaturized" (less than full-frame) photographic image mark off spaces or areas of difference (representational difference; cultural diference; personal difference) that, in combination with each other and contained by the frame, comprise several identities: the formal identity of the frame itself; the identity of the object of representation (Oscar); the identity of the narrative or story; and perhaps in some sense the identity of the narrator as well. These discrete visual and temporal elements paradoxically cohabit a field of temporal simultaneity: the speed of film projection.

The separate and drifting nature of these visual components is in some ways reminiscent of the heterotopic photographic spaces that occur in *La Ofrenda;* in *The Devil,* however, they are uprooted and mobile. The arbitrary quality of this uprootedness gives the photograph in *The Devil* a dystopian inflection reinforced by the use of the family photograph to recount family dysfunction. In any case, the photograph in *The Devil* is not a space within which identity is consolidated, authenticated, or confirmed, but is one of several partitioned-off components into which identity fragments and decomposes. These discrete elements of the visual field, perhaps like the identity features of the "contradictory Latina subject," are separate, coexistent, and cannot necessarily be resolved into one another.

As Portillo uses it, the stilled image can lean either toward the transparency/self-presence of the fictional narrative or toward the opacity of the unnarrativized (material) film. The photograph tends more and more to *return* to this opacity in *The Devil:* it reverts from the character of animation it has at the start to an opaque materiality at the end: a final unreadability. Toward the end of *The Devil* several people, perhaps family members, sit around a table in semidarkness, inspecting, shuffling, and circulating family photographs. These are the black-and-white family photographs we've been shown in the course of the film. The narration tells us that instead of yielding telltale evidence, they still conceal the secrets "held tight" by the family. Retaining their silence and returned to their constitutive materiality, they are once more opaque lifeless objects instead of performers in a family drama. The narrator says, "I came back to Mexico with a naive idea that if I pursued all the clues and uncovered the facts, I'd uncover the truth, just like in the movies."

Perhaps *The Devil* can be regarded as a film that, as Rosa Linda Fregoso says of *La Ofrenda,* moves away from the representation of fixed identity categories (and all forms of fixed meaning) toward a representation of identity as continuously "under production": contested, negotiable, and always changing. Perhaps in doing so *The Devil* necessarily moves away from traditional documentary genres toward a unnarrativized blend based, even more than *La Ofrenda,* on contingencies and processes. Perhaps Portillo's inconclusive, fragmented construction of Tío Oscar is meant to reflect the problematic nature of complex identities along lines suggested by Stuart Hall:

> Identity is . . . not transparent; it is not unproblematic; it is no guarantee of authenticity. Perhaps then instead of thinking of identity as an already accomplished historical fact . . . we should think of identity as a production which is never complete, which is constituted inside, not outside representation.[18]

However, I believe there are also other readings to extract from Portillo's construction of Oscar as a story and as a set of identity concerns, and I would like to turn toward those now.

Third Meanings, Deviant Leanings

Considered alone, *The Devil* seems to be a film about the construction and representation of Tío Oscar as a postmodern identity, and the "unfixability" or complexities and unknowabilities of both identity and truth as such. However, considered in a context including *Las Madres* and *La Ofrenda* and the identity concerns of these earlier films, what other readings of *The Devil* emerge? To begin to answer this, we might want to ask ourselves, why is this the only film into which Portillo makes a personal intervention? We might also want to take note of the fact that in *Las Madres* the photographic image as a fixer of identities functions in two ways. As a surveillance tool, in the hands of a repressive state government, it is the means by which political "deviants" are identified and trapped, to be tortured and killed. As a signifier in an iconic liberatory political language, it is the means by which the body before torture is reclaimed, and identity rewritten, not in terms of subversion and punishment but of relationality (biological and communitarian), participation, and resistance. The fixing of identity cuts two ways: toward death and toward "freedom."

We might also want to remember that in *La Ofrenda,* sexual diversity and gender-bending are tolerated in apparently different degrees and under different circumstances on the northern and southern sides of the international border. Traditional Mexican society, as the narration emphasizes, tends toward strict compartmentalization and narrow definitions of sex roles, gender, and sexuality. Departures from these definitions are permitted only on designated days, under specific conditions. Even then, gender deviance is treated as a disguise, a form of masquerade, the unusual and extraordinary, not an ordinary feature of everyday social interaction. San Franciscan attitudes are different: more open and permissive. North of the border it is possible to openly display an AIDS altar. The implication is that in Old Mexico, open acknowledgment of queer identity (let alone queer community) would be impermissible. Given the binary structure of *La Ofrenda, The Devil* represents a kind of interpolation of one-half of the binary into the other. Portillo's trip down to Mexico to investigate her uncle's death poses an intervention of the permissive attitudes north of the border into a sex- and gender-conservative social context south of the border.

Portillo establishes in the opening sequences of *The Devil* the nature of her film as a personally conducted guided tour of the "inner workings" of her extended family. She takes us to her childhood home and we peek, as it were, through the keyhole. She points out the landmarks, like the Cine Azteca, of her hometown, Chihuahua, Mexico. She remarks on the conservative attitudes that prevail in the provinces of Mexico:

> The provinces have long been the stronghold of conservative values. In Chihuahua, as I found out, these values were a thin veneer which obscured the sordid details of my uncle Oscar's death.

We see her at intervals in phone conversations with her aunt Ofelia. Sometimes her film crew surrounds her and comments; sometimes she's alone. She brings her own social environment with her, an environment clearly distinct from the social landscape through which we are conducted on our "tour."

Portillo's personal textual interventions are important in several ways. First, in combination with the identification with Tío Oscar that she claims for herself at the outset of the film ("He was my favorite uncle . . ."; "I loved that about him . . ."; etc.), they invite us to assume she has a particularly *personal* stake in the telling of *this* man's tale over other family members'. Also important is the fact that these interventions always, for Portillo, assume the forms of auditory or moving images, exclusively. She herself never offers her own image in the form of a photographic representation; she is, instead, always in motion. Portillo's own cinematic identity, unlike Oscar's, thus remains in the realm of the unfixed, the unstatic, and, in a sense, the unnamed. Oscar's condition (as a dead man) is overdetermined, not so much by the number of identifications that cluster around him, as by their nature and their ordering within the film. One is, perhaps, able to accept the possibility that his activities as an overzealous entrepreneur, a politician, a millionaire, a corrupt businessman, a "bad father," the youth-seeking husband of a manipulative woman twenty years his junior, etc. might in one way or another have led to his death. But there is also the overriding implication that Portillo's final explanation is the most compelling: that Tío Oscar was a gay man in a stridently homophobic milieu, trapped in a loveless arranged marriage, blackmailed for his sexual orientation by his second wife, and infected with AIDS. At least, this construction of Tío Oscar occupies a privileged explanatory place: by being held out to the end Portillo makes it foundational to his (and her?) story. For if Portillo identifies herself with Tío Oscar, how are we to read these interviews with his (also her) family, where the mention of queerness prompts shrill outcries of horror? The homophobia in Mexico's provinces is underscored by the overwrought reactions of family members to any mention of the "H" word, as well as by their final, solemn responses to speculations concerning Tío Oscar's HIV status:

> Raúl: Saying he had AIDS is the biggest lie you could perpetrate.

> Historian: Traditionally we treat the dead with generosity. We try to remember only their good side.

Portillo aligns herself, affectively and physically, with Tío Oscar. She puts herself both in his place and under his charge when she lies down on the acupuncture table and, like Saint Sebastian, accepts the "wound," an empathic piercing of the skin while, tellingly, ruminating on the nature of sin. Portillo's priest may generously exclude suicide from his definition of sin, but, we learn, Oscar may be guilty of other sinful activities not so readily forgiven (as may be Portillo herself: "Sin . . . Ouch! That really hurts for a Catholic, even a lapsed one").

Portillo never locates her own sexuality one way or another. This is not, it seems, the ostensible subject of the film. What does, however, become its tacit subject are the dangers surrounding queer identification in the environment which is Portillo's extended family. This is clearly not a setting in which one could safely come out. Tío Oscar is dead. The final revelations surrounding his sexuality are embedded in representations by his closest family members (his children) of his profound loneliness, unhappiness, and isolation. When Portillo puts out the possibility of AIDS and homosexuality to his siblings (including her own father) and others, they comment on the unfortunate way the dead tend to be dishonored instead of honored, as they should be when they're gone. Dishonor, horror, isolation, shame, guilt complexes, and finally death: this is the baggage the homosexual tag carries with it in the social environment of Portillo's extended family.

Beneath its shifting postmodern surface, then, *The Devil* also engages, at least subtextually, with a problem of *fixed* identity: the violence and danger that continue to cling to homosexual identification in certain strata of Mexican society. The dangers of gender-crossing are implicit in *La Ofrenda* as well, where they are strictly and neatly contained in traditional

Mexican culture: there is a safe place for them, but this is the safe place of the masked identity, donned and doffed on special occasions, but un-named and unframed in the flow of ordinary social time. In San Francis-can Mexican-American culture, sexuality and gender identity may be more open and fluid, the second half of *La Ofrenda* (and its shift to same-sex voice-over narration) suggests, but this is, again, a tolerance contin-gent on a specific social, geographic, and historical location—and a re-stricted location, at that.

Portillo does not make her intervention into the provinces of Mexico alone. She includes shots, as mentioned, of her whole film crew. Since (as we learn in *Las Madres*) safety against repression is ensured by community, and by numbers, it is significant that we see Portillo in these shots sur-rounded by friends, who are themselves engaged and responsive, both to Portillo and to the unfolding events in her family story. Even if this group context is conveyed telegraphically, in one or two shots, its inclusion at all is important.

Conclusion

Las Madres documents an extreme instance of the use of the photographic image in a state-sponsored project of social control. As we know from re-cent histories of the semantic categories "homosexual" and "heterosex-ual," they are nineteenth-century constructions roughly corresponding to the period of the invention of photography. One of the early uses of pho-tography was precisely to place individual faces within a social taxonomy, often for purposes of surveillance and control. In *Las Madres* history, the photograph is the means by which potential "subversives" are identified and exterminated by the Argentine government. Throughout Western history (even before the medical category "homosexual" was invented), sexual deviance has frequently been punished with a severity comparable to the disappearing of political dissidents in Argentina. This punishment proceeds directly from the fixing of identification, pinning a name and an image to the suspect individual. In *Las Madres* this process of identification works in two ways. Histories of the oppression of political dissidents and of sexual minorities are in important respects overlapping histories, an overlap that extends to methods of social control involving surveillance, identification, and punishment. As Stuart Hall says in his essay "Deviance, Politics, and the Media":

> In many cases the "numbers" of deviant groups and of politically ac-
> tivist minorities are one and the same. This process of coalescence
> is attested to in the widespread convergence of criminal and ideo-

logical labels applied, without much distinction, by labeling agencies to dissenting minorities of both a "deviant" and "political" type.[19]

Though this specific overlap is not broached in *Las Madres,* it is important to bear in mind in surveying the whole field of Portillo's films and the role played therein by still photography. It is also important to the trajectory of inflections of the photographic image in her work from utopic (*Las Madres*) to heterotopic (*La Ofrenda*) to dystopic (*The Devil*). The inscription of the photograph in *La Ofrenda,* as a heterotopic space-off from conventional social spaces, aligns it with Barthes' "third meaning," insofar as the countertextuality of the third meaning constitutes a space-off from narrative, intersecting with or interrupting its flow.[20] *La Ofrenda* is ostensibly about the reorganization of cultural and national identities across the divide of the U.S.-Mexico border. It is also, and equally, as Rosa Linda Fregoso suggests in *The Bronze Screen,* concerned with the reorganization of gender identities.

From early cinema on, the story of the heterosexual family has been the "stable" story which aheterosexuality intrudes into, disrupts, and destabilizes. The classical cinema story is invariably a story of the formation or preservation of the heterosexual family or couple and the infinitely multipliable circumstances under which this formation is interrupted, threatened, and restored, thus "resolving" the plot. Heterosexuality has been identified with the very prototype or model of narrative progression.[21] Within this circumstance, the argument could be made that whatever interrupts this flow is describable as the counter or alternative thrust of a queer(ed) narrative; a flow in one direction interrupted by a potential flow in another. One of the ways the "fixed moment" can operate in film, then, is as the initiating moment of a countertext that issues from a break or gap in the performance of forward narrative motion.[22] Formally, the element of disruption for the medium of moving pictures happens also to be the constitutive basic unit of the medium itself: the still(ed) photographic image. Perhaps the still image, by introducing a break into cinema's spaced and timed forward motion, unsettles perception and causes the film image to "waver between fixity and movement."[23] In any case, to be reminded of the still image is to be pointed back toward the discrete elements out of which the illusion of movement is itself produced: the "bones" and "ashes" of the "dead body" from which movement is conjured. The photographic image makes the illusion of narrative movement possible, but only on condition that its ontology, its actual "terms of existence" (as not-moving; as still) remain unpresentable, in the same way that the "teleology" of classical narrative progression is possible only on condition that it always displaces the third meaning. It is the moment that disrupts the iterative performance of gender (the "excess") that makes the delimiting of gender identification both possible and always at risk.[24] Similarly, the photographic image is the constitutive unit and the "excess" or "inadmissible extra meaning" out of which the formal identity of cinema is produced, but which always also threatens this identity with interruption and collapse. In relation to "deviant" sexuality in Portillo's films, the photograph is developed into a general trope for specifying, or fixing identity—and in the case of *The Devil,* a trope for a taxonomic or naming device that cannot speak its name. So we never *really* know who or what Tío Oscar was: some forms of identity, under the circumstances that prevail in the provinces, become dangerous, elusive, and fugitive—as hard to pin down as a moving butterfly.

Selena fans kneeling over the tombstone of her grave in Corpus Christi, Texas, during the shooting of *Corpus: A Home Movie for Selena.* Courtesy of Lourdes Portillo.

Interviewing Selena fans for *Corpus: A Home Movie for Selena.* Courtesy of Lourdes Portillo.

Scenes from *Corpus: A Home Movie for Selena* of Selena fan and member of the Tejano Academy of Fine Arts, a dance studio directed by George Balli in Corpus Christi. Courtesy of Lourdes Portillo.

Imiko Omori (left) filming a scene for *Corpus: A Home Movie for Selena*. Courtesy of Lourdes Portillo.

Sarah Chin (sound recordist, right) during the filming of Cherríe Moraga (center) for *Corpus: A Home Movie for Selena*. Courtesy of Lourdes Portillo.

Selena fan Armando Peña displaying his recent purchase of a Selena doll. Photo by Renée Tajima-Peña.

PART THREE

PRODUCTION MATERIALS

The materials compiled in the following section represent a sampling of documents used by filmmakers in organizing a film—items which I earlier termed the "invisible seams in the production process." Included is the storyboard for Portillo's *Columbus on Trial*. In many ways, the storyboard works like a draft for the technicians and actors. It is a visualization of what the filmmaker plans to do after she has examined the location and familiarized herself with the actors. Portillo storyboards most of her films, including documentaries. The first document included here is the script notes for *Después del terremoto;* they are the script supervisor's notes of what actually got done during the process of filming. Other documents pertaining to Portillo's first film—the cast list and the funding application—follow. For those who have never seen an Oscar nomination letter, I have included the letter Portillo received from the Academy of Motion Picture Arts and Sciences for *Las Madres: The Mothers of the Plaza de Mayo*. Other items of archival value contained in this section include the written transcript of the Spanish and English narration and the transcript for interviews for the documentary *La Ofrenda;* and the screenplay and the floor plans for the set design for *Columbus on Trial.*

SCRIPT NOTES

DATE	SCENE–TAKE	COMMENTS	S	R	TIME	LENS	ACTION
1/25	31A –1	good	1 MOS	✓			insert on Irene standing outside TV. Store — insert on TV
							end of camera roll end
							new camera roll new sound roll
			2	2		zoom	slate d w flashlight
	3-5 –1	we slate good					inside bus MCU. profile Irene looks out window
	–2	OK.					Miss [sketch] in prof. 6 bus from (25th to 16th going North)
	–3						then straight on [sketch]

<u>SCRIPT NOTES</u>

DATE	SCENE—TAKE	COMMENTS	S	R	TIME	LENS	ACTION
4/278	1 - 1		17 ✓	19	1:25	12mm	Master from side ~~to~~ Irene leafing thru marriage manual
	—1	cue trk					
	1-2						Master from reverse enters frame left → through leaving door
	—1	noisey cue trk					
	1-2A					T 2.8. 25mm	C.U. on manual getting it from drawer?
	—1						
	—2	entering frame rt.					
	—3	without pull focus			:40		

SCRIPT NOTES

DATE	SCENE-TAKE	COMMENTS	S	R	TIME	LENS	ACTION
4/2/78	1 - 3						M.C.U. for beginning of film ~~Irene~~ Irene enters frame Rt. looks in to mirror
	- 1	too fast eyes moving	17 MOS	19	.		
	- 2	better					
	- 3	OK.					
	⟵7 - 4 (no slate)	good			.		hand held not to get reflection in window
	1 - 4						MCU. on putting on coat
	- 1	good					
	not slated 4		all WILD effects				C.U. on pictures Pans twice on photos on mirror
	1 - 5						C.U. on door knob
	1	false start					

SCRIPT NOTES

DATE	SCENE-TAKE	COMMENTS	S	R	TIME	LENS	ACTION
4/2/78	1 - 6		17	19			Master WIPE Irene ~~leaving~~ house down stairs in wipes under vase
	- 1	good snd.			1:40	9.5	w/o snd [effects on 1-5]
	- 2	Too much expression Irene re: flowers			1:45		
	- 3	camera noise louder (roll change)		20			
	1 - 7						
	- 1	w. wate	MOS				C.U. on wiping under vase
	- 2	w. water					
	- 3	w. Kleinix					
	- 4	without water					

SCRIPT NOTES

DATE	SCENE-TAKE	COMMENTS	S	R	TIME	LENS	ACTION
4/2/78	2 - 1 - 1		MOS				Medium Wide Irene exits house down stairs
	2 - 2 - 1	w. snd					
	— 2	w. snd new roll good	18	20			
	— 3	OK					
	2 - 3 — 1		18	20		15 mm	lower angle coming down stairs
	2 - 2 — 4	good on snd + pix					coming down stairs again like beginning

SCRIPT NOTES

DATE	SCENE–TAKE	COMMENTS	S	R	TIME	LENS	ACTION
4/21/78	2 - 4						M.L.S. Irene walks down street after leaving house
	-1						
	-2	need more time	18	20			
	-3	cut OK					
	-4	good					
		+ WILD SND OF walking with bad wind					

SCRIPT NOTES

DATE	SCENE–TAKE	COMMENTS	S	R	TIME	LENS	ACTION
1/25	3–1 1	nervous ?	✓	1	:25	4 / 9.5	Hand held (wide) Walking beside Irene as she walks past young Bros and stops to store into T.V. set. (zenith) 3 tags (coat unbuttoned) green thing in lap walks into store (hand on purse) left
	3–1 2	bad on sound motor cycle w cant hear toddlers		1	:26		→ NEED insert on T.V.
	scene 3–1 3	good	✓	1	:30	T– 12mm	(WIDE) on high hat Irene walks into store towards camera out frame left looks at T.V.
	3–2					4	open / closed door
	–1	look action call camera not ready (she came forward she should 10 pic at 2ND set)			:20		TV on TV on
	–2	false start then good			:25		

SCRIPT NOTES

DATE	SCENE–TAKE	COMMENTS	S	R	TIME	LENS	ACTION
1/25	3-3		✓	1		12	wide 2
	—1	n.g. actor not ready			:05	F 4	Medium shot
	—2	O.K. but actor nervous need more volume for snd.	✓		:40	12mm F 4 should be (28-4)	until she starts to sign (turns book there is one... something
	—3	want another line reading "today or tomorrow" on delivering TV O.K. on snd. not good	✓		:60	12mm F 2.8- 4	here) forgot to tell (you) with that model here... yours sues new until "bye bye" she doesn't exit.

Front T.V.'s in background back Irene couch

200

<u>SCRIPT NOTES</u>

DATE	SCENE–TAKE	COMMENTS	S	R	TIME	LENS	ACTION
1/25	3-3 · 4	n.g actor too nervous	√	1	:20	4-28 12 mm	Med wide 2 shot seated in front of T.V Irene's back couch new action: to shake hand at end and he kisses her hand
	-5	slated as 4 actor looks ½ camera			:60		
	-6	(good) on Snd & camera	√	1	:60		"here" turns so I will be yours — gives pen ok. starts to sign. hands back when ,

<u>SCRIPT NOTES</u>

DATE	SCENE–TAKE	COMMENTS	S	R	TIME	LENS	ACTION
1/25	3-4 −1	not enough time on Irene listening (Landed $20.00)	✓	1	!45	25 mm / .21f	M.C.U. on Irene listening to T.V. salesman he doesn't talk until she asks when will you deliver it — then action continues— he Kisses her hand she walks out of frame
	−2	O.K, good	✓	1	:45	28	
	+	WILD SND Salesman sync cutaway on cartoon W. Camera					+ ~~unstated~~ inserts on sync, mike T.V. ① Takes, int. pops 2, n.s. ③ ¿ ext.

CAST LIST

Arlene - Young maid (recent immigrant from Nicaragua).

Salesman - T.V. store (speaks Spanish with American accent).

Magali - Young community worker - best friend to Arlene - (born in Nicaragua, raised in San Francisco).

Serafin- Magali's younger brother - street kid (born and raised in San Francisco).

Bobby - English speaking child (5 or 6).

Johnny- English speaking child (5 or 6).

Julio- Young political exile from Nicaragua - arrived only days ago in S.F. with slide show.

Aurora- Julio's cousin, Mother of Bobby and Johnny. In her 30's. Bi-lingual - has lived in San Francisco a long time.

1st Man- Managua, Nicaraguan - torturer - Police Dept.

2nd Man- Managua, Nicaraguan police torturer.

3rd Man- Managuan, Nicaraguan police torturers.

4th Man- Managuan, Nicaraguan police torturer.

Tia Juanita- Arlene's religious aunt - over 50.

Tia Cuca- Arlene's aunt - who cooks a lot - head of household- over 50.

Tia Raquel- Arlene's aunt, over 50 - a little synical.

Liliana- Raul's wife. Has young children. Has been in U.S. for a few years.

Raul- Went to Univ. with Julio - married to Liliana - is a Father - in U.S. for a few years - is an accountant.

(cont'd)

PARTY   Three couples, four babies & toddlers, etc -
GUESTS-   Some single men (30's), young and teenage singles -
              Some older people.

Guillermo-   Boyfriend of Magali   also a community worker -
              raised in U.S., bi-cultural.

Dona Mercedes- Over 65 - hard of hearing, married to Don Felipe.

Don Felipe-   Over 65, married to Dona Mercedes.

Mike-   Aurora's husband - an American, Father of Bobby and
              Johnny. In his 30's - a worker, drives meat truck.

Raul-   Friend of Julio's from the University of Managua.
              Has been in U.S. for a few years. An accountant.
              Married to Liliana. Has young children (same age
              as Julio).

SPEAKING ROLES

1. Arlene-   Spanish-English (20's)
2. Salesman-   Spanish-(American accent).
3. Magali-   English - Some Spanish - 20's.
4. Serafin-   English - late teens 16-19.
5. Johnny -   English - 5 or 6 - child.
6. Bobby-   English - 5 or 6 - child.
7. Julio-   Spanish - 25-30.
8. Aurora-   English-Spanish - 30-36.
9. 1st Man-   Spanish.
10. 2nd Man-   Spanish.
11. Tia Juanita - Over 50 - Spanish.
12. Tia Cuca-   Over 50 - Spanish - experienced cook.
13. Tia Raquel-   Over 50 - Spanish - experienced cook.
14. Liliana-   24 - English accented Spanish.
15. Guillermo-   English/Some Spanish - 23-30.
16. Dona
    Mercedes-   Spanish - over 65.
17. Don Felipe-   Spanish - over 65.
18. Mike-   English - familiar with Spanish - 36.
19. Raul-   25-36 - Spanish - English (accented).

<u>NON SPEAKING</u>

<u>Party Guests</u>-   Bi lingual
                        Babies
                        Toddlers
                        Teenagers
                        Couples - young singles
Can double   ⎧Single males (30 --   )
                        ⎨Older people
Torturers-   ⎩Two men

○   EXHIBIT "A"   ◌   II

Name Lourdes Portillo-Scarlata &   Project Title "Despues de un Temblor"
      Nina Serrano
Amount requested from AFI $10,000.00

              For complete budget ( )
              Finishing funds for a total budget of $_____
              Part of a larger budget totalling $18,000.00

Approx. length 28 mins. B&W (X) Color (X) Gauge (16mm) Animated ( ) Dramatic (X)
Documentary ( ) Experimental ( ) Other (define) _____

SYNOPSIS OF PROJECT

The Mission, "la mision," is the Latin barrio in San Francisco where many Mexicans, Chicanos, Los Salvadorenos, Guatamalans, Nicaraguans, Peruvians, and Cubans live. People walk, talk and "visit" on the sidewalk in front of their over-crowded Victorian apartment buildings. Music can be heard emanating from car radios and transistors. In addition, every few blocks bands can be heard rehearsing in garages. The young people have painted street murals of history, culture and community problems. Drug abuse and poverty are common themes seen depicted in panoramic vistas on the sides of many buildings throughout the neighborhood.

The population is an ever-growing one, for every day new immigrants from all over Latin America arrive to begin new lives. "Despues de un Temblor" is the story of young Nicaraguan immigrants who have come to San Francisco after the massive earthquake that devastated their country in 1972. Since that time, Nicaragua has been in a state of seige. The situation has even been called "civil war, " as the forces of the President, General Somoza, whose family has been in power for forty years, clash with the growing opposition against him. There are two million people living in Nicaragua; 50,000 Nicaraguans have come to live in the United States. A large number have settled in San Francisco in hopes of creating better lives for themselves.

The main character in "Despues de un Temblor" is a young woman, Arlene, who is earning money to support herself, as well as lending a hand to her family back in Nicaragua. She lives with her aunts in the Mission district, Arlene faces and sorts out the difficulties of her new environment. The film investigates the effects of the North American society on the Indio-Hispanic culture, as it is played out in this simple drama about family life, romance and community.

This fifteen minute 16mm. film will be bi-lingual and subtitled. The actors will use English and Spanish interchangeably. It will be filmed in the actual homes and streets of the Latin community in San Francisco. It is intended for both English and Spanish speaking people across the country.

Also include a complete script for dramatic project.

EXHIBIT "B"   V

Name ___Lourdes Portillo-Scarlata &___ **Project Title** _"Despues de un Temblor"_

Nina Serrano

BUDGET

For projects requesting finishing funds ( ); partial funding ( ) from AFI,
itemize budget under the following headings:

	Amount Requested from AFI	Additional funds needed (X) Funds already spent ( )	Total
Production			
Crew 5 people for 11 days x $40.00		$2,200.00	
Cast 4 actors for 11 days x $40.00		$1,760.00	
Misc. Prod. Wardrobe, phone copying, packaging, shipping.		$ 900.00	
Stock			
25 400' rolls of 7247 x $40.00-	$1,000.00		
¼' - 30 rolls x $3.00	$ 95.00		
Equipment Rental			
Camera - 11 days x $125.00	$1,375.00		
Sound - 11 days x $ 50.00	$ 550.00		
Grip & lites 11 days x $75.00	$ 825.00		
Lab Processing			
Editor $200.00/wk. x $12.00		$2,400.00	
Coding 11200 x $.02	$ 250.00		
Editing machine/3 months	$1,800.00		
Supplies	$ 300.00		
Post Production			
Develop & print 11200' x $20.26 plus tax	$2,151.00		
Transfer & stock mag. film 1200 x $.04	$ 500.00		
Mixing			
6 hrs. x $100.00	$ 600.00		
Rights			
There is no charge for rights.			
Three Release Prints for AFI	$ 470.00		
Contingency	$ 89.00	$ 740.00	
TOTALS	$ 9,911.00 _10,000.00_ (Must not exceed $10,000)	$ 8,000.00	$ 18,000.00

EXHIBIT "C"   VI

Name   Nina Serrano
         Lourdes Portillo Scarlata   Project Title   "Despues de un temblor"

PRODUCTION AND PAYMENT SCHEDULE

Production must begin within ninety days of receiving a grant from AFI and projects must be completed within 18 months from the grant date.

Payment request dates should be estimated for three weeks prior to the start date of each phase of production.

Date   Feb. 20 1978   Beginning photography payment request $ 2,833.00

Date   March 1, 1978   Beginning post-production payment request $ 2,834.00

Date   June 1, 1978   Completion of rough cut payment request $ 2,833.00

Upon delivery of three release prints to the AFI the final payment will be made.

Date   Aug. 1, 1978   Delivery of three release prints payment request
                       (not less than 15% of total) $ 1,500.00

Copyright and artistic control remain at all times with the filmmaker

COMPLETE IF APPLICABLE

Additional Funds
     have been obtained from Comm. Theatre arts in the amount of $ 8,000.00
     are being sought from _____ in the amount of $
            (please cite specific sources-use additional page if necessary.)
I understand that I must obtain all additional funds necessary to complete the project before AFI funds can be released. If said additional funds are not obtained within ninety days of receiving grant, the grant money automatically reverts to the AFI's Independent Filmmaker Program fund.

Date   July 12, 1977   Signature Lourdes Potillo-Scarlata

Send application to: The American Film Institute
                       Independent Filmmaker Program
                       501 Doheny Road
                       Beverly Hills, California 90210

ACADEMY OF MOTION PICTURE ARTS AND SCIENCES

8949 Wilshire Boulevard • Beverly Hills, California 90211-1972 • (213) 278-8990

Telex: 698-614

February 10, 1986

Ms. Lourdes Portillo
981 Esmeralda Street
San Francisco, CA 94110

Dear Ms. Portillo,

CONGRATULATIONS!

On behalf of the Academy I am delighted to inform you, in case you have not already heard, that you have been nominated for an Academy Award for Best Documentary Feature for LAS MADRES The Mothers of Plaza de Mayo.

As you may know, the Board of Governors annually hosts a luncheon honoring our nominees in all categories. It's one of the most enjoyable side-benefits of an Oscar nomination, and we expect this year's edition to be every bit as warm and memorable as its predecessors. I hope you'll be able to be with us to recieve your certificate of nomination and to meet the Academy board members and your fellow nominees.

The luncheon will take place at Noon on Thursday, March 13, in the International Ballroom of The Beverly Hilton hotel. Please reply before March 6th by returning the enclosed card, and be sure to let us know if you will be accompanied by a guest. If you have any questions please call Cheryl Behnke at (213) 278-8990.

The 58th annual Academy Awards Presentation will be held on Monday, March 24th, 1986 at the Dorothy Chandler Pavilion of the Los Angeles Music Center. You will be receiving a formal invitation soon.

I hope to see you at both events!

Warm regards,

Robert E. Wise
President

REW:cb

"LA OFRENDA / THE DAYS OF THE DEAD" .

TRANSCRIPTS

1.- GRANDMOTHER PUTTING SHAWL ON / ABUELITA PONIENDOSE EL REBOZO

ENGLISH NARRATION / NARRACION EN INGLES

What seemed unimportant then, has now possessed my memory.

SPANISH NARRATION / NARRACION EN ESPANOL

Lo que entonces no me parecia importante, ahora se ha apoderado de mi memoria.

2.- GRANDMOTHER WALKING / ABUELITA CAMINANDO

ENGLISH NARRATION / NARRACION EN INGLES

How we treated one another, how we lived, takes on great significance.

SPANISH NARRATION / NARRACION EN ESPANOL

Como nos tratabamos los unos a los otros, como viviamos --ahora adquiere un significado especial.

3.- CLEANING THE GRAVES / LIMPIANDO LAS TUMBAS

ENGLISH NARRATION / NARRACION EN INGLES

In Mexico, the ancient celebrations for the dead take place on the first and second day of November, when the souls of the dead return to visit the living. The preparations are given long and elaborate attention, marking the sacredness of the visit.

SPANISH NARRATION / NARRACION EN ESPANOL

En México, las antiguas celebraciones dedicadas a los difuntos ocurren el primero y el segundo de noviembre. Es cuando las almas vienen a visitar a los vivos. Los preparativos son largos y elaborados, definiendo el carácter sagrado de su visita.

4.- GRANDMOTHER SWEEPING THE GRAVE / ABUELITA BARRIENDO LA TUMBA

ENGLISH NARRATION / NARRACION EN INGLES

I remember the lullabies of my childhood: they weren't of fairy tales of imaginary elves, but lullabies of that constant presence, death.

SPANISH NARRATION / NARRACION EN ESPANOL

Recuerdo los cuentos de mi ninez. No eran cuentos de hadas acerca de duendes imaginarios, sino eran historias acerca de aquella presencia constante, la muerte.

5.- GRAVEYARD CLEANING MONTAGE / MONTAJE LIMPIANDO EL CEMENTERIO

ENGLISH NARRATION / NARRACION EN INGLES

Octavio Paz wrote:
"In its celebrations, a culture steps outside time, to acknowledge enduring truths. Time is no longer succession, and becomes what it originally was; the present, in which past and future are reconciled. In celebrating death, we step outside time and so transcend the eternal cycle of life and death."

SPANISH NARRATION / NARRACION EN ESPANOL

Octavio Paz escribió:
"En sus celebraciones, una cultura da un paso más allá del tiempo, para reconocer la verdad que permanece a través del tiempo. El tiempo deja de ser una sucesión, para convertirse en lo que era originalmente: el presente, en el cual el pasado y el futuro se reconcilian. Al celebrar la muerte damos un paso más allá del tiempo, transcendiendo --aunque solo sea brevemente-- el eterno ciclo de la vida y la muerte."

6.- FLOWER MARKET / EL MERCADO DE LAS FLORES

ENGLISH NARRATION / NARRACION EN INGLES

The ancient Mexicans called this day the feast of "Death and Flowers", celebrating the transitory and flowering nature of life.

I still smell the aroma of the zempazuchil filling the air with expectation. On the Day of the Dead, you, grandmother, scattered petals to mark a path to the door so that our dead could find their way home.

Food specially cooked for the souls is placed on the altar offering, so that they too can enjoy its aroma.

SPANISH NARRATION / NARRACION EN ESPANOL

Los antiguos mexicanos conocian esta celebración como "La Fiesta de la Vida y las Flores", debido a que ellos celebraban la naturaleza transitoria y florida de la vida.

Todavia puedo sentir el aroma de las flores de zempazuchil llenando el aire con expectaciones. En el Dia de Muertos, tú, abuela, esparcias los pétalos marcando el camino, a fin de que nuestros muertos pudieran encontrar la casa.

En el altar de las ofrendas, se coloca comida cocinada especialmente para las ánimas para que ellas también puedan disfrutar de su aroma.

7.- SHOPPING / COMPRANDO

ENGLISH NARRATION / NARRACION EN INGLES

Before the arrival of the Spanish, the Indians dedicated an entire month to honoring the dead. The last days of the celebration coincided with the Catholic feast of All Saints and All Souls. The Indians incorporated the Catholic rituals into their ancient celebrations for the dead, today known as Los Dias de Muertos or The Days of the Dead.

SPANISH NARRATION / NARRACION EN ESPANOL

Antes de la llegada de los espanoles, los indios dedicaban un mes completo a rendir homenaje a los difuntos. Los últimos dias de la celebración coincidian con las fiestas católicas del Dia de Todos los Santos y del Dia de los Difuntos --el primero y el el segundo de noviembre. Cuando las celebraciones se mezclaron, estas se convirtieron en lo que se pasó a conocer como "Los Dias de Muertos".

8.- SUGAR SKULL / CALAVERA DE AZUCAR

ENGLISH NARRATION / NARRACION EN INGLES

A gift of a sugar skull with my name pasted on its forehead was a playful reminder of that fearful end.

SPANISH NARRATION / NARRACION EN ESPANOL

El regalo de una calavera de azúcar con mi nombre en la frente era una manera de recordar aquel temido final.

9.- FAMILY DINNER / CENA FAMILIAR

ENGLISH NARRATION / NARRACION EN INGLES

The dead return on this night to visit and to become, once again a part of the family, sharing in the everyday life of those who remember them.

The family lives not in anticipation but in memory...

SPANISH NARRATION / NARRACION EN ESPANOL

Los difuntos regresan esta noche. Nos visitan, y se convierten --una vez más-- en parte de la familia, compartiendo la vida cotidiana con aquellos que los recuerdan.

La familia vive no de expectaciones sino de recuerdos...

10.- <u>GRANDMOTHER</u> / <u>ABUELITA</u>

SPANISH DIALOGUES / DIALOGOS EN ESPANOL

Te pido Heleodoro, que le pidas a Dios de que yo viva otro poquito, siquiera para que acompane yo a tus hijos. Tu eres alma juzgada por El. Pidele que yo viva más.

ENGLISH SUBTITLES / SUBTITULOS EN INGLES

Dear Heliodoro,
please ask God-

on my behalf, that I live a
bit longer,

so that I can be here with
our children.

You're a soul who's been
judged by God.

Ask him that he let me live
a little longer.

11.- <u>MITLA</u>

ENGLISH NARRATION / NARRACION EN INGLES

I am obsessed with the past...with things that were only hinted at, in my school textbooks.

The concepts of sin and hell were alien to the Indians. They believed that it was the way one died. and not the way one lived, that determined which afterlife one would go to.

Persons who died of a natural death went to the Mictlan, the underworld, which they entered thru a tunnel situated now under the church of San Pablo. The company of a small dog was granted to the dead person; to guide them through a number of obstacles in the the underworld. After four years the souls reached their final resting place, Mitla.

Mitla means "place of the dead", and is regarded as the gathering place not only for the souls of those nearby, but for all the souls.

Under the veneer of Westernization, the cultures of the Indian world --that have existed for 30,000 years, continue to live, sometimes in a magical way, sometimes in the shadows.

SPANISH NARRATION / NARRACION EN ESPANOL

Estoy obsesionada con el pasado...con aquellas cosas que casi no se menciona-ron en mis libros de escuela.

Los conceptos del pecado y del infierno eran desconocidos para el indio. Ellos creían que la manera que uno moría y no la manera que uno vivía era lo que determinaba el destino final.

Las personas que morían de muerte natural iban al Mictlan --el inframundo. Entraban a través de un tunel --situado abajo de la iglesia de San Pablo. Al difunto se le concedia la compania de un perrito, para que este lo guiara a través de los obstáculos del inframundo. Después de cuatro anos las almas alcanzaban el lugar del reposo final, Mitla.

Mitla significa "lugar de los muertos", y se considera el lugar de reunión no solo de las almas de aquellos que están cerca, sino de todas las almas.

"Bajo el barniz de la cultura occidental, las culturas del mundo indigena --que han existido por más de 30,000 anos, continuan vivas; a veces, má- gicamente, y a veces, en la sombra."

SPANISH DIALOGUES / DIALOGOS EN ESPANOL

Pregunta: Quién le hablo de San Pablo? Cómo es?

Hombre joven: Las gentes más grandes, vaya, antiguas, ves, gentes grandes dicen ahí es cabecera de las ánimas.

Pregunta: Tienen que ver algo también con las ánimas estas ruinas? Usted cree?

Hombre joven: Sí.

Anciano:· Sí, lo creo.

Pregunta: Por qué cree?

Anciano: Porque aquí las ánimas, dicen, em un sueno que viene a visitar las ánimas.

Pregunta: Asi lo vió en sus suenos?

Anciano: Sí.

Pregunta: Aqui vienen las ánimas?

Anciano: Sí, aqui dicen.

Pregunta: Dónde estamos nosotros? En la iglesia?

Anciano: No. Aqui, aqui. Aqui dicen.

Pregunta: Entonces nosotros estamos entre las ánimas?

Anciano: Como usted tiene aparato, entonces puede ver que es cierto, que aqui están las ánimas, vaya. Aqui se ve entonces, el infierno, y el purgatorio.

Pregunta: Pero no le da miedo?

Anciano: No, por qué?

ENGLISH SUBTITLES / SUBTITULOS EN INGLES

Question: Who told you about Mitla?

Young man: The elders.

They said this is the
resting place of the souls.

Question: These ruins have something
to do with the souls?

Young man: Yes.

Old man: Yes.

Question; Why do you think so?

Old man: Because in my dream

the souls asked me to
come and honor them.

Question: You saw that in your dreams?

Old man: Yes.

Question: So the souls live here?

Old man: That's what people day.

Question: Here in the ruins
or in the Church?

Old man: Here in the ruins.

Question: So we are among the dead
now?

Old man: You have that apparatus so
you can see the souls—

and the entrance to
purgatory and hell.

Question: Aren't you affraid?

Old man: No...Why?

12.- THE SUN / EL SOL

ENGLISH NARRATION / NARRACION EN INGLES

To my ancient ancestors, life and death were cycles of nature; and duality,
the essence of life. Life is destroyed to be reborn.

SPANISH NARRATION / NARRACION EN ESPANOL

Para mis antepasados indios, la vida y la muerte eran ciclos de la naturaleza; y la dualidad, la esencia de la vida. La vida termina para volver a
crearse.

13.- AZTEC SCULPTURES / ESCULTURAS AZTECAS

ENGLISH NARRATION / NARRACION EN INGLES

What is there in me of my Indian past? Even greater than the stone sculptures.
I carry inside of me the strengh and weigh of a brilliant and terrible past.

SPANISH NARRATION / NARRACION EN ESPANOL

Qué es lo que queda de mi pasado indio, dentro de mí? Aún más grandioso que
las esculturas de piedra. Llevo conmigo la fuerza y el peso de un pasado
brillante y terrible.

14.- SPANISH MURALS / MURALES ESPANOLES

ENGLISH NARRATION / NARRACION EN INGLES

The Spanish wanted riches for themselves, land for their King, and souls for
their Church. What is it in me, today, of that conqueror of yesterday?

SPANISH NARRATION / NARRACION EN ESPANOL

Los espanoles querian riquezas para ellos, tierra para su rey, y almas para
la iglesia. Qué queda dentro de mí, de aquel conquistador del pasado?

15.- CUILAPAN MURALS / MURALES DE CUILAPAN

ENGLISH NARRATION / NARRACION EN INGLES

Hernan Cortes, the conquistador of México, wrote to the Kings of Spain:
"Their principal idols, the ones they have the most faith and belief in,
I overthew their thrones and pushed them down the stairs of their temples.
I had their places of worship cleaned because they were filled with the
blood of their sacrifices; instead I placed images of our Lady and other
saints."

SPANISH NARRATION / NARRACION EN ESPANOL

Hernan Cortés --el conquistador de México-- escribió a los Reyes de Espana:
"Derribé los tronos de sus idolos más importantes --aquellos en los que
creian con más fervor. Los arrojé por las escaleras de sus templos. Hice
limpiar sus lugares de culto, porque estaban impregnados con la sangre de
sus sacrificios. En su lugar coloqué imagenes de nuestra Senora y otros
santos."

16.- WALL OF SKULLS / PARED DE CALAVERAS

ENGLISH NARRATION / NARRACION EN INGLES

The images of death that so horrified the Spanish, were destroyed and buried,
surviving only in ancestral memory.

SPANISH NARRATION / NARRACION EN ESPANOL

Las imágenes de la muerte que tanto horrorizaban a los espanoles fueron des-
truidas y enterradas, sobreviviendo únicamente en la memoria ancestral.

17.- <u>MEXICO CITY / LA CIUDAD DE MEXICO</u>

ENGLISH NARRATION / NARRACION EN INGLES

Dreaming of the past, I weep at the fall of Tenochtitlan, the destruction
that made way for Hernan Cortés to build his capital, México City.

SPANISH NARRATION / NARRACION EN ESPANOL

Estaba sonando con el pasado, cuando sollozé con la caida de Tenochtitlan,
destrucción que abrió el camino a Hernan Cortés para construir su capital,
la ciudad de México.

18.- <u>JOSE GUADALUPE POSADA</u>

ENGLISH NARRATION / NARRACION EN INGLES

In the late 1800's, Jose Guadalupe Posada brought to México City a provincial
appreciation of the imagery of death. He sparked in the art world the ancient
recognition of the skull --the calavera, as the icon of our dual existence.

Posada breathed life into the imagery of death. His engravings mock the van-
ities of the living.

SPANISH NARRATION / NARRACION EN ESPANOL

En el siglo XIX, José Guadalupe Posada volvió a introducir con una inspiración
vital --dentro del mundo del arte-- el reconocimiento de la antigua calavera
como simbolo de nuestra existencia dual.

Posada animó con vida la imagen de la muerte. Sus grabados representan una
burla de las vanidades de los vivos.

19.- <u>MAN COVERING HIS FACE WITH NEWSPAPER / HOMBRE CUBRIENDOSE LA CARA CON UN PERIODICO</u>

SPANISH MONOLOGUE / MONOLOGO EN ESPANOL

Presidente de la Madrid quisiera que viniera otro temblor para llevarse el
dinero a Suiza, pai ı vivir como rey, en unas hamacas de seda, como está
López Portillo viviendo. Aquí está la información de las calaveras, las
"calacas" de los funcionarios; los grandes ‑uncionarios que se encuentran
enterrados en el pabellón general.

ENGLISH SUBTITLES / SUBTITULOS EN INGLES

Here is the calavera of the priest

President de la Madrid,
wishes that there would be

another earthquake so that
he could steal the money and

take the money to Switzerland to
live like a King in a

silk hammock like Lopez
Portillo is living now.

Here are the calaveras
of the politicians,

the great politicians that
are buried in the cemetery

20.- <u>PEDRO LINARES</u>

ENGLISH NARRATION / NARRACION EN INGLES

In ancient México, artistic endeavor was called "song and flower". In creating, the good artist was believed to be deified or closed to God.

ENGLISH SUBTITLES / SUBTITULOS EN INGLES

"The good painter, knowing,
with God in his heart
creates things in his heart,
converses with his own heart...
as he were a toltec
he paints the colors of all the flowers."

SPANISH NARRATION / NARRACION EN ESPANOL

En el México antiguo, se conocia la creación artistica como "flor y canto".
Se creia que el buen artista estaba endiosado ó cerca de Dios.

"El buen pintor, entendido,
Dios en su corazón
diviniza con su corazón a las cosas,
dialoga con su propio corazón...
como si fuera un tolteca
pinta los colores de todas las flores."

SPANISH MONOLOGUE / MONOLOGO EN ESPANOL

Los inventé, vaya, de un sueno que tuvé, un sueno muy feo, allá por donde según anduve yo, le dicen el lugar de la eternidad. En el sueno vi a los "alebrijes", que eran unos unos animales muy feos, como las nubes, cuando van caminando que van tomando diferntes formas. Asi eran los alebrijes. Venian encima de mi, como queriendo devorarme, e iban cambiando formas, como por ejemplo, una cabeza de toro, una cabeza de vibora. Se iban transformando.

ENGLISH SUBTITLES / SUBTITULOS EN INGLES

I invented them from a bad
dream that I had,

a very ugly dream.

There in my dream,
called the place of
eternity,

I saw the alebrijes, these
ugly animals.

They were like the clouds
when they pass by,

and take on different shapes,
that's how the alebrijes look.

They hovered over me
trying to devour me.

They would transform

From a bull's head to
a snake's head...

21.- TOURISTS / TURISTAS

ENGLISH DIALOGUES / DIALOGOS EN INGLES

Guide voice: Yes, it's original made by the Aztecs. Yes. Any other question?
               No?

Woman's voice: Sir, what do you think about the Aztec's concept of death?

Tourist man: Oh, young lady, I'm up at this age now, where I have to start
               worrying about death. Maybe this is a good idea, then. You
               now? I mean, this whole group, we are up the age we have to
               start worrying about death.

Tourist woman 1: They were poor. They didn't have anything. So, they have
               something to look forward in another life. And they prom-
               ised them these things. So, they gave them a reason for
               living. And they make them want...that death wasn't some-
               thing you have to be affraid of. No to fear. We fear death,
               but the Indians didn't.

Tourist woman 2: When my husband died, I tried to ...I wanted to talk about
               it. And I went to my uncle's, who I thought he could help
               me. And when I started talking about my husband, he shrugged
               the shoulders, and left the room. He didn't want to hear
               about it. And people need to deal with their grief. They
               need to talk about it. They need to understand it. And
               there is a grief period that...It's just awful if you don't
               talk about it. It's just heartbreaking.

SPANISH TRANSLATIONS OF THE ENGLISH DIALOGUES / TRADUCCION AL ESPANOL DE LOS DIALOGOS EN INGLES.

Voz del guia: Si, es original, hecho por los aztecas. Si. Alguna otra pregunta? No?

Voz de mujer: Senor, qué piensa del concepto azteca de la muerte?

Hombre turista: Ay, senorita, estoy en la edad, ahora, en la que tengo que empezar a preocuparme de la muerte. Entonces quizás esto sea una buena idea. Sabe? Quiero decir, todo este grupo estamos en la edad en la que nos tenemos que empezar a preocupar acerca de la muerte.

Mujer turista 1: Eran pobres. No tenian nada. Asi que de esta manera, tenian algo en que esperar en la otra vida. Les prometieron estas cosas. Asi que les dieron una razón para vivir. Y les hicieron querer...que la muerte no era algo que habia que tenerle miedo. Que no habia que temerla. Nosotros le tenemos miedo a la muerte, pero los indios no

Mujer turista 2: Cuando mi esposo se murió, traté...Queria hablar de ello. Y fui a casa de mi tio, el cual crei que me podia ayudar. Y cuando empecé a hablar de mi esposo, se encogió de hombros, y salió de la habitación. No queria oir hablar de ello. Y la gente necesita hablar de su dolor. Necesita entenderlo. Y hay un periodo de aflicción que ...Es horrible si no se habla de ello. Es simplemente descorazonador.

22.- RURAL PEOPLE / GENTE DEL CAMPO

ENGLISH NARRATION / NARRACION EN INGLES

To my Indian ancestors, time was a wheel: the risings and settings of the sun and the moon were evidence of its eternal turning. The universe was a single, unified whole. Within it took place the endless struggle of opposites: night and day, light and dark, life and death.

SPANISH TRANSLATION / NARRACION EN ESPANOL

Para nuestros antepasados indios, el tiempo era una rueda en continuo movimiento. La salida y puesta del sol y de la luna manifestaban este girar continuo. El universo era una única y simple unidad. Dentro de ella tenia lugar la lucha sin fin de los opuestos: el dia y la noche, la luz y la oscuridad, la vida y la muerte.

23.- FLOWER MAKER / ARTESANO DE LAS FLORES

SPANISH DIALOGUES / DIALOGOS EN ESPANOL

Artesano: Este es un perrito. Se le llama "matachin". El matachin se le ha
            puesto porque anteriormente eran cantantes que con un canasto iban
            de casa en casa, a cantar. Entonces tenia usted que regalarle al-
            go de pan, de fruta. Entonces casa por casa iban cantando alaban-
            zas.

Pregunta: Qué significa la calavera en el valle de Oaxaca?

Artesano: Es una semejanza. Es una realidad, como se ven a las calaveras es
            como vamos a terminar.

ENGLISH SUBTITLES / SUBTITULOS EN INGLES

Flower maker: We call them matachines
               because there were singers,

               that went from house to
               house with their baskets.

               And people would offer
               them food for their songs.

Question: What's the meaning of the
            skull in Oaxaca?

Flower maker: It is a likeness, a reality,

               the way these skeletons look
               is how we all will end up looking.

ENGLISH NARRATION / NARRACION EN INGLES

In this Day of the Dead celebration, people mock death and gender, and whatever else needs a little push...We remember the dead by celebrating life...

In the general disorder of a fiesta everyone forgets himself, and enters into otherwise forbidden situations and places.

Music and mere noise are united, not to recreate or recognize themselves,
but to swallow each other up.

SPANISH NARRATION / NARRACION EN ESPANOL

En esta celebración del Dia de Muertos, la gente se burla de la muerte, y de
cualquier otra cosa que necesita un pequeno empujón...Recordamos la muerte
celebrando la vida.

En el desorden general de la fiesta, todos se olvidan de si mismos, entrando
en lugares y participando en situaciones prohibidas.

La música y el ruido se unen, no para crear ó para reconocerse a si mismos,
sino para devorarse mutuamente.

24.- OAXACA DANCING / BAILE EN OAXACA

ENGLISH NARRATION / NARRACION EN INGLES

In the rigidity of Mexican society --where rules of behaviour have been pre-
scribed for thousand of years, it's in the fiesta and the comparsa that we
can allow ourselves to be free momentarily, to expose our inner selves to
the rest of the community.

SPANISH NARRATION / NARRACION EN ESPANOL

En la rigidez de la sociedad mexicana --en las que las reglas de comporta-
miento han estado prescritas por miles de anos, es en la fiesta y en la comparsa que nos sentimos libres momentariamente, mostrando nuestra intimidad
ante el resto de la comunidad.

25.- STREET THEATER PERFORMANCE / REPRESENTACION TEATRAL EN LA CALLE

SPANISH DIALOGUES / DIALOGOS EN INGLES

Hija: Caporal, por favor!

Caporal: A ver, qué se le ofrece?

Padre: A ver quiero que me des cuenta de mi ganado.

Caporal: Se están muriendo algunos.

Padre: Aquí necesitamos hacer un trabajo. Que aquí mi hija, que ahorita se
        acordó de mi...

Hija: Qué chulo está tu caporal, papá.

Padre: Pero hija...

Hija: Está moribundo.

Padre: Pero ahorita lo revivimos.

Hija: Doctor viene con una brocha. Parece condenado, también.

Padre: A ver diga lo que se lo ofrece.

Hija: Guapo!

Padre: Aquí quiero que hagas dos ó tres brujerias a mi yerno, que se me está
        yendo, hombre.

Doctor: Cuanto estoy ganando? Porque en esta cosita...

Padre: No te preocupes del dinero. Aquí está mi hija que todavia aguanta.

        Bueno, que ya está un poquito acabada, pero te la acabas de acabar.

Hija: Ay, doctor. Tan bueno y tan carinoso. Virgen Sagrada María!

Doctor: No llores mujer, no llores! Calmate esos sollozos.

        Hm! Ya no se puede hacer nada por él senor!

ENGLISH SUBTITLES / SUBTITULOS EN INGLES

Daughter: Foreman, come over here!

Foreman: Yes, little old man.
           How can I help you?

Father: How are my cows?

Foreman: Not so good.

Father: My daughter needs help.
         Her husband is sick.

Daughter: Your manager is cute, father.

Father: Please, your husband is right here.

Daughter: So, what! He's half-dead.

Father: Well, now we're going to revive him.

Daughter: This one doesn't look that healthy, either.

Doctor: How can I help you?

Daughter: Handsome!

Father: I want you to do some
         witchcraft.

Doctor: How much will you pay me?

Father: Don't worry about money.

         I'll give you my daughter.

         She's a little worn out, but
         you can finish her off.

Daughter: Dear doctor, please help him.

           I have happy memories of
           him, he was so sweet.

           Holy Virgin,
           please help him.

Doctor: Don't cry woman,
         Calm down!

         There is nothing we can
         do for him.

26.- <u>MAURO</u>

MONOLOGUE IN SPANISH / MONOLOGO EN ESPANOL

Mauro:

Este disfraz lo usan en la mayoria de las comparsas, en la mayoria de los espectáculos, los Muertos.

Siempre sale una mujer enlutada, y sin colores, de mascaras. Solamente con rayones, con efectos oscuros.

Existe la burla de la gente que las conoció en el matrimonio. Siempre se rió de ellas, porque el marido ó era celoso, ó las golpeaba mucho. Pero ellas no viendo eso, ellas amaban, y amaban...

Hay viudas demasiado alegres, demasiado coquetas. En pleno velorio, en pleno entierro ya anda buscando otro.

Desde el momento que se llama ofrenda, pues se le ofrenda parte, pues ofrendar-le a los muertos, toda la tradición del altar, todas las cosas. Se le ofrenda eso, recordarlos, haciendo memoria, la muerte, queriendo mucho a la muerte. Porque al fin y al cabo, acabamos en eso, con la muerte.

Hasta el más humilde siente la obligación de la ofrenda. Es como cuando aga-rran y te ofrecen una manzana. Te la ofrecen con la mejor de las sonrisas. Te dan y no esperan nada más. Te dan, comparten, te invitan. Eso es tradi-ción. Eso es leyenda.

La palabra ofrenda tiene un significado muy profundo, dentro de las raices tanto indigenas en si, en todas las culturas.

La ofrenda es una palabra de amor, y el amor no tiene precio. Creo que nada tiene que acabar con la tradición en México, porque la ofrenda sigue.

ENGLISH SUBTITLES / SUBTITULOS EN INGLES

Mauro:

This costume is used

in the plays of the Days of the Dead.

There is always a woman in mourning.

dressed in black with no make-up.

People mock her because in her marriage

her husband was either
jealous or abused her.

And in spite of that,
she continues to love him.

And love him.

Some widows are too
happy, too flirtatious.

and even at the funeral

they are looking for a new husband.

It is called an altar
offering because

on the Days of the Dead one
offers

all the traditional
remembrances to the dead.

Thus keeping their memory
alive,

appreciating death, loving
death,

because that's how we'll
all end up.

Even the very poor feel an
obligation

to make an offering...

Like when they offer you an
apple.

They do with a smile.

They give it expecting
nothing in return.

They share it with you.

That's the tradition, that
is the legend.

The word offering has a
very special meaning

in our indian culture and in
all cultures.

The word offering means
love,

and love has no price.

I believe that this
tradition

that Mexican people have deep inside
will never end.

The offering continues.

27.- CONCHA SAUCEDO

ENGLISH MONOLOGUE / MONOLOGO EN INGLES

Concha Saucedo:

For us Dia de los Muertos is the day in which our ancestors visit us. And
is the day that connect us to our cultural past. It is the connector of
5000, 6000, 10000 years. So, in that way it acts as a reinforcer for the
cultural elements that people want to keep. And for people that they are
separated from homeland, from, in certain way, from their culture, because
they are in a forign culture, even those of us who are born here; so, it
becomes a central way of reinforcing that, and reinforcing it among the
community itself, in connecting each other to one another through that
culture, and through the acknowledgement that we all share the same ancestors
whether is an ancestor who died yesterday or who died thousand of years ago.

SPANISH TRANSLATION OF THE ENGLISH MONOLOGUE / TRADUCCION AL ESPANOL DEL MONO-
LOGO EN INGLES

Concha Saucedo:

Para nosotros el Dia de Muertos, es el dia en el que nuestros antepasados nos
visitan. Y es el dia que nos conecta con nuestro pasado cultural. Es la
conexión desde hace 5000, 6000, 10000 anos. Conexión que reinforza los elementos culturales que se quieren conservar. Y para aquellas personas que se
encuentran separadas de su tierra, de su cultura --incluso para aquellos que na-
cimos aquí-- por el hecho de estar en una cultura extranjera, esta tradición
se convierte en el medio más importante de reinforzar esta cultura dentro de
la comunidad. Esta tradición nos conecta los unos a los otros, a través del
pensamiento de que todos comparimos los mismos antepasados. Bien puede ser
un antepasado que murio ayer ó hace mil anos.

28.- <u>AMELIA MESA-BAINS</u>

ENGLISH MONOLOGUE / MONOLOGO EN ESPANOL

Amalia:

I think the evolution has really been a movement from a very internal and
close small community celebration of people --reafirming the Day de los
Muertos tradition of folk art and honoring their own family members-- to
a very large movement now that involves people outside of the Latino or
Mission community.

This sort of Western world that we live in, it doesn't give people a lot of
opportunity to deal publically with death. It is something you don't talk
about it, you get over it very quick.

And the aspect of building the altar, for instance, involves time, and is a
"recuerdo" of remember every year, so death is not like a close chapter in
a book; it's something that you think every year, that you come back to;
and you bring the spirit of the person you love back with you.

What gives it power, I believe, is that it is a group process that involves
people, and makes them stronger.

SPANISH TRANSLATION OF THE ENGLISH MONOLOGUE / TRADUCCION AL ESPANOL DEL
MONOLOGO EN INGLES

Amalia:

Pienso que el Dia de Muertos empezó siendo una celebración interna dentro de
una pequena comunidad, con el objectivo de rendir homenaje a los familiares,
y de reinforzar esta tradición. Ahora se ha convertido en un movimiento, en
el que participan personas fuera de la comunidad Latina ó de la Misión.

Este mundo occidental en el que vivimos no ofrece la oportunidad de tratar
de la muerte públicamente. Es algo de lo que no se habla. Se termina con
el tema rápidamente.

Y el altar requiere tiempo. Es un "recuerdo" anual. De esta manera, la
muerte no es algo como el capítulo final de un libro. Es algo en lo que
se piensa cada ano. Algo a lo que se vuelve, con el espiritu de la persona
querida.

Lo que le da fuerza, yo pienso, es el hecho de que es un proceso de grupo, en
el que las personas se envuelven, haciendose más fuertes.

ENGLISH NARRATION / NARRACION EN INGLES

Chicanos have revived and adapted Dia de Muertos. For them, the past is a
never ending source of active nostalgia. Here our celebrations maybe different in form of those in México, but the spirit of the tradition lives on.

SPANISH NARRATION / NARRACION EN ESPANOL

Los Chicanos han revivido y adaptado el Dia de Muertos. Para nosotros el
pasado es una fuente inagotable de nostalgia. Nuestra celebración aqui
puede que sea diferente de la de México, pero el espiritu de la tradición
permanece vivo.

29.- <u>HERMINIA</u>

SPANISH MONOLOGUE / MONOLOGO EN ESPANOL

Herminia:

Por cada muerto se pone una vela, y se visten con sus monos.

Cuando hay uno que se murió recientemente, se le hace una vela especial, más grande y más gruesa. Y se le pone un pan más grande, y se le adorna con lágrimas. Las personas nombran a esas figuritas lágrimas.

Se hacen figuritas en el pan, distintas figuritas, de animalitos, angelitos, y munequitos.

Se pone agua. El agua de preferencia no debe de faltar. Creo que el agua y el copal --el somerio-- son muy importantes. Eso es lo que atrae lo bueno.

Nosotros tenemos fé en que en este dia vienen nuestros seres en espiritu. Creemos que a media noche ellos llegan. Y pués, ellos, pensamos que agradecen que nosotros les dedicamos este dia, y hacemos todo lo posible de poner comida, y fruta, todo lo que ellos acostumbraban a comer.

Adornamos con flores de zampasuchil, que es la flor natural de este tiempo. Tiene un olor muy especial, la flor. El olor de la flor con el olor del copal mezclados dan un olor como de ozono, algo asi como el olor del hueso.

Ya sea aqui ó en otro lugar nuestros seres queridos, ellos vienen, en cualquier lugar. Además ahora se está dando a conocer nuestra cultura, que es muy importante. Y es algo que nunca debemos de olvidar, aunque estemos muy lejos de nuestra patria. Pero la importancia es hacerlo donde sea.

ENGLISH SUBTITLES / SUBTITULOS EN INGLES

Herminia:

For each dead person one
places a candle.

They are decorated with ribbons.

If there is a recent death,

You place a larger and
thicker candle,

as well as a larger bread
on the altar.

The bread is decorated
with tears.

One can make bread in the
shape of people,

angels or small
animals.

There must be
water and incense on

the offering because
it attracts what's good.

We believe that the spirits of
our loved ones

return on these days.

We also believe that they
come back at midnight,

and they appreciate
our efforts on this day.

We make every effort

to place food or whatever
they like on the offering.

We decorated with
marigold flowers,

the flowers of the season.

The marigold has a very
special odor...

The odor of the incense
combined

with the odor of marigolds
smell very much like bone!

Our dead return,

even if we are far from our
country.

They visit, wherever we
are.

Now that our culture is
becoming known here,

it is very important

that we don't forget to celebrate
wherever we are.

30.— AMALIA MESA-BAINS

ENGLISH MONOLOGUE / MONOLOGO EN ESPANOL

Amalia:

Life and death are truly the core experiences that will, in fact, bind people together, and that to me, there is a kind of space between life and death, and that space is healing. Art is about healing. When people participate in art, when they make it, when they viewed it, it is the same as making yourself well.

SPANISH TRANSLATION OF ENGLISH MONOLOGUE / TRADUCCION AL ESPANOL DEL MONOLOGO EN INGLES

Amalia:

La vidá y la muerte son realmente las experiencias más profundas que unen a las personas. Existe un espacio entre la vida y la muerte. La curación. El arte cura. Cuando las personas participan en una actividad artistica, bien creando ó participando como espectadores, estas experimentan una mejoría.

31.— CARLOS

ENGLISH DIALOGUES / DIALOGOS EN INGLES

Carlos:

Well, traditionally I started making altars through my grandmother who was from Jalisco. Her name was Teresita Diaz.

And this is her.

This is my grandfather, Wescenlao Diaz.

And they come from Jalisco. And they were religious. And they have been cele-brating Dias de los Muertos for a long time. And I made this altar at home to commemorate some of my friends who died of aids, this year.

And at the very top, it's here, I have a calavera. It says SIDA. It repre-sents AIDS in Spanish.

And then we have la Virgen de Guadalupe that I made as a calavera, because she is the symbol not only of the Catholic Virgen , but also Toranci, the Aztec godmother.

And also in my altar I have my friend Carol Nunez, who died in a traffic accident, when were teenagers.

And my cousin, Roxana Mares, from Denver, Colorado, and she was run over, when were teenagers.

And this year Amaro, and my friend Rene, who passed away, in September, of Aids.

SPANISH TRANSLATION OF ENGLISH MONOLOGUE / TRADUCCION AL ESPANOL DEL MONOLOGO
EN INGLES

Carlos:

Empecé haciendo altares con mi abuela, que era de Jalisco. Se llamaba Teresita Diaz.
Y esta era ella.

Este es mi abuelo, Wescenlao Diaz.

Eran de Jalisco. Muy religiosos. Hemos estado celebrando el Dia de los
Muertos durante mucho tiempo.

Este ano hice el altar en mi casa para conmemorar a algunos de mis amigos que
murieron de Sida, este ano.

Y aqui arriba tengo una calavera. Dice SIDA. Quiere decir AIDS, en espanol.

Y aqui tenemos la Virgen de Guadalupe, que he hecho como una calavera. Es un
simbolo no solo de la Virgen católica, sino también de Toranci, la diosa madre
de los aztecas.

También en mi altar tengo a mi amiga Carol Nunez, que murió en un accidente
de automobil, cuando teniamos diecisiete anos.

Y también tengo a mi prima, Roxana Mares, de Denver, Colorado. Fué atropellada
cuando teniamos diecisiete anos.

Y aqui Amaro, y mi amigo Rene, que murieron de Sida, este ano.

32.— AMALIA

ENGLISH MONOLOGUE / MONOLOGO EN ESPANOL

Amalia:

Death is almost like an obscenity in this culture. And among Latinos, and
Chicanos, and particularly in the Mission district community around the time
of Dia de los Muertos, death is made to be lovable, and life giving, and
joyful; ironic; all the things that --I think-- other people can't have.
I believe that is why it has grown in highly proportion numbers outside the
communities joining in.

SPANISH TRANSLATION OF THE ENGLISH MONOLOGUE / TRADUCCION AL ESPANOL DEL MONO-
LOGO EN INGLES

Amalia:

La muerte, en esta cultura, es casi como una obscenidad. Pero durante la
celebración del Dia de Muertos, la muerte --entre los latinos, los chicanos,
y en general en el distrito comunitario de la Misión-- se representa como algo que se ama, que da vida, que es divertido, irónico. En general representa
todo aquello que las personas no pueden tener. Creo que esta es la razón por
la que esta celebración se ha extendido rápidamente a otras comunidades.

33.- <u>WOMAN AT THE PARADE / MUJER EN LA PROCESION</u>

MONOLOGUE IN ENGLISH / MONOLOGO EN INGLES

Woman:

Y eso es muy importante que haiga de todas las razas, porque asi comprende uno, y ve uno que nos estamos solos, que estamos unidos, los unos a los otros. Para mi es importante. Y estoy contenta porque habia de todas las razas. Y para mi es beautiful.

ENGLISH SUBTITLES / SUBTITULOS EN INGLES

Mujer:

It is very important
that people

from all races are here.

That way, we
are not alone.

We are united.

For me that's important,

and I am happy because
here we have all the races.

and that's beautiful!

ENGLISH NARRATION / NARRACION EN INGLES

The fusion of our past and present has created a new art form: altars drawn as much from imagination as from custom.

SPANISH NARRATION / NARRACION EN ESPANOL

La fusión de nuestro pasado con nuestro presente ha creado una nueva forma de arte: la creación de altares. Altares cuya inspiración radica tano en la imaginación como en las costumbres.

34.- <u>CONCHA SAUCEDO</u>

ENGLISH MONOLOGUE / MONOLOGO EN INGLES

Concha:

Bueno, "la cultura cura" means it we were to translate literally that "culture heals", and esentially what it means is that there are elements in all cultures that give health to people if they retain those elements; and particularly for Latinos, we have, sometimes we have to separate ourselves from that culture, and that separation, that dislocation has created an imbalance, which in effect is "unhealth". And when we are saying "la cultura cura", we are saying "return to your culture", maintain your culture, because the base of your health is there. You will be able to find within the richness of the culture that what you need to live today.

SPANISH TRANSLATION OF THE ENGLISH MONOLOGUE / TRADUCCION AL ESPANOL DEL MONO-LOGO EN INGLES

Concha:

Bueno, "la cultura cura" quiere decir que la cultura ayuda a mejorarse. Y esencialmente quiere decir que hay elementos en todas las culturas que pueden curar a las personas, siempre que dichos elementos se conserven. En particular, nosotros, los latinos, hemos tenido que separarnos de nuestra cultura, y esta separación, esta "dislocación" ha creado una situación de desequilibrio, de enfermedad. Y cuando decimos "la cultura cura", estamos diciendo "vuelve a tu cultura", conserva tu cultura, porque la fuente de tu salud está ahí. Serás capaz de encontrar dentro de la riqueza de la cultura todo aquello que necesitas para vivir hoy.

35.- WOMAN TEACHER / MAESTRA

ENGLISH MONOLOGUE / MONOLOGO EN INGLES

Woman teacher:

The altar this year is been dedicated to all the children that have died in wars, in all the countries like Iran, Irak, Afganistan Central and South America, and Africa, South Africa, where they dying also for freedom.

And the children started bringing their toys, their favoring toys, because they thought that if they were dead and they were, wherever they go, heaven, they would like to play with toys. So they just started bringing toys for these children.

One of the little girls brought this egg, Marta Murillo. Her mother died. and she says that this is the last thing that her mother gave her before she died. She brought it, and she says that she thinks that a child would like to play with it, in heaven, or wherever they go.

SPANISH TRANSLATION OF THE ENGLISH MONOLOGUE / TRADUCCION AL ESPANOL DEL MONO-
LOGO EN INGLES

Maestra:

Este ano el altar está dedicado a los ninos que murieron en la guerra. Deci-
dimos hacer este altar en conmemoración a los ninos que murieron en la guerra.
En Irán, Irak, Afganistan, y Latinoamérica; en Africa y Sudafrica, donde también están muriendo en la lucha por la libertad.

Y los ninos empezaron a traer sus juguetes favoritos. Pensaron que si ellos
se hubiesen muerto, y estuvieran en el cielo, les gustaría jugar con juguetes.

Una de las ninas, Marta Murillo, trajo este huevo. Ella dice que es la última
cosa que su madre le regaló antes de morir. Así que ella lo trajo pensando
que algún nino en el cielo le gustaría jugar con él.

36.- SONG / CANCION

SPANISH SONG / CANCION EN ESPANOL

De colores,
de colores se visten los campos en la primavera,

De colores,
de colores son los pajarillos que vienen de fuera,

De colores,
de colores es el arco iris que vemos lucir,

Y por eso los grandes amores de muchos colores,
me gustan a mí (bis)

Canta el gallo,
canta el gallo con el kiri kiri kiri kiri kiri.

La gallina con el kara kara kara kara kara.

Los polluelos con el pio pio pio pio pi.

Y por eso los grandes amores de muchos colores,
me gustan a mí (bis)

ENGLISH SUBTITLES / SUBTITULOS EN INGLES

In colors

The fields are dressed in
colors in the spring.

In colors

The little birds come from
far away in all colors.

In colors

The rainbow that flow is
made of all colors.

That is why my great loves
come in all colors (bis)

And that is why I love them.

The rooster sings kiri-kiri-kiri-kiri.

The chicken sings kara-kara-kara-kara.

The chicks sing pio-pio-pio-pio.

That why my great loves
come in all colors.

37.- MAN TEACHER / MAESTRO

ENGLISH DIALOGUES / DIALOGOS EN INGLES

Teacher: I asked you to think about two different things. Either a wish for
yourself before you die or a wish for a friend's family, or a friend
whose mother died on Tuesday. I know that even though he is not
here, he'll feel good to hear these things, and he may somehow feel
it. Ok?

Camilla?

Camilla: I wish that our friend will feel better when he comes back to school.

Teacher: George?

George: I wish that before I die that my sons or daughters stay healthy or
something?

Teacher: It's a nice wish. Vanessa?

Vanessa: I wish that before I die, my little brother will take care of my
mother.

Teacher: It's a beautiful wish. Brian?

Brian: I wish before I die, nobody else dies, all my family.

Teacher: Patricia?

Patricia: I wish before I die, to see my best friend again.

Teacher: Who is your best friend?

Patricia: Vanessa.

Teacher: Carlos?

Carlos: I wish before I die, Chito to be married already.

Teacher: That Chico to be married already. He's a good friend. Ah?
Anybody else? Thea?

Thea: I wish before I die, I could have a reunion with all my friends.

Teacher: That will be nice. Will you invite me?

SPANISH TRANSLATION OF THE ENGLISH DIALOGUES / TRADUCCION AL ESPANOL DE LOS DIALOGOS EN INGLES

Maestro: Les pedí que pensaran en dos cosas diferentes. Una, cúal sería el
último deseo después de su muerte. Y la otra, que es lo que más
desean para la familia de un amigo, ó para su amigo cuya madre
murió el martes pasado. Sé que aunque él no esté aquí ahora, el
oir estas cosas le haría sentirse muy bien. Incluso, puede que
él lo sienta. De acuerdo?

Camila?

Camila: Deseo que nuestro amigo se encuentre mejor cuando vuelva a la escuela.

Maestro: Jorge?

Jorge: Mi último deseo sería que mis hijos se encontrasen en buen estado de
salud. Algo así?

Maestro: Es un buen deseo. Vanesa?

Vanesa: Antes de morirme, me gustaría que mi hermanito cuidase de mi madre.

Maestro: Es un deseo precioso. Brian?

Brian: Antes de que yo me muera, me gustaría que nadie de mi familia se hubiese
muerto.

Maestro: Patricia?

Patricia: Deseo que antes de morirme, pueda ver otra vez a mi mejor amiga.

Maestro: Quién es tu mejor amiga?

Patricia: Vanesa.

Maestro: Carlos?

Carlos: Me gustaría que antes de que yo me muera, Chito ya se hubiese casado.

Maestro: Que Chito ya se hubiese casado. Es un buen amigo. Verdad?

Alguién más? Thea?

Thea: Antes de morirme, me gustaría reunirme con todos mis amigos.

Maestro: Será agradable. Me vas a invitar?

SPANISH NARRATION / NARRACION EN ESPANOL

Para el habitante de Nueva York, Paris ó Londres,
la muerte es la palabra que jamás se pronuncia,
porque quema los labios.
El mejicano. en cambio,
la frequenta,
la burla, la acaricia,
duerme con ella, la festeja,
es uno de sus juguetes favoritos
y su amor más permanente.

ENGLISH SUBTITLES / SUBTITULOS EN INGLES

The word death is not pronounced
in New York, Paris or London,
because it burns the lips.
The Mexican, in contrast,
is familiar with death,
jokes about it, caresses it,
sleeps with it, celebrates,
it is one of his favorite toys
and most steadfast love.

Octavio Paz

ROLL #1

VISUALS	AUDIO
Cl-up newspaper	Aquí está la información de las calaveras, las "calacas" de los funcionarios; los grandes funcio-narios se encuentran enterrados en el pabellón general.
Pedro Linares making calaveras	Los ————➤ inventé, vaya de un sueño que tuve, un sueño muy feo, allá por donde estaba; le dicen el lugar de la eternidad. En el sueño ví a los "alebrijes"; pero son unos animales muy feos, como las nubes, cuando pasan y toman formas diferentes; así eran los alebrijes. Venían encima de mí, tratando de devorarme; cambiaban de forma, de cabeza de toro, de serpiente...
He is showing a skeleton	Ahorita les voy a enseñar una cosa como esta. Primero se hace el cuerpo con la cabeza; ya que están hechos, se vacían los moldes, se cierra, entonces se coloca el cuello, lo segundo; y luego lo tercero, se le hacen las manos, los pies, y se les va colocando...
Interview with "el viejito": 2 men and 2 children standing next to San Pablo rúines	Q- Quién le habló acerca de San Pablo, ? su madre, su padre? Younger Man- La gente mayor; dicen que este es el lugar de las ánimas. Q- Tienen que ver algo con las ánimas estas ruinas? Viejito- Sí Q- Por qué cree? V- Porque aquí ? Q- Lo vió en sus sueños? V- Sí, yo Q- Aquí vienen las ánimas? V- Sí. Aquí dicen. Q- Aquí donde estamos? No en la iglesia? V- No. Aquí, aquí. Aquí dicen.

239

ROLL # 1   page 2

VISUALS	AUDIO
Interview with "el viejito":cont.	Younger Man: Aquí es la cabecera de las ánimas.
	Q- Entonces nosotros estamos entre las ánimas?
	V-
	?
	Q- Pero No le da miedo?
	V- No.
Pan shot left to right on flower shop. Medium shot of flower maker working M-shot of flower maker (after Cl-up of hands making flower)	Flower maker- Este es un perrito. Se le llama "matachín". El matachín se le ha puesto porque anteriormente eran cantantes que con un canasto iban de casa en casa a cantar. Entonces tenía usted que regalarle algo de pan, de fruta. Entonces casa por casa iban cantando alabanzas.
	Q- Qué significa la calavera en el valle de Oaxaca?
	FM- Es una semejanza, es una realidad cómo se ven a las calaveras, como vamos a terminar.

ROLL # 2

VISUALS	AUDIO
"Widows walking by	Mauro: Este disfraz es usado en el Día de Muertos. Siempre sale una mujer enlutada, sin colores, aún mascaras,
M-shot of Mauro wearing a costume, next to altar	No es una viuda que triunfó ni que fracasó, simplemente es una mujer que amó, y que se quedó ahí. Entonces cuando se tapa la cara no lo hace por hipocresía ni por nada, sino simplemente porque la gente que las conoció en el matrimonio siempre se ríe de ellas, porque el marido ó era celoso ó las golpeaba mucho; pero ellas no viendo eso, ellas amaban y amaban, y amaban...
M-shot of widow holding a cross	Hay viudas demasiado alegres, demasiado coquetas, pintadas; esa es la viuda alegre; la llaman
Mauro taking off his wig	"la casquivana", "la cascoligera", "la facilita". Tiene muchos nombres, que dan a conocer a una mujer que no le tiene respeto al marido, sino que en pleno velorio ya anda buscando otro. Desde el momento que se llama ofrenda, se le ofrenda el Día de Muertos toda la tradición, eso, recordándoles, haciendo memoria, queriendo a la muerte; al fin y al cabo, así es como todos terminamos, muertos...
Deep shot of "la abuelita" with another woman filling out a basket	Hasta el más humilde siente la obligación de la ofrenda. Si te ofrecen una manzana con la mejor de las sonrisas
They walk away from the camera	te dan, no esperan nada, eso es tradición. Siempre será lo mismo, ofrenda, tradición, leyenda;
They put the basket on the table and over it with a piece of cloth	porque al fin y al cabo, la palabra ofrenda tiene un significado especial en todas las culturas.
They walk away with the covered basket	La ofrenda es amor, y el amor no tiene precio.

241

ROLL # 3

VISUALS	AUDIO
Interview with Herminia: She stands in front of an altar. She points out at different objects as she talks about them	

Herminia: Por cada muerto se pone una vela, y se viste con sus monos. *más gruesa*
Cuando hay uno que se murió recientemente, se le ~~pone~~ una vela especial más grande, y se le pone
un pan más grande, y se ~~le~~ adorna con lágrimas, *las personas nombran esas*
figuran lágrimas
Se hacen figuras en el pan, distintas figuritas, de animalitos, *anfelito y muñequito*
Se pone agua, *de preferencia y el agua no debe de faltar*
Creo que el agua y el copal son ~~muy importantes~~. Eso es lo que atrae lo bueno.
Nosotros tenemos fé que en este día vienen nuestros seres, *creemos* que a media noche ~~ellos~~ llegan
~~aquí.~~ Pues, ellos, pensamos que agradecen que nosotros les ~~dedicamos~~ este día. Hacemos todo lo
posible de poner comida, y fruta *todo lo que ellos acostumbraban* ~~en el altar~~. *a comer*
Adornamos con flores de zampasuchil, que es la flor natural *de este tiempo*
Tiene un olor muy especial ~~esta~~ flor. El olor de la flor, y el olor del copal mezclados dan un olor
como de ozono, algo así, como ~~de muerto~~. *el olor*
Ya sea aquí ó en otro lugar *nuestros seres queridos ellos vienen no*
en cualquier lugar que
y además ~~ahora que~~ se está dando a conocer nuestra cultura, es muy importante. ~~Eso es~~ algo que ~~nunca~~
~~nosos~~ debemos de olvidar, *aunque estemos lejos de nuestra patria*
la importancia en
~~lo importante es hacerlo donde sea.~~

el ~~total~~ sombrero no debe de faltar. Porque eso
a la

AFTERNOON - INT. SOMEWHERE IN THE AMERICAS.

SC. 1 THE HALLS OF JUSTICE. A LONG SHADOWY CORRIDOR.

An explosion of energy and people bustle down the corridor. It is a mob of press people walking ahead of a man that wears a feather on his hat. The mob asks questions relentlesly.

Through the hubbub of activity, in the center of the storm we see; DON CRISTOBAL COLON, THE ADMIRAL, CHRISTOPHER COLUMBUS. He glides across the corridor, as if floating.

COLUMBUS, dressed in full costume of his day (plume feather, tights, Spanish ruffles, French ridges, knee -high boots) dominates his wimpy attorney and somewhat enjoys his celebrity status. He is vain. And very concerned about his appearance .

Smoking a cigar, loud, trying to control an uncontrollable situation, moving about Colombus like some nervous fly is his lawyer BOB OSO

> OSO
> (pushing them back)
> My client has no comment. No comment!
> Back up... Back up.

> ANITA
> (Without missing a beat)
> ...Any comment for our viewers?
> (while she looks at the camera and
> holds the microphone to C. He leaves
> the frame)

In the same shot COLUMBUS reappears closer to the camera , leaving ANITA in the lurch behind him. Microphones are once again shoved close to his face.

> COLUMBUS
> (with an Italian accent)
> Wha...What ? murder...Wha, rape. Querida,
> (Anita comes into frame) do I look like a
> killer?... like a rapist? Why dat ungrateful
> prosecuting son of a bitch. . Read the history
> books. He ain't got shit on me , Baby!

> OSO
> (gets in front of C.)
> My client has no comment...back up you
> animals...you hear me?...Security!!...

A few steps down the hall. Reporters fight to ask questions. OSO is going crazy. COLUMBUS leads the pack into the courtroom.

SC. 2 CORRIDOR

STORM CLOUD is impeccably dressed in a suit and tie. He wears a vest of war beads. He turns, walks down the corridor to the courtroom revealing a foot-long braid with a small feather attached. As he walks down the corridor he is approached by Mr. X who steps in his path.

                    STORM CLOUD
        What do you want?... Who are you?

                    Mr. X
                (getting in his way)
        Just call me "X"

                    STORM CLOUD
                (trying to get away)
        So, what do you want from me X?

                    Mr. X
        I want nuthin' man. I have pertinent
        information concerning the case that I think
        will be of great interest to you. You are about
        to break open a great historical conspiracy. I
        have important dates and facts.

                    STORM CLOUD
        Why are you doing this?

                    Mr. X
        Because the black man, the red man and the
        brown man, we all in the same situation. All
        right, case in point. It's 1451. Columbus and
        Queen Isabella are born. Five years later
        Haley's Comet streaks across the sky!

                    STORM CLOUD
        So?

                    Mr. X
        Don't you get it? Extermination is a thirteen-
        letter word. Columbus would string up and
        burn groups of thirteen Taino Indians at a time.
        In honor of our Redeemer and his twelve
        apostles; thirteen. Leonardo Da Vinci's Last
        Supper depicts the same number... Four
        hundred and fifty years later the Cleveland
        Indians beat the Yankees in the World Series
        and Halley's Comet once again streaks the
        sky!

                    STORM CLOUD
        Excuse me Mr....

                    MR. X
Call me X.

                    STORM CLOUD
Yes, X what does this information have to do
with my prosecution?

The opening music from DRAGNET over STORM CLOUD'S last line.

STORM CLOUD turns away. BLUESCREEN in the background is a panoramic
view of L.A. on fire. In closer view, at store fronts Latinos are looting, running away
with milk cartons , TV sets, whatever.

                    MR. X
                (insulted)
Don't walk your silly long hair ass away form
me. Hey! I'm takin' to you, Tonto! if ya'll
indians wouldn't have died like flies and been
lazy and shit, the white man would have never
brought us from Africa to cut sugar cane and
pick cotton!

Storm Cloud heads for the courtroom Mr. X is left behind as he shouts his final
command to Stormy.

                    MR. X
Don't forget, ese, remember the shit man. You
represent us all. 500 years my mestizo
bro...500...

SC. 3 COURTROOM

From the position of the JUDGE'S bench we see a monitor on her desk that reads;
Justicia Diaz, Hispanic, Stanford Law School. Magna cum Laude, Miss Hispanic
Values etc. etc. The Judge comes towards the bench and sits, her black robe
creates a wipe on the screen .

Close on pounding gavel

JUDGE JUSTICIA DIAZ, an upper class "Hispanic", obviously a mestiza with a
complex, she looks over some legal briefs. THE JUDGE presides over the
courtroom with grace and an air of superiority.   She looks up to scan her court
room skeptically.

                    JUDGE
This court will come to order.
                (pounds gavel once, motions for
                counsel to approach the bench)

I don't know what you two have in mind, (fake smile) but let me remind you I will not let my courtroom be turned into a circus. Glares at them .

Apprehensive looks from the Lawyers. She looks at Columbus on her monitor. He's sitting as if posing for a painting, satisfied with himself. **On the background is the blue sea and the caravels sailing towards us**.. STORM CLOUD pulls out a braid of sweetgrass from his inside jacket pocket. He begins to light it with a Bic lighter which produces a rather large flame. The Judge is trying her best to avoid the smoking braid . STORM CLOUD crosses the screen twice. THE JUDGE puts a delicate handkerchief to her nose, gives STORM CLOUD a dirty look.

> STORM CLOUD
> To all my relations!! Ho!!

> JUDGE
> Ho?!

> OSO
> Ho?

Storm Cloud crosses the screen.

Judge Justicia is already impatient with them. She gathers herself , mustering up all the dignity she can.

> JUDGE JUSTICIA
> (fake charming))
> We Hispanics have struggled in this country long and hard... we no longer have to resort to witchcraft.... Try to act civilized ! Stop burning weeds in my courtroom!!

COLUMBUS smiles a paternalistic smile. STORM CLOUD is annoyed with her.

FADE OUT

FADE IN

SC. 4 COURTROOM

OSO is pacing around in an ill-fitting polyester suit, presenting his case.

> OSO
> (confidently)
> First of all, I'd like to say that the discovery of America was inevitable... and and it was a sort of accident if you will.. My client was on his

way to Japan! He was a fearless explorer
embarking on an adventure unlike any other.
Quote;

COLUMBUS is surrounded by beautiful white clouds on a blue sky.

> OSO V.O.
> "Christopher Columbus, a skilled Italian
> seaman, now stepped upon the stage of
> history. A man of vision, energy,
> resourcefulness, and courage, he managed,
> after heartbreaking delays to gain the ear of
> the spanish rulers." and from there discover
> our America!

A few rotten tomatoes fly at OSO, plop, plop. plop, he ignores them.

> OSO
> If my client had not set sail, other Europeans
> would eventually have done it. So there!!
> (tugging at his shirt sleeves,nervously)
> Allow me to read from a history books. I quote
> "Care and trouble had turned his hair white.
> His temper was naturally irritable, but he
> subdued it by the benevolence and generosity
> of his heart. Of a great inventive genius, a lofty
> and noble ambition, his conduct was
> characterized by the grandeur of his virtues
> and the magnanimity of his spirit"...

COLUMBUS dreaming of gold coins flying around his head.

> OSO

> Your honor, he was the first... The first to bring
> religion to this godless people... One of the
> main reasons was to save their souls. (OSO
> moves from behind an exhibit table ladden
> with chocolate, tabacco tomatoes potatoes
> and avocados) My client did not commit a
> crime, he in fact introduced Europe to
> America, (with a bar of chocolate in one hand
> and a bottle of spagetti sauce in the other) one
> world to the other, now tell me is that a crime?

On the Bluescreen is the fabulous cathedral of Mexico City and other stunning
colonial buildings as seen from a visitors point of view. The Ave Maria is on the
soundtrack.

> OSO
> Columbus presence meant the beginning of
> the end of all the barbarism that reigned in the

Americas... (looks at Storm cloud) such as human sacrifice!!

                    SEVERAL VOICES V.O.
OH!! OHHH!! Hissing.

          OSO
(questioning COLUMBUS on the stand)
Would you kindly explain to the Judge, whom I
believe is Spanish by way of Mexico! (he grins
at her, she nods back) what you were doing in
the Carribbean.

               COLUMBUS
(takes out a cross and points it towards
STORM CLOUD) Heathen!! ... I brought
European civilization. Think of where they
would be now... with their tribal wars.
They didn't have horses or knew how to use
the wheel..Thanks to me they have a single
language, Spanish. I brought them
Christianity... It was a beautiful meeting of two
worlds..

SOUNDTRACK --MORE MUSICA SAGRADA

               STORM CLOUD
Objection, your honor. It was not religious
fervor that brought him here but the
uncontrollable lust for gold. Gold. Gold , gold!
This man was a traveling salesman, a self
promoter!! What he calls a discovery was
nothing but a lucrative business with free labor
thrown in!

               JUDGE
Order!! I demand order! Don't you see he
brought Hispanic Culture to the Americas? .

          OSO
We must be related!

On the JUDGE'S computer: migration patterns of the Europeans to the Americas;
statistics, etc.

A CU of the Judge's complacent smile.

FADE OUT

FADE IN

SC. 5 COURTROOM

Sometime later... It is STORM CLOUD's line of questioning he struts around
confident, full of himself... COLUMBUS is on the stand.

> COLUMBUS
> (with an italian accent, romantic)
> I had to cross that big ocean, I came here to
> explore...The Indians had it easy, for
> chrissakes. Running around naked,
> swimming, lounging. They thought they were
> at Club Med. They lived without religion, why
> don't you accuse me of having saved their
> souls! or accuse me of having discovered the
> new world! Ha, Haaa...

BLUES CREEN projection of US. stamps, from the Indians Point of view first, then
from the European. Storm Cloud illustrates.

> STORM CLOUD
> (turning to the judge)
> Objection your honor, the terms "discover"
> and "New World" must be
> stricken from the record. He did not discover
> a new world. In fact, these so-called "Indians"
> discovered him .

He continues his cross examination. COLUMBUS IS ON THE STAND.

> STORM CLOUD
> What was the deal that you cut with the Queen
> of Spain?

> COLUMBUS
> My terms were one tenth of all the wealth that
> would arrive from Japan along the new route,
> not only for myself but for anyone else. For all
> time, for myself and for my heirs. Mind
> you...ultimately, I got screwed on the deal.

> STORM CLOUD
> You said Japan? This is not Japan. This is
> what you call America.

> COLUMBUS
> Fer God's sakes, is that a serious accusation?
> Anyone can make a mistake! some people
> call me Spanish but I am really Italian.. and so
> what, what I am is the great discoverer.

A Hatchet flies across the screen and lands close to Columbus. He looks around
suspiciously.

                    STORM CLOUD
                (taking the hatchet off and caressing it)
        Isn't it a fact that you treated these supposed
        "indians" like animals?

                     COLUMBUS
        It depends what you mean by animals, for
        example, I love dogs, Dobermans, German
        shepards; hunting dogs. We brought many to
        the Caribbean... Here poochy, pooch.

BLUES CREEN dogs barking ferociously, fighting over a peice of meat, tearing it
apart, growling.

                    STORM CLOUD
        The dogs were fed the flesh of the natives on
        your instructions... to get them used to "Indian
        flesh"... You didn't see Indians as fellow
        human beings. You enslaved them and in a
        few years exterminated every last one on the
        Island of Hispaniola.

COLUMBUS DANCES A MAMBO ON a Map of the Caribbean from the 15th
century, as if it were a rug. Quote underneath" The propagation of faith and the
submission to slavery are idissolubly linked."   signed, C. C. The soles of his feet
leave bloody marks on the map.

                      OSO
        He is a dicoverer!

                    STORM CLOUD
        He is a rapist!

                      OSO
        He is a giver!

                    STORM CLOUD
        He is a taker!

                     COLUMBUS
                   (ON THE MAP)
        He's powerful and that makes him sexy!

                      OSO
        He is a visionary!

                    STORM CLOUD
        He's Hannibal Lector!

                      OSO
        He's Gerard Depardieau!

The Judge calls for order in the court, hitting the gavel several times.

JUDGE
Order! Please continue... Storm Cloud.

Columbus BLUESCREEN goes deep in his fantasy world dreaming of the
Caravels bobbing up and down in the ocean.

STORM CLOUD
(looks maliciously towards the Judge.)
Your Honor, I would like to quote the
Colombus Journal " I have sent men to the
river. They have brought me back seven head
of women, girls and adults, and three infants'"
entered on 12/11/1492... As one can see your
honor that to be an indian and a woman
inmediately puts you on the same level as
cattle. If I were you I'd banish him from all the
history books!

This catches the Judge's attention, she looks at COLUMBUS, he is not very happy.
THE JUDGE's nails drag slowly across the desk.. OSO is sweating profusely. CU
of the JUDGE frowning.

JUDGE
We will adjourn for a fifteen minutes break .

COLUMBUS looks grim, ill-fated. He and OSO exchange whispers. They get up
and move towards the center of the courtroom and come face-to-face with the
prosecutor. As they all turn to exit, COLOMBUS tries to strike a deal with STORM
CLOUD.

COLUMBUS
Hey tonto, let's just forget about this whole
mess. No harm, no foul. Listen Kid, you know,
I got a reputation to uphold. I am known
throughout the New World and the Old World,
the whole universe, as the great explorer.
Don't ruin it!

OSO
(cleaning the sweat of his face)
With a guilty verdict, think how hard it will be to
rewrite all them history books, the street signs,
the city in Ohio.

COLUMBUS
Tell you what I am gonna do, kid. I'm willing to
share my damn holiday with an Indian. Gray
Horse or somethin". Whadaya say? I am not
such a bad guy. I loved Dances with Wolves.
It was a beautiful movie.

OSO
Drop all charges, Storm Cloud.

STORM CLOUD
Sure enough! I am not a damn fool. We've
been waiting for five hundred years, forget it.

STORM CLOUD walks ahead confident leaving them behind.

FADE OUT

FADE IN

SC. 6 - IN THE COURTROOM

JUDGE
The bench has deliberated and found Mr.
Christopher Columbus not guilty of any crime
whatsoever. There is insufficient evidence to
find him guilty beyond all reasonable doubt...
He will remain the Adventurous explorer and
hero of all Italian Americans and the icon of
all the America.......
Furthermore he will not be banished from the
History books. Court Adjourned.

STORM CLOUD'S jaw drops, he leaves the room in a huff. CHRISTOPHER
COLUMBUS smiles mockingly, OSO is jumping up and down.

OSO
My career is zooming ahead! The best
Hispanic lawyer in the U.S.

SC. 7 TILE BACKGROUND, BATHROOM.

C.U. of Xochitl, a young woman putting on black war paint.

STORM CLOUD is defeated, crying. XOCHITL sports a Huelga tattoo as she tries
to console him.

XOCHITL
Don't worry honey, I'll fix it.

SHE slips a gun under her belt and puts a trenchcoat and hat on.

SC. 8 BACK IN THE COURTROOM

A jubilant OSO smoking a big cigar, and COLUMBUS open the courtroom double
doors and continue walking into the hallway.

SC.9 OUTSIDE THE COURTROOM DOORS

Suddenly, a JACK RUBY type in a trenchcoat rushes into the middle of the crowd and shoots Colombus. The crowd reacts with alarm. Columbus falls to the ground, Oso by his side. Chaotic commotion. Anita tries to inch in for some comments. Oso is going crazy.

                    OSO
          Oh my God! Jesus, Mary and Joseph! He's
          shot. Call an ambulance...Somebody, my
          master...

                    ANITA
          Mr. Columbus ... Mr. Columbus, any final
          comments?

COLUMBUS is lifted and dropped on the stretcher. He's loaded into the back of the ambulance headfirst. We see the door shut. OSO falls on the door in a dramatic style.

                    OSO
          (grabbing the ambulance door)
          You didn't pay me...Ritcheee!

SC. 10 THE AMBULANCE.

Sirens are blaring, an attendant working over a dazed and almost dead Columbus who appears to be hallucinating, as the ghosts of 500 years seem to be haunting him through the windows of the ambulance. The FLATLINER RYTHM of Columbus 's fading hearbeat. The urgent voices of the attendants on the ambulance radio communicating to the hospital.

BLUESCREEN in the windows of the ambulance. Engravings from the <u>Cruelties of the Spanish</u> by Thodore de Bry. Sounds of dogs growling. Gold coins, Julio Iglesias sings as the sound of the gold coins comes out of his mouth.

                    ANITA
          (at one of the windows of the
          ambulance)
          Any final thoughts, Mr. Columbus?

Camera person squeezes into the window crowding Anita, she turns to the camera person.

                    ANITA
          For our viewers who have just joined us, the
          famed Italian explorer was shot today in the
          corridors of the courthouse. He is here
          live...Uh barely live...

Anita sticks the microphone out to Columbus for response. Columbus moans... At another window.

                    JUDGE
              (talking to the camera)
        It's a shame when violence comes into the
        courtroom. But sometimes emotions run high
        and certain things cannot be avoided.

A BOY of ten pops into frame alongside the judge.

                    JUDGE
        This is my hijo Quetzalcuatl. Say hi, mijo. He
        wants to be a judge one day too, just like his
        mommy, huh mijo?

                    KID
              (pointing to Columbus))
        What's that?

                    JUDGE
        That's Christopher Columbus mijo. You read
        about him in your history books, te acuerdas?
        He's almost dead, so say goodby mijo.

                    KID
        Bye.

THE WAVES, UNIMPRESSED BY ALL THE COMMOTION.
IN THE AMBULANCE

We hear only the sound of COLUMBUS'S short breaths and the Flatliner heart rate
machine. The driver is on the radio speaking to the hospital. A few short breaths.

MR. X is singing "You got the right one baby, Ha Ha" (Ray Charles),
Behind him are three Indias in huipiles singing back Ha, Ha.

STORM CLOUD appears in the ambulance window. Their eyes lock for a moment.

                    STORM CLOUD
        Payback's a bitch, ain't it?

Kid Frost rap, "Run Indio Run" is heard over the credits. Sirens.

BLUESCREEN INSERTS

SC. 11 BLUESCREEN - JUDGE AND ANITA AND JUDGE AND KID

SC. 12 BLUESCREEN - X AND BACKUP INDIAS

SC. 13 BLUESCREEN - THE CITY GOES BY COLUMBUS SALAME FACTORY, COLUMBUS STREET.

THE END

C.COLOMBUS LOURDES PORTILLO PRODUCTION   S.F. 7/10/1992

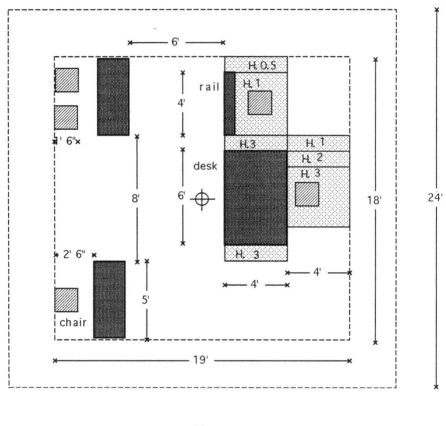

COURT ROOM floor plane

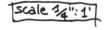

scale 1/4": 1'

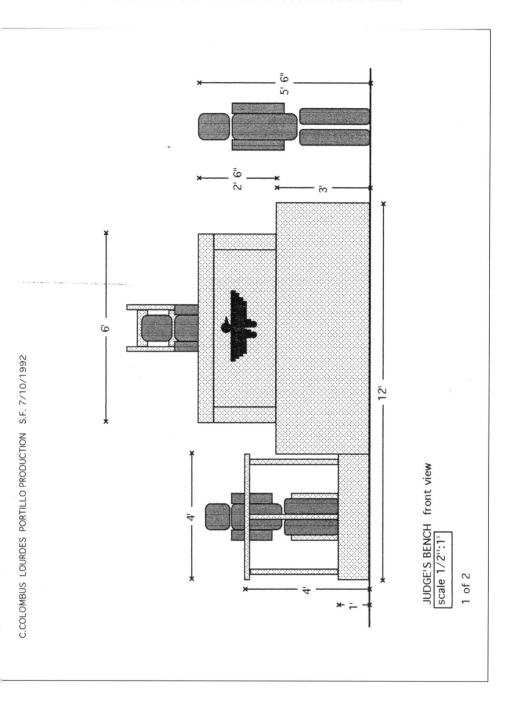

C.COLOMBUS LOURDES PORTILLO PRODUCTION S.F. 7/10/1992

JUDGE'S BENCH front view

scale 1/2":1'

1 of 2

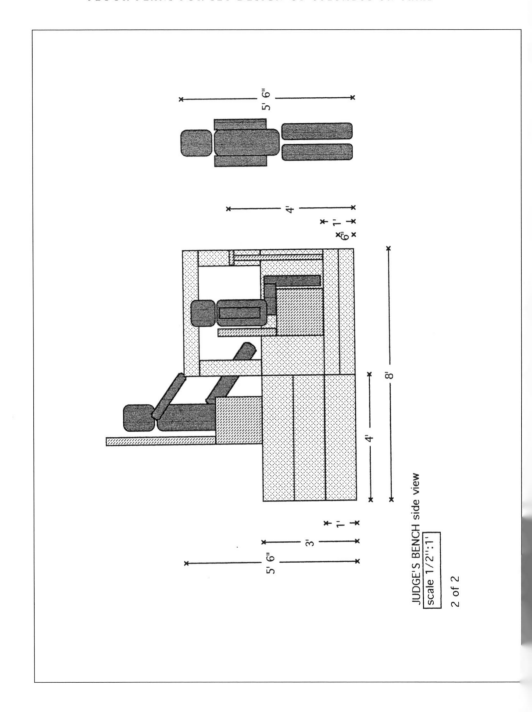

JUDGE'S BENCH side view

scale 1/2":1'

2 of 2

wide of Them

Pto.

CC. Smiles Serdonically
Storm cloud crosses the screen &
turs to look at her   fode out

Fade out

58 Storm Cloud despondent w/girlfriend

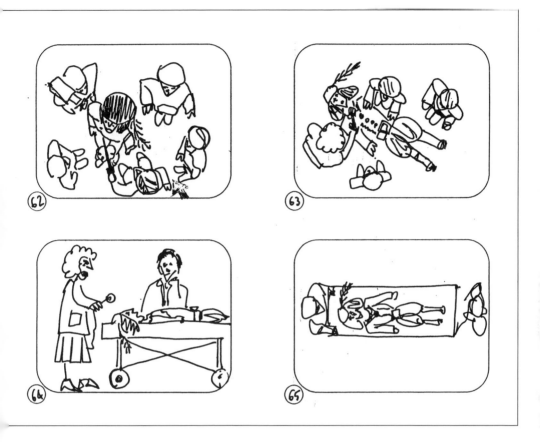

Norma Iglesias Prieto

Appendix

¿QUIÉN ES EL DIABLO, CÓMO Y POR QUÉ DUERME? LA LECTURA DE UNA PELÍCULA CHICANA EN MÉXICO

Desde el punto de vista del espectador mexicano, el trabajo cinematográfico de Lourdes Portillo, especialmente su documental *El diablo nunca duerme,* juega un papel muy importante en la deconstrucción de México y de su cultura. *El diablo nunca duerme* es un documental que tanto en forma como en contenido rompe con los cánones establecidos de su género y revela aspectos casi secretos de la cultura mexicana. Por estas características este documental constituye un material interesante para el estudio de la relación que se establece entre una película y sus audiencias, fundamentalmente porque obliga a que el público hable y debata sobre algunos de los aspectos más privados de la cultura mexicana y de la subjetividad de quien interpreta. Es la discreta invitación a la reflexión cinematográfica, la sutileza de su crítica social y política, e incluso su carácter de intriga, lo que le da el tono singular y crítico a este documental que versa sobre un evento —la muerte en México del tío de la realizadora— que es al mismo tiempo asunto personal y privado como también público. Sin duda, *El diablo nunca duerme* es de varias formas transgresor e innovador, pero desde el punto de vista de los auditorios mexicanos, uno de los aspectos más transgresores es el hacer público aspectos que pertenecen al mundo de lo privado, al mundo de lo familiar.[1] En otras palabras, la película no respeta el popular refrán mexicano que señala que la ropa sucia se lava en casa. Y es todavía más importante el hecho de que sea una chicana quien quebrante la tradición, ya que generalmente en México (especialmente en el centro y sur del país) la figura del chicano o la chicana lleva implícito el sentido de que se trata de una persona que de algún modo se avergüenza de o traiciona a México por el simple hecho de haber dejado el país y por vivir más vinculado a otra realidad económica, política y social. El mismo hecho de vivir en Estados Unidos es visto como una traición, pero al mismo tiempo es algo secretamente envidiado por la importancia que el estilo americano de vida tiene a lo ancho del planeta, donde lo americano se ha convertido en el modelo a seguir. Por estas razones, el documental de Lourdes Portillo es para las audiencias mexicanas doblemente transgresor, porque no quebranta, cuestiona y critica una arraigada tradición mexicana (los secretos de familia), sino que esta transgresión es llevada a cabo por una chicana.

En este documento se analizan algunas cuestiones como por ejemplo, ¿qué pasa con la lectura de una película que cuestiona una serie de convenciones, costumbres y tradiciones que son tanto cinematográficas como sociales y culturales? ¿Cómo estas transgresiones son interpretadas por las audiencias mexicanas? ¿Cómo, en la reconstrucción discursiva de los eventos presentados en el documental, se diferencia lo mexicano y lo chicano, lo personal y lo político, lo propio y lo ajeno? ¿Quién, para los jóvenes auditorios mexicanos, es el diablo? ¿Cómo y por qué duerme? En otras palabras, el interés central de este ensayo es el estudio de esa parte de los procesos de recepción cinematográfica en donde los auditorios se interpretan al interpretar una película, es entrar al mundo de la apropiación de una película por parte de personas concretas para reconocer la relaciones que una película establece con sus espectadores.

En este ensayo se analiza la interpretación que de este documental hacen varios grupos de estudiantes de posgrado de El Colegio de la Frontera Norte en Tijuana. Se llevaron a cabo tres grupos de discusión con estudiantes de distintos programas de maestría (Economía, Desarrollo Regional y Administración Integral del Ambiente) con el objeto de que vieran y discutieran libremente la película. El primer grupo estuvo conformado por estudiantes originarios de la frontera norte de México, o bien con muchos años de residencia en esta zona del país. El segundo y tercer grupo estuvieron constituidos por estudiantes que recientemente habían llegado a la frontera norte provenientes del centro y sur de México.[2]

Los grupos de discusión y la presentación de la película

Entrar al mundo de la recepción de cine es un reto para cualquier investigador porque exige la búsqueda de una técnica que recupere a los sujetos y sus subjetividades, pero que al mismo tiempo respete, en la medida de lo posible, la naturaleza del acto de recepción cinematográfica. En este proyecto se tuvo que trabajar fuera de las salas de exhibición ya que el cine de Lourdes Portillo, como el de cualquier otra chicana cineasta, no tiene canales regulares de exhibición en México. Se decidió entonces a trabajar con la técnica de grupos de discusión que no son precisamente los tradicionales *focus groups* puesto que no se trata de entrevistas grupales, sino de la convocatoria de un grupo selecto de personas para que sin ninguna guía de preguntas elaboren una discusión en torno a la película que se les acaba de mostrar. En los grupos de discusión no existe en realidad la figura del moderador, sino que la discusión va tomando el rumbo que el grupo en su conjunto quiera darle, lo que permite la producción de discursos con cierto grado de espontaneidad.

La fuerza metodológica de la técnica de grupos de discusión, es que el discurso que se genera puede ser verosímil porque ha sido producido en grupo, es su producción imaginaria. El respaldo del discurso y del grupo que lo elabora está en el consenso. Se reconoce que el discurso del grupo de discusión es una representación del discurso social, o de la ideología en su sentido más amplio — conjunto de producciones significantes que operan como reguladores de lo social. Uno de los puntos importantes del grupo de discusión, es que en la situación discursiva que el grupo de discusión crea, las hablas individuales tratan de acoplarse entre sí al sentido social, y por eso se puede decir que el grupo opera en el terreno del consenso, que puede ser entendido como el resultado de las sumas de negociaciones intersubjetivas.

Los integrantes de los grupos de discusión saben que son invitados para hablar y opinar sobre una película. Su dinámica, en ese sentido, simula la de un equipo de trabajo. Y como en todo grupo de discusión se dan dos tensiones, por un lado el trabajo-discusión (razón de su existencia porque se les ha invitado a opinar sobre una película), y por otro lado, el placer de charlar en grupo sobre una película. Así el grupo de discusión instaura un espacio de reconstrucción grupal de la película y de opinión grupal de temas derivados de la misma.

Durante la convocatoria de los grupos de discusión, se les dijo a los estudiantes que se les invitaba a ver una película de una realizadora chicana, lo que marcó de manera notoria el rumbo de la discusión ya que se empezó discutiendo lo chicano y lo mexicano.

Una película chicana

Hay que recordar que los participantes de dos de los tres grupos no eran originarios de la zona fronteriza por lo que lo 'chicano' o lo 'mexicoamericano' no les era algo cotidiano o vivencial, sino que se enmarcaba más en una imagen muy estereotipada, fundamentalmente creada a partir de los medios de comunicación.

De esta forma se dijo, por ejemplo, después de ver la película, que les había sorprendido porque no parecía una película chicana, ya que para ellos la característica del cine chicano es la aparición de 'cholos', de gente pobre y con muchos problemas, y de un exceso de violencia.

> En muchas películas chicanas yo he visto mucha violencia; muestran
> y hablan de la ignorancia de la gente y destacan no tanto los paisajes

> sino la esencia y la problemáticas de las personas, de los estratos sociales más bajos, del tema de las drogas, y en general sus temas siempre son alrededor de esa gente. (Grupo de Discusión [GD] 2)

> Yo he vivido también por acá por el norte y tengo la imagen de que cuando se habla del chicano, y muchas veces son inclusive los mismos chicanos los que se han dado a la tarea de ponerse el paliacate, de dejarse el bigotito aquí y andar con el pantalón, el zoot-suit. (GD2)

> Yo estaba mentalizada a otro tipo de película, no a ésta. (GD2)

> Cuando supe que era una película chicana pensé que iban a salir las bandas, los cholos y cosas así. (GD2)

Las anteriores citas muestran las construcciones que se han hecho de lo chicano en el centro y sur de México. Este tipo de comentarios no se dieron entre los fronterizos, lo que hace suponer que estos tienen una idea más amplia y compleja de la problemática chicana. Sin embargo, a pesar de que dos de los tres grupos partieron de una imagen muy estereotipada de lo que es el cine chicano, y la cultura chicana en general, los auditorios abandonaron ese nivel para hablar de lo que les parecía uno de los principales aportes de *El diablo nunca duerme,* así también como de algunas críticas.

En primer lugar los grupos opinaron que se trataba de un documental distinto y novedoso porque habla y cuestiona muchas cosas, pero también recupera las tradiciones mexicanas desde el punto de vista de alguien que es parcialmente de afuera. Es decir, a pesar de que se trata de una persona muy vinculada a México y su problemática, es alguien que vive fuera de la cotidianidad mexicana, así como de las redes familiares y de sus reglas. Pero, que sin embargo, tiene la 'capacidad cultural' de entender y compartir los códigos, no sólo lingüísticos sino culturales, para comprender, plasmar y cuestionar una amplia gama de problemáticas que se viven en México incluyendo incluso distintos niveles analíticos. A esta audiencia le llamó poderosamente la atención el hecho de que no sea un documental que habla de lo mexicano en Estados Unidos, que no sea tampoco un documental que hable de los mexicanos en aquel país y de su problemática, sino que lo novedoso, desde el punto de vista de las audiencias mexicanas, es que es un documental sobre México visto desde la perspectiva de una realizadora chicana, y esto es justamente lo que enriquece el trabajo pero también, a juicio de las audiencias, en ocasiones limita y marca su perspectiva, o por lo menos no termina de gustar a algunos mexicanos.

En términos generales, lo que parece más enriquecedor, novedoso y transgresor de *El diablo nunca duerme* es que rescate—para bien y para mal—muchos elementos de la cultura mexicana a través de hablar de su familia, el que hable y muestre públicamente estas formas tan enraizadas de relaciones familiares, que reflejan a su vez, formas de relaciones sociales en el país. Pero esto está relacionado con el hecho de ser una realizadora chicana. Las audiencias aseguran que ella pudo hablar de todo esto justamente por ser una persona que aunque parcialmente forma parte de esa realidad, se encuentra fuera de las redes cotidianas.

> Lo muestra porque no está inmersa en la misma problemática, y esa es la ventaja que le da el ser de afuera. (GD2)

> Tiene la ventaja de regresar, de poder entrar sin ser extraña, de entender los códigos y las reglas, eso sí, sin los estereotipos gringos, pero también sin tener que vivir las consecuencias de haber abierto el tema. (GD2)

> Ella puede ser muy crítica porque ve las cosas desde afuera. La visión que tiene ella—por el hecho de haber crecido en un lugar y en un entorno cultural muy distinto al que se está enfrentando—le hace ver las cosas o el mundo de manera diferente. (GD3)

> Por venir de afuera la carga moral y los compromisos son menos fuertes, y por ello tiene menos limitaciones. (GD1)

> Lourdes no sólo quiere investigar la muerte de su tío; ella quiere hacer un documental y eso le permite hacerla un poco de inspector, porque ella con la cámara y el micrófono puede preguntar, y a los otros les toca contestar. Pero ella sin la cámara y el micrófono seguramente tendría otra fuerza y quizá otra manera de preguntar las cosas. (GD1)

> A lo mejor si ella se hubiera quedado en Chihuahua, o incluso se hubiera ido a vivir a otra parte de México, y tampoco hubiera visto a su tío y a su familia por muchos años, pero no hubiera salido del país, es muy probable que su visión y su forma de abordar el problema hubieran sido muy distintas, seguramente no se hubiera manejado sin tantos tabúes. (GD1)

Se reconoce de esta forma que Lourdes Portillo puede ser más crítica puesto que tiene la ventaja de mirar desde fuera, de ser la realizadora, pero también entendiendo y compartiendo los códigos desde adentro.

> Ella va sacando lo mexicano, porque ya conoce y ha vivido aquí [México], pero su posición y experiencia de vivir ahora allá [E.U.] la hace saber cuáles son esos contrastes. (GD1)

Sin embargo, estoy convencida que ella nos ve de afuera, además tiene la ventaja de que puede decir: "Yo no vivo aquí, yo me voy a ir". Ella tiene un sentido de pertenencia a la familia, pero siempre está viendo desde afuera, y hasta cierto punto, desde una perspectiva muy distinta. (GD1)

Finalmente ella ya es parte de una cultura muy distinta, además viene de afuera, viene a hacer su trabajo, viene a preguntar. (GD2)

Su condición de chicana, tan importante para su nivel de crítica y para poder lograr la transgresión, fue también en un principio vista por los distintos auditorios como una limitación, o por lo menos, como un sesgo en su descripción de lo mexicano.

El México que muchos perciben todavía, sobre todo los que emigraron, es un México muy romántico, un tanto folklórico, en donde todavía se canta ranchero, se usa sombrero, un México muy tradicionalista, y no creo que realmente sea así.(GD3)

Ellos vuelven a lo que sienten realmente perdido, ven un México destacando las cosas que añoran, un México que se les fue y que quieren recordarlo así, muy tradicional, por eso cuando vienen les gusta ir a los barrios tradicionales, oír la música también tradicional, recordar a los héroes más clásicos, pero el México actual ya no es sólo así, es visual y socialmente más complejo, pero las imágenes de Lourdes recurren a lo más tradicional y a veces incluso al estereotipo. México aparece como un rancho, pone música e imágenes de Pancho Villa, se oye el mariachi y bolero, sale la bandera nacional, y en México hay mucho más que eso. (GD3)

Incluso en el documental ella misma plantea el shock que le provocó el reencontrarse con ese México que es distinto al de sus recuerdos, es decir, ya nada más le quedan sus recuerdos porque la realidad física y social es otra. (GD3)

Es importante hacer notar que en general los espectadores nunca antes habían visto ninguna película de Lourdes Portillo, ni siquiera habían oído hablar de ella. Sin embargo, los espectadores logran establecer un vínculo importante con la película e inclusive con ella, a pesar de nunca haberla visto. Este vínculo probablemente se debe a la presencia tan evidente de Lourdes y de su punto de vista en el asunto de la muerte de su tío; por esta razón los espectadores, a pesar de las anteriores críticas, se sintieron totalmente vinculados a ella, de tal forma que en su manera de hablar se referían a Lourdes Portillo con una familiaridad sorprendente que haría pensar a cualquiera que la conocían de años. De esta forma, y siguiendo el tipo de discurso tan coloquial y familiar que se muestra en el documental, en sus discursos se referían a ella como "Lulis" o como "Lourdes", reproduciendo de alguna manera el tipo de discursos coloquiales que se dan dentro de una familia. Y este tipo de vínculo que se entabla con la ausente realizadora y su trabajo, y no solamente con su documental, como producto que se les ha pedido que comenten, permite al público un tipo de análisis muy amplio que abarca tanto el contenido, el ritmo, el formato, el tema y la problemática que el documental abarca, como también que se hable de la realizadora, de sus intenciones, sus búsquedas, su postura, así como de cuestiones morales y éticas que la realizadora, suponen, tuvo que plantearse al tocar y desarrollar el tema de la muerte de su tío, un tema que en un principio fue calificado por los auditorios como propio del ámbito privado.

De esta forma, algunas de las preguntas, no siempre explícitas, que guiaron los comentarios de estas audiencias fueron: ¿qué y para qué Lulis (como comúnmente se refirieron a la realizadora) quiere hacer un documental sobre la muerte de su tío? ¿Qué es en realidad lo que ella está buscando? En primer lugar, este tipo de problemáticas o de preguntas muestran que el auditorio reconoció y problematizó sobre el hecho de que se trate de un material que intencionalmente descubre y critica las convenciones del cine documental y que muestra a la realizadora como un elemento más incluido en la trama, de tal forma que su propuesta y sus intenciones son objeto de discusión, cosa que no se haría de un documental tradicional en donde la intención no se discute ya que se parte de la idea de la objetividad y neutralidad del metadiscurso documental.

Algunas de las respuestas más generales a estas preguntas sobre la intención, y que abarcan gran parte de la problemática desarrollada en los grupos de discusión sobre esta película, fueron que a través de la muerte de su tío, Lourdes quiere ver y entender a su familia y sus relaciones, porque a través de ello, se puede ver y entender a sí misma, en una especie de juego de espejos. Que al tratar de entender las relaciones familiares, se entiende y se captura ella misma, y de paso, entiende y muestra el país de donde proviene.

> Puede tratarse de una búsqueda que tiene Luli por encontrarse, entonces para encontrarse hay que voltear para atrás, y para voltear para atrás hay que ir a tus orígenes, a tu familia, y el pretexto o la forma de ver a su familia fue la muerte de su tío Oscar. (GD1)

> Luli quiere regresar a sus raíces y lo hace por medio de un hilo conductor que es su tío y los misterios de su muerte. (GD1)

> Es que para ella, entender a su familia y a México, parece una necesidad. (GD1)

En el primer grupo de discusión constituido principalmente por mujeres y por fronterizas, uno de los primeros comentarios tuvo relación con los distintos posicionamientos identitarios que Lourdes Portillo tuvo a lo largo de su película. Se dijo entonces que se posicionaba de distintas formas, como chicana, como sobrina, como investigadora, como realizadora, como mujer, como católica, etc. Y que gracias a esta complejidad mostrada en su persona, se podía entender la complejidad de la vida de las mujeres, en una problemática típicamente de género, pero también que este juego evidente y explícito de posicionamientos identitarios de la realizadora cuestionaban no sólo las relaciones de género, sino fundamentalmente al género cinematográfico documental y la problemática más amplia de la objetividad del conocimiento.

Esta discusión llevó también a las mujeres a hablar del sexismo de la sociedad mexicana que es fundamentalmente reproducido a través de las relaciones de poder en las familias y que es claramente mostrado en *El diablo nunca duerme,* cuestión que por ejemplo fue totalmente ignorada y no tratada en los otros dos grupos formados fundamentalmente por hombres. De esta forma una de las mujeres del primer grupo dijo:

> El documental retrata de manera muy particular muchas de las prácticas y patrones culturales de los mexicanos, algunos de los rasgos más generales de nuestra cultura y uno de ellos es el machismo. A través de la problemática de las esposas del tío Oscar, Lourdes habla del machismo, de algo tan evidente, y que puede dar risa cuando lo vemos en el documental, pero que es terrible—por ejemplo, la enfermedad de la primera esposa como justificación de la infidelidad del tío Oscar, como ahí dijeron, qué va a hacer, son necesidades. Entonces vemos como siempre hay justificación para el machismo, y son incluso las mujeres las que lo justifican porque parece que las más machistas son las mujeres, o como dicen, el machismo se mantiene por las mujeres que lo reproducimos y lo toleramos. (GD1)

> El documental muestra y nos recuerda del machismo exagerado que hay en nuestra cultura. (GD1)

La riqueza temática alrededor de la muerte del tío Oscar

Otra de las cuestiones a la que los grupos hicieron referencia, fue la riqueza temática y los distintos niveles de abordaje que se dan en este documental. La problemática de la muerte es una de ellas, tanto en el sentido de ser un tema importante en las tradiciones mexicanas, como por el trato cultural que se le da al recuerdo de una persona fallecida, así como al problema de la justicia en este país que se ve reflejada en los casos no aclarados de muertes de personajes reconocidos o no.

Uno de los grupos señala entonces que el entrar a discutir los rasgos culturales a través de la muerte como se hizo en *El diablo nunca duerme,* es un recurso muy mexicano, por lo que el sólo hecho de que Lourdes Portillo decidiera abordar la problemática desde ahí, demuestra que participa fuertemente de la cultura mexicana, y éste es otro de los elementos que hacen que el público mexicano se sienta muy vinculado como se dijo— no sólo a la problemática tratada, sino a la persona quien lo realiza.

> Es algo muy curioso como los mexicanos desarrollamos y fincamos muchas cosas, inquietudes y proyectos alrededor de la muerte. (GD1)

> Nos distingue una cultura alrededor de la muerte. (GD1)

Se señaló también que fue poco común el trato que se le dio a la memoria del tío Oscar, ya que dicen que en México, la gente no habla mal de los muertos y sobre todo si son de su familia (GD1). Se reconoció con mucho detalle como es común que no se hable mal del muerto, que por el contrario, existe en México una tendencia a convertirlos en una especie de santos (GD2), a simplificar su personalidad, a olvidar sus defectos y que en el afán de perdonar y olvidar, a veces nos hace perder la dimensión de lo que realmente fueron (GD1). Por eso es tan usual oír decir: Tan bueno que era, pobrecito (GD3).

Pero en el caso del tío Oscar, al empezar a tratar de entender quién fue y cómo murió, al dar pie y de alguna manera presionar para que la gente hable, empezó a dar paso a todo lo contrario, cada vez se le atribuían más defectos y problemas, y desaparecían las cualidades tan señaladas en el inicio del documental. Pero al mismo tiempo, surgía un tío Oscar más de carne y hueso, más complejo y visto desde distintas perspectivas, que la simple idea inicial de un tío excepcional y feliz. Un tío Oscar que encarnaba las múltiples contradicciones, conflictos e intereses no sólo de una persona, sino de todo un país. Las variadas imágenes del Oscar Ruíz Almeida nos hablan de la intriga, del chisme, del rumor, y del peso de todo esto en la construcción y reconstrucción de la realidad.

> El documental nos muestra cómo los rumores llegan a convertirse en verdades y cómo estas supuestas verdades marcan el rumbo de una persona y de un país. (GD2)

Su muerte, como la de otras figuras públicas que aparecen en el documental (la de Colosio, por ejemplo) nos adentra a la tradición del silencio, del secreto y de la impunidad que se vive en este país.

El segundo aspecto ligado a la muerte que fue discutido por los grupos fue precisamente el del silencio, la impunidad y falta de justicia que caracteriza a México. Al vincular la muerte de su tío con la de otros personajes públicos el documental adquiere un tono político y de crítica social.

> En la película se le da un tinte político cuando menciona la muerte de Pancho Villa y se ve la foto de cuando lo balacearon, el impacto de bala en el carro, y también el asesinato de Colosio. En ese momento, hay la imagen de una casa en donde aparece un florero arriba de la televisión y la sombra parece el perfil de Salinas, las orejotas y la cabeza. (GD3)

Es a partir del caso del tío Oscar que el documental habla de un problema serio de la sociedad mexicana, el silencio, la corrupción, la impunidad y los secretos a voces.

> Esta forma de pensar explica en mucho el porqué muchos ilícitos no se denuncian, por ejemplo, las violaciones, la violencia doméstica, el maltrato a menores, etc. Hay tantas cosas que se callan, pero no se olvidan, ni resuelven. (GD2)

Conforme las distintas personas que aparecen en el documental van hablando del tío Oscar, éste se va complejizando y parece que el público se va sorprendiendo de la misma forma en la que ellos suponen Lourdes también se fue sorprendiendo durante su investigación.

> Me parece muy interesante cómo se propone redescubrir a una persona, cómo quiere reencontrar a su tío y al final de cuentas se topa y nos topamos con muchas realidades muy distintas, que ella, ni nosotros nos imaginamos. (GD2)

La realidad melodramática mexicana

Otro de los aspectos del documental que fue recuperado por los espectadores fue el que recurriera a las telenovelas para describir a la cultura mexicana.

> Otra cosa que se me hizo super interesante, me gustó muchísimo, fueron las imágenes de las telenovelas porque es cierto que forman parte de la cultura nacional, así somos, bien melodramáticos. Es como una analogía, la vida es un melodrama, la vida es una telenovela. Las situaciones que veíamos en las telenovelas eran las que se iban construyendo en los diálogos del documental. Y así es. La nueva esposa es la mala, se casa con él por dinero, tienen que cuidar las apariencias, tienen amantes pero hay que ser discretos, etc. La verdad es que se conoce tanto de la forma de ser de los mexicanos en las telenovelas; nuestras vidas son verdaderos melodramas sólo que sin actores famosos. (GDI)

El tema de las telenovelas dio la oportunidad de hablar de las convenciones sociales y culturales en México, como por ejemplo, el clasismo y las diferencias entre clases sociales; la preocupación por guardar las apariencias y la imagen en los sectores sociales medio y alto y no tanto una verdadera postura ética y moral; la infidelidad de alguna manera aceptada en los hombres pero no en las mujeres; los tabúes sobre la sexualidad; el rol de la religión y el poder de la Iglesia Católica; el malinchismo o preferencia de lo extranjero frente a lo mexicano que se manifestó en la insistencia de los familiares del tío Oscar por señalar, como un punto favorable a la familia, el que la primera esposa era de descendencia yugoslava, etc.

> Yo no creo que el enojo de la familia se deba a que él se haya casado de nuevo y de manera tan rápida, sin haber guardado el debido luto, sino que se debe a que se casa con la amante que es de una familia pobre y no educada. Si él se hubiera casado con una mujer de su mismo nivel social, de su clase, de su círculo, no hubieran hecho tal escándalo. (GDI)

El debate sobre "La ropa sucia se lava en casa"

En los tres grupos se dio un fuerte debate sobre la cuestión de haber hecho público los asuntos familiares, sobre la violación del tabú cultural que prohibe el hablar de los secretos familiares. El debate incluyó preguntas como: ¿Qué era lo que Lourdes estaba realmente buscando? ¿lo que ella hizo es ética y moralmente correcto? ¿qué es lo que finalmente el documental nos muestra? ¿qué es lo que los espectadores toman o aprenden de este evento familiar y social?

Sobre las intenciones de la realizadora, hubo dos grandes posiciones que se derivan del hecho de que el documental obliga a los espectadores a manifestarse de manera muy radical, diluyendo posiciones neutras o poco criticas. Por esta razón se encuentran posturas polarizadas que defienden o critican de manera explícita a la película y al trabajo de Lourdes como realizadora. De esta forma tenemos por un lado una postura de defensa de la película, y por otro lado, una postura que la critica fuertemente.

Aquellos que defendían la película argumentaban que Lourdes Portillo hizo el documental como una necesidad para explorar y abrir a la discusión la muerte de su tío Oscar porque ella estaba verdaderamente interesada en entender lo que en realidad pasó. Por lo que ella utilizó el cine y el documental como un instrumento para averiguar lo sucedido. Y lo hizo a través del cine y del vídeo porque éstos son sus campos y áreas de trabajo. Se dijo entonces que si ella hubiera sido escritora seguramente hubiera escogido la novela o el cuento para tratar de resolver un asunto que le preocupaba personalmente. Además, quienes defienden esta postura aseguran que la investigación y la producción de la película le permitieron a Lourdes Portillo expresar su punto de vista al respecto, le permitieron comprender a su familia y sus relaciones, le permitieron contribuir al conocimiento de las tradiciones y la cultura mexicana, le permitieron también comprender y confirmar su propia identidad cultural así como deconstruir al género documental explorando nuevas formas narrativas. Las múltiples contribuciones de *El diablo nunca duerme* para esta posición se pueden resumir en el siguiente comentario.

> La película muestra las bases en las que se sostiene la familia como una institución, y en las que se sostiene la sociedad en general. También muestra las creencias y los prejuicios que se dan alrededor de la familia y de sus relaciones. (GD2)

Esta posición de valoración positiva del documental reconoce también una serie de logros de la misma. Se reconocen las dificultades que se tuvieron en la creación, desarrollo y producción de la película, dificultades que no sólo fueron de carácter técnico, sino también de carácter social. Lourdes Portillo tuvo que crear una atmósfera de confianza para que los distintos miembros de la familia, amigos y otros actores sociales se animaran a hablar de la vida y muerte del tío Oscar.

> Debió de haber sido muy difícil para ella y para su familia hablar de esos aspectos tristes y dolorosos. Ella tuvo que presionarlos para que hablaran y para que ellos mismos se confrontaran con sus propios secretos. Ella removió muchos sentimientos, muchos recuerdos sobre varios eventos en la vida del tío. Debió haber sido como abrir una coladera. (GD1)

> Seguramente fue doloroso pero también fue una experiencia enriquecedora y fascinante. (GD1)

> Como que no le importó el que se dijeran muchas cosas de su familia, cosas no muy gratas, ella se sostuvo en la ética de la verdad, aunque la verdad a veces duela. (GD1)

Otro aspecto importante de la película que esta posición de defensa reconoce, es la forma en la que el documental fuerza a los espectadores a pensar acerca de sus propias familias, problemáticas y secretos. Se reconoce que la película mueve fibras sensibles y aspectos de la intimidad que confrontan no sólo a la familia de la realizadora, sino a las audiencias con sus propios secretos.

> Es verdad que los asuntos privados y los secretos son aspectos muy fuertes de nuestra cultura, pero, ¿por qué negarnos a hablar de nuestros padres o de nuestros abuelos, cuando eso es realmente lo que somos? Es necesario hablar de esas cosas para reconocernos. (GD2)

Los espectadores también señalaron que lo transgresor de la película fue algo interesante pero que sin embargo había que admitir que de alguna manera les incomodó ya que no es común que se revelen los secretos familiares, y que al hacerlo, la película generaba una sensación de compromiso e involucramiento de los espectadores.

> No estamos acostumbrados a hacer público lo que pasa en casa, lo que pasa en la familia. (GD2)

El reconocimiento de ese sentido de incomodidad de los espectadores frente a la revelación de aspectos privados, hizo reconocer también la dificultad que para Lourdes Portillo debió de haber significado la producción de una película sobre los secretos y enredos de su propia familia, y en ese sentido, se le reconocía un gran valor tanto al material documental, como a su labor como directora de la película.

> A todos nos gustaría tener algún material como un libro o un vídeo sobre la historia de nuestra familia, pero lo que seguramente no nos gustaría es que este material se presentara en público porque eso implica otro nivel. Hablar de nuestras familias, de sus conflictos y secretos, nos genera mucho conflicto porque aunque lo quisiéramos, quién sabe si tuviéramos el valor o el coraje para enfrentarnos a hacerlo público. Estamos limitados por nuestra propia cultura, nuestros principios y nuestros prejuicios y es muy difícil romper con ellos. (GD2)

Por otro lado, la argumentación de crítica sobre este material documental fue mucho más sencilla que su defensa. En general la postura de crítica de *El diablo nunca duerme* se sostuvo argumentando que Lourdes Portillo en realidad usó la muerte de su tío Oscar para hacer un documental que les pareció interesante pero morboso, por lo que esta postura pone en duda la ética de la realizadora.

> Yo creo que ella como documentalista sólo tomó la muerte de su tío como un pretexto para hacer algo atractivo, pero que en realidad a ella no le importó el daño que pudiera causar a su familia. A ella sólo le importó su película y conseguir su información. (GD2)

> Ella ofendió públicamente a su familia y también a la audiencia porque hay cosas que nadie debe de saber. (GD2)

> Está mal porque la ropa sucia se lava en casa. (GD2)

> Esta película lo único que hace es reforzar la cultura del chisme; de hecho la película es un chisme y además viola la intimidad. (GD3)

> Como que metió cizaña, saca información que no es necesaria— ¿qué sentido tiene enterarse de los chismes de una película? (GD3)

De esta forma, se vio que la postura que no valora positivamente la película más que elaborar una crítica bien sustentada, tendió a ignorarla a través de no hablar de ella. Es decir, que de nuevo la crítica se mantuvo y se guardó en el silencio, lo que demuestra en parte la fuerza del silencio de la cultura mexicana.

Para concluir

Tal como lo señaló uno de los espectadores, la discusión grupal generada a partir de ver *El diablo nunca duerme* reprodujo el tema, los aspectos, las formas, las estructuras, los temores, los tabúes y los prejuicios que marcan a la cultura mexicana.

> En esta sala estamos reproduciendo el tema del documental; hemos demostrado cómo la cultura mexicana es funcional al régimen político, económico y social en el que vivimos. Conforme escucho la discusión me gusta más la película porque aquí nosotros reproducimos los debates y los prejuicios que se dan en las familias y en la sociedad, y se puede llegar a defender la intimidad o la vida privada más que la aclaración de un crimen. Nos incomoda que nos vean, que nos analicen, o más bien, nos incomoda vernos y analizarnos y entonces es más importante que no se sepa y no sepamos de nosotros que aclarar un crimen o cualquier otra injusticia. (GD2)

A través de este ejercicio sobre la relación de *El diablo nunca duerme* y el público, se pudo dar cuenta de la relación que la película establece con un grupo de espectadores mexicanos, así también como la forma en la que los espectadores se apropian y reconstruyen la película. En otras palabras, este ejercicio muestra lo que la película hace a los espectadores y lo que los espectadores hacen a la película.

Una de las principales contribuciones de *El diablo nunca duerme* es su capacidad de mostrar la complejidad y los diferentes niveles de la realidad social, así como la capacidad del cuestionamiento de la lógica binaria en donde algunos aparecen como los malos y otros como los buenos, es decir, donde sólo se reconoce lo blanco o lo negro. Este documental presenta la complejidad social y nos permite descubrir varios diablos y ángeles, así como las diferentes caras y momentos de una misma persona que a veces puede parecer un ángel y en otras un diablo. Si en ocasiones y para algunas personas, el diablo es Ofelia —la segunda esposa del tío Oscar—, para otras el diablo es Lourdes, o su tío Oscar, pero también en otros momentos de la película y de la discusión el diablo puede ser el comandante de policía, los familiares, los amigos o los diferentes grupos sociales que rodean la vida de Oscar Almeida. La relación que *El diablo nunca duerme* pudo establecer con el público, lo mismo que su transgresora forma y contenido, producen el efecto de hacer sentir a los auditorios que inclusive ellos mismos podrían ser los diablos, por lo que el dicho popular de "El diablo nunca duerme" cobra un especial sentido en la recepción e interpretación de esta película.

Por ello se puede afirmar que el documental de Portillo cuestiona varios aspectos de la vida social, y no sólo a partir de los actos de una persona, sino a través de las actividades de un grupo social. En su crítica, la realizadora reconoce que ella misma es parte de ese grupo social y que no está exenta de responsabilidad.

El diablo nunca duerme nos obliga a reflexionar sobre la realidad chicana y mexicana, sobre los límites entre una y otra cultura, sobre los límites de lo público y lo privado, de los asuntos familiares y los públicos, de la muerte y el dolor, pero también sobre los límites y posibilidades del género documental y del vínculo entre una película y su realizador. Como auditorios necesitamos redescubrir los múltiples y variados diablos y ángeles que nos rodean. Es necesario continuar debatiendo y cuestionando sobre estos y otros límites que nos imponen nuestras respectivas sociedades.

Filmography

1999 Producer/Director/Writer: *Corpus: A Home Movie for Selena.* Broadcast nationally in 1999.

1997 Producer/Director: *Sometimes My Feet Go Numb* (performance video).
Multimedia Director: *13 Days,* a nationally toured play by the San Francisco Mime Troupe.

1994 Producer/Director: *The Devil Never Sleeps/El diablo nunca duerme* (82-minute documentary).

1993 Producer/Director/Writer: *Mirrors of the Heart* (60-minute documentary). Produced by WGBH in Boston for PBS series "Americas." Broadcast nationally in 1993.

1992 Producer/Director: *Columbus on Trial* (experimental video). Broadcast nationally in 1992.

1989 Director: *Vida* (short narrative film). Produced by John Hoffman.

1988 Producer/Codirector/Writer: *La Ofrenda: The Days of the Dead* (60-minute documentary).

1986 Producer/Codirector/Writer: *Las Madres: The Mothers of the Plaza de Mayo* (60-minute documentary).

1979 Producer/Codirector/Cowriter: *After the Earthquake/Después del terremoto* (short narrative film).

Major Awards and Honors

Recipient of CalArts/Alpert Award in the Arts, 1999

Corpus: A Home Movie for Selena (1999)

- Golden Spire, San Francisco International Film Festival, 1999, San Francisco, California

The Devil Never Sleeps (1994)

- Best Five Documentaries of the Year, Independent Documentary Association, 1996, Hollywood, California
- Golden Gate Award, San Francisco International Film Festival, 1995, San Francisco, California
- Best Feature-Length Documentary, San Juan Cinemafest, 1995, San Juan, Puerto Rico
- Best Documentary, San Antonio CineFestival, 1995, San Antonio, Texas
- Best Documentary, Mostra Internacional de Filmes de Dones, 1995, Barcelona, Spain
- New Directors/New Films, The Film Society of Lincoln Center and the Museum of Modern Art, New York, 1995, New York City
- Most Promising Latino Film, The Independent Feature Project, 1994, New York City

Mirrors of the Heart (1993)

- Silver Hugo, Chicago Film Festival, 1994, Chicago, Illinois
- Silver Apple, National Educational Film and Video Festival, 1994, Berkeley, California

Columbus on Trial (1992)

- Best Video, second place, Visual Artist Third Annual Film and Video Festival, 1993, San Jose, California
- Honorable Mention in Native American Studies, American Film and Video Association, 1993, Illinois
- The 1993 Whitney Museum Biennial, New York, New York

Vida (1989)

- Cine Golden Eagle, 1990
- Special Mention, San Antonio CineFestival, 1990, San Antonio, Texas

La Ofrenda: The Days of the Dead (1988)

- Blue Ribbon, American Film and Video Festival, 1990, San Francisco, California
- Honors, International Documentary Association, 1989, Los Angeles, California
- Director's Choice Selection, Black Maria Film and Video Festival, 1989, West Orange, New Jersey
- Outstanding Cinematic Achievement, Best of Category, Documentary Film, National Latino Film and Video Festival, 1991, New York City
- Special Jury Prize, Sinking Creek Film Festival, 1990, Greeneville, Tennessee
- Best Exploration of Belief Prize, VISTAS, A Film Festival of Contemporary Folklife and Popular Culture, 1990, Los Angeles, California
- Best Feature Documentary, Athens Film Festival, 1989, Athens, Ohio

Las Madres: The Mothers of the Plaza de Mayo (1986)

- Emmy Nomination, News and Documentary, 1986, The National Academy of Television Arts and Sciences
- Academy Award Nomination, Best Documentary, 1986, Academy of Motion Picture Arts and Sciences
- Special Jury Prize, Sundance Film Festival, 1986, Park City, Utah
- Grand Prix Ex-Aquo, Certamen Internacional de Cine Documental y Corto Metrage, 1986, Bilbao, Spain
- Coral Prize, Feature Documentary, Festival Internacional de Nuevo Cine Latinoamericano, 1986, Havana, Cuba

- Second Place, Documentary, Sydney Film Festival, 1986, Sydney, Australia
- Prix du Public and Prix du Presse, Women's Film Festival, 1986, Creteil, France
- Blue Ribbon, American Film and Video Festival, 1986, New York City
- Best Film, Global Village Documentary Film Festival, 1986, New York City
- First Prize, International Catholic Organization for Cinema and Audio-visuals, 1995, Havana, Cuba
- Among Six Best Films, International Documentary Association, 1986, Los Angeles, California
- Caracol Prize from Union of Writers and Artists, International Film Festival, 1985, Havana, Cuba
- Best of Northern California, National Educational Film Festival, 1986, Oakland, California
- Golden Gate Award, San Francisco International Film Festival, 1986, San Francisco, California
- Best Film, Sinking Creek Film Festival, 1986, Greeneville, Tennessee
- Women Journalists' Association Prize, Women's International Film Festival, 1986, Creteil, Paris

After the Earthquake/Después del terremoto (1979)
- Diploma of Honor, Cracow Shorts Film Festival, 1979, Cracow, Poland

Notes

Introduction

1. Ruth Behar, *Vulnerable Observer: Anthropology That Makes Your Heart Break* (Boston: Beacon Press, 1996).
2. Sonia Saldivar-Hull, *Feminism on the Borderlands* (University of California Press, 2000.
3. Julia Lesage, "Feminist Film Criticism: Theory and Practice," in *Sexual Stratagems: The World of Women in Film,* ed. Patricia Erens (New York: Horizon, 1979), 144–155.
4. "Sacando los Trapos al Sol (Airing Dirty Laundry) in Lourdes Portillo's Melodocu-mystery, *The Devil Never Sleeps,*" in *Redirecting the Gaze,* ed. Diana Robin and Ira Jaffe (Albany: State University of New York Press, 1999), 307–330.
5. Hannah Ngala, *Point Last Seen: A Woman Tracker's Story* (Boston: Beacon Press, 1997).

Chapter Four

1. Alexandra Juhasz, "'They Said We Were Trying to Show Reality—All I Want to Show Is My Video': The Politics of the Realist Feminist Documentary," *Screen* 35, no. 2 (summer 1994): 173.
2. See pp. 50–51, above.
3. See discussion in my chapter in *The Bronze Screen: Chicana and Chicano Film Culture* (Minneapolis: University of Minnesota Press, 1993), 96–105.
4. See Angela Davis, *Women, Race and Class* (New York: Vintage Books, 1983); Mary Romero, *Maid in the U.S.A.* (New York: Routledge, 1992); Evelyn Nakano, "Racial Ethnic Women's Labor," *Review of Radical Political Economics* 17:3 (1983), 86–108.
5. Romero, *Maid in the U.S.A.,* 48–65.
6. Liz Kotz, "Unofficial Stories: Documentaries by Latin American Women," in *Latin Looks: Images of Latinas and Latinos in the U.S. Media,* ed. Clara E. Rodriguez (Boulder: Westview Press, 1997), 211.
7. Judith Mayne, *Cinema and Spectatorship* (London: Routledge, 1993), 158.
8. Social Development Division, Women and Development Unit of Economic Commission for Latin America and the Caribbean, *Refugee and Displaced Women in Latin America and the Caribbean* (Santiago, Chile: United Nations, April 1991).
9. See p. 66, above.
10. John Simpson and Jana Bennett, *The Disappeared and the Mothers of the Plaza* (New York: St. Martin's Press, 1985), 158.

11. See Simpson and Bennett, *The Disappeared and the Mothers*, esp. pp. 155–170.

12. Quoted in Simpson and Bennett, 169.

13. Avery Gordon, *Ghostly Matters: Haunting and the Sociological Imagination* (Minneapolis: University of Minnesota Press, 1997), 194–195.

14. Simpson and Bennett, *The Disappeared and the Mothers*, 169–170.

15. Antony Faiola, "Argentina Dictator Runs Out of Pardons," *Washington Post,* July 8, 1998, A24.

16. Newman and Rich.

17. Frances Negrón-Muntaner, "Drama Queens: Latina Gay and Lesbian Independent Film/Video," in *The Ethnic Eye: Latino Media Arts,* ed. Chon A. Noriega and Ana M. Lopez (Minneapolis: University of Minnesota Press, 1996), 62.

18. Some aspects of this discussion are also examined in Rosa Linda Fregoso, "Sacando los Trapos al Sol (Airing Dirty Laundry) in Lourdes Portillo's Melodocumystery, *The Devil Never Sleeps,*" in *Redirecting the Gaze: Gender, Theory, and Cinema in the Third World,* ed. Diana Robin and Ira Jaffe (Albany: State University of New York Press, 1999).

19. Valerie Smith, "Telling Family Secrets: Narrative and Ideology in *Suzanne Suzanne,* by Camille Billops and James V. Hatch," in *Multiple Voices in Feminist Film Criticism,* ed. Diane Carson, Linda Dittman, and Janice R. Walsh (Minneapolis: University of Minnesota Press, 1994), 381.

20. Denise Segura and Jennifer L. Pierce, "The Chicana/o Family Structure and Gender Personality: Chodorow, Familism, and Psychoanalytic Sociology Revisited," *Signs* 19 (August 1993): 72.

21. Jean Franco, "The Incorporation of Women: A Comparison of North American and Mexican Popular Narrative," in *Studies in Entertainment: Critical Approaches to Mass Culture,* ed. Tania Modleski (Bloomington: Indiana University Press, 1986), 135.

22. bell hooks, "Dialogue between bell hooks and Julie Dash," in Julie Dash, *Daughters of the Dust* (New York: New Press, 1992), 31.

23. Michel Foucault, *Herculine Barbin: Being the Recently Discovered Memoirs of a Nineteenth-Century French Hermaphrodite* (New York: Pantheon Press, 1980), 82.

24. Cited in Jeanne Allen, "Self-Reflexivity in Documentary," in *Explorations in Film Theory,* ed. Ron Burnett (Bloomington: Indiana University Press, 1991), 109.

25. Allen, "Self-Reflexivity in Documentary," 103. Allen makes these comments about self-reflexive documentaries in general.

26. Juhasz, "'They Said We Were Trying to Show Reality,'" 177.

27. Judith Mayne, *The Woman at the Keyhole* (Bloomington: Indiana University Press, 1990), 51.

Chapter Five

1. Sylvia Molloy, "Of Quotes and Queers" (presentation in Spanish and Portuguese Department, Stanford University, October 22, 1998).

2. José Limón, *Dancing with the Devil: Society and Cultural Poetics in Mexican-American South Texas* (Madison: University of Wisconsin Press, 1994).

3. Other elements in *La Ofrenda* that anticipate *Diablo* are the transnational approach to the art forms of the Days of the Dead, both in the United States and Mexico, and the queering of the altar tradition in San Francisco's Mission District. See Rosa

Linda Fregoso's *The Bronze Screen* (Minneapolis: University of Minnesota Press, 1993) for an analysis of the film.

4. Rosa Linda Fregoso, "Sacando los Trapos al Sol (Airing Dirty Laundry) in Lourdes Portillo's Melodocumystery, *The Devil Never Sleeps*," in *Redirecting the Gaze: Gender, Theory, and Cinema in the Third World,* ed. Diana Robin and Ira Jaffe (New York: State University of New York Press, 1999), 309.

5. In *A Line around the Block,* Marga Gómez spoofs the over-the-top emotions of telenovelas, performing a few lines from typical scenarios ("¡¡Déjame!!" ["Leave me alone!!"] and "¡¡No puedo tener hijos!!" ["I can't have children!!"]) and then commenting: "And those are just the comedies" (unpublished ms.; excerpt in *Contemporary Plays by Women of Color,* ed. Kathy A. Perkins and Roberta Uno [New York: Routledge, 1996], 197–198).

6. Fregoso, "Sacando los Trapos," 313.

7. This relativizing "framing" technique (that of the TV or that of the stage) coexists with unambiguous visual images that frame in the sense of "incriminate" from LP's point of view. In her search for Oscar's killer, images of predation and death, evil and cruelty, point a finger at Ofelia as well as Oscar's business associates and debtors: the shark (Ofelia), the snake (Ofelia and Spriu), the butterfly of death/*mariposa de muerte* (Caballero), and the cactus (Ofelia).

8. Fregoso states that "in searching for the truth behind [Oscar's] death, Portillo discovers that there is no singular truth or singular meaning, that the hierarchical organization of knowledge is neither plausible nor possible" ("Sacando los Trapos al Sol," 309).

9. Immediately after Luz's insistence on Oscar's thinness, LP begins the series of interviews that responded to the question of his queerness.

10. As when the police official is looking for Oscar's file in a context that implies that the police have intentionally lost his record. In reality, this segment preceded the earliest police scene in *Diablo.* Portillo, interview by author, San Francisco, October 27, 1998.

11. The queering of Villa recalls the other context of betrayal: the moral hypocrisy of the Catholic Church and the provinces associated with Villa's image and music.

12. Compare this example of LP's quoting from Mexican popular music to ironically frame her subject to Lebanese Mexican singer and performer Astrid Hadad, whose performances "out" the sexism and misogyny of the lyrics. See her video *Corazón sangrante* by Ximena Cuevas (Mexico City: Management Astrid Hadad, 1998).

13. When Catalina, Oscar's first wife, was on her deathbed, her children brought the dying woman some fish to amuse her. But Catalina became hysterical when, right in front of her, one fish attacked another and bit it in half. Juxtaposed to this voice-over narration is the visual image of a swimming shark. Coupled with the knowledge that Ofelia was Oscar's mistress before Catalina's death, the indictment of Ofelia is clear.

14. Jeffrey Burton Russell, *Mephistopheles: The Devil in the Modern World* (Ithaca: Cornell University Press, 1986), 158–189. Quoted in Limón, *Dancing with the Devil.*

15. For a detailed study of how LP dominates her family through manipulation of public and private knowledge, see Fregoso's article "Sacando los Trapos al Sol."

16. Portillo, interview by author, San Francisco, October 27, 1998.

Chapter Six

1. Bill Nichols, *Representing Reality* (Bloomington: Indiana University Press, 1991), 120–121.
2. Thomas Vaugh, "Walking on Tippy Toes: Lesbian and Gay Liberation Documentary of the Post-Stonewall Period, 1969–84," in *Between the Sheets, in the Streets: Queer, Lesbian, Gay Documentary,* Visible Evidence Series, vol. 1, ed. Chris Holmlund and Cynthia Fuchs (Minneapolis: University of Minnesota Press, 1997).
3. Judith Mayne, *Cinema and Spectatorship* (London: Routledge, 1993), 155.
4. Rosa Linda Fregoso, *The Bronze Screen* (Minneapolis: University of Minnesota Press, 1993), 54–55.
5. Judith Mayne, in a chapter entitled "Spectatorship Reconsidered" in *Cinema and Spectatorship,* provides a critical discussion of various models being used to approach the question of spectatorship: "empirical" (cognitive and ethnographic studies); "historical" (historicizing of film exhibition and reception, but often bypassing gender distinctions); and "feminist" (some critics moving away from psychoanalysis in favor of a "historical subject"; others, in particular Di Lauretis, exploring the tensions between "woman" and "women"). I find especially relevant to the goals of my study Mayne's remarking that the focus on the exhibition context offers the opportunity to examine "the combination of individual fantasy and social ritual" (p. 66). I explored this intersection by using fragments of textual analysis: insofar as spectators' individual fantasies are perceptible in their comments (mine included), they are expressed in part through their appropriation of certain fragments or layers of the film.
6. See Fregoso "Mestizaje (Hybridity) in Cultural Politics," in *The Bronze Screen;* and Chéla Sandoval, "Mestizaje as Method," in *Living Chicana Theory,* ed. Carla Trujillo (Berkeley: Third Woman Press, 1998).
7. In 1994: Toronto, Independent Feature Project (Most Promising Latino Film). In 1995: Sundance; San Antonio CineFestival (Best Documentary); Chicano Film Festival, Chicago; San Francisco International Film Festival (Special Jury Award); Sydney, Melbourne, Wellington, Taos Talking Pictures Festival; New Directors/New Films, New York; Muestra de Cine Mexicano en Guadalajara. In 1997: Lussas Etats Généraux du Documentaire, France; Hong Kong, etc.
8. In 1995 it was awarded Best Documentary by the International Documentary Association in the United States.
9. Best Documentary at the Mostra International de Films de Dones in Barcelona; it was also shown in France at the Films de Femmes Festival of Creteil.
10. Xochtitl Films is Lourdes Portillo's production company, based in San Francisco; Women Make Movies, a New York–based distributor.
11. Deborah Martin, "Film Society Wild about *El Diablo,*" *El Paso Herald-Post,* September 25, 1995.
12. French-born, living in New York, where I am pursuing a study of American contemporary documentaries, I also must add that the *Devil Never Sleeps* came early to my attention because my husband, Kyle Kibbe, was its cameraman. I began recording public discussions in January 1996 at Context Studios, an independent venue in

New York City, where I curated two documentary series and presented *The Devil Never Sleeps* as part of the series "Of Families and Global Events"; it was introduced by Latin Americanist Electa Arenal, to whom I wish to express here my gratitude. I recorded audience discussions later in 1996 at New York University and the Brooklyn Museum, and in 1997 at the French documentary festival of Lussas. This study benefited immensely from Lourdes Portillo's kindness in sharing information about the film's reception: she passed on to me several papers written by students in Chicano Studies and the 1995 recording of a discussion in San Francisco, and she remembered in several conversations the many screenings that she had attended. I am most thankful for her help.

13. The pleasure of and desire for knowledge associated with the documentary have been highlighted and commented on at length by Bill Nichols in *Representing Reality*. The entertainment aspect of the film was highlighted by *TV Guide* in New York in these terms: "Was it suicide or murder? Filmmaker Lourdes Portillo investigates her wealthy uncle's 1990 death in Mexico in *The Devil Never Sleeps*." It was picked that day along with a fiction film, TV series, and another documentary ("*When We Were Kings* [Muhammad Ali], presented on Pay Per View). *TV Guide*, Manhattan ed., September 27–October 3, 1997, 181.

14. "She, more importantly, educates her audience on Mexican culture, the institution of family, and the politics of a corrupt government. Indeed, *El Diablo Nunca Duerme* is rich with Mexican culture in the form of music, religion, and 'novelas.'" Sylvia Galvez, *"El diablo nunca duerme": A Short Critical Analysis* (unpublished student essay, 1996).

15. This observation is followed by: "Has the world been turned upside-down by this 'suicide,' or does the filmmaker assert that even when it appears 'topsy-turvy' there is stability in the world through truth?" Patricia Marcus, unpublished student essay.

16. Julia Favela, *Text Criticism* (unpublished student essay, February 1996).

17. Isela Mendez, unpublished student essay, February 1996.

18. Ibid. It was interpreted this way by other students.

19. Patricia Marcus, unpublished student essay.

20. Isela Mendez, in her unpublished student essay, makes reference here to Rosa Linda Fregoso's discussion in *The Bronze Screen* of films "made by, about, and for Chicanos."

21. As I am pursuing a comparative study, my highlighting the particulars of each performance also emphasizes their cultural specificity. Furthermore, I left aside the discussion of other prisms: other Latinas/os looking at Chicanos/as and Mexicans, Mexico City residents looking at residents of northern Mexico, etc.

22. Lourdes Portillo, question and answer session, April 1995, Pacific Film Archives, Berkeley.

23. Lourdes Portillo, question and answer session, Center for Media, Culture and History, New York University, March 1996.

24. "In the film's initial moments, the viewer is led to believe that this will be another journey into Mexican culture's fascination with death. We are, however, mistaken, for this film goes beyond such cultural archetypes," David Cid, unpublished student essay, 1996.

25. The first question after a screening at New York University, it was also asked at the

Brooklyn Museum and was followed by laughs in the audience. Many questions about the family members were raised at the Museum of Modern Art, where *The Devil Never Sleeps* was presented in March 1995 as part of the New Directors/New Films Festival screening.

26. I am thinking of the O. J. Simpson trial and the development of "infotainments" and talk shows, as many of these debates were recorded in 1995–1996, prior to the investigation of President Clinton's affair with Monica Lewinsky. Regardless of any particular scandal, the ongoing telenovelization of U.S. TV programs has probably contributed to changes in audience responses; Portillo continued to present the film several years after its release and noted, as the years went by, a greater acceptance of her filming private feuds in her family. U.S. spectators were not as concerned by the infringement on ethics of the documentary; in particular, the taping and reenactment of phone conversations with Ofelia did not bring the reaction it had previously, even from students of journalism at Berkeley (Portillo, phone conversation with author, April 1998). This suggests there is a historical dimension to the spaces of exhibition.

27. Lourdes Portillo, Center for Media, Culture and History, New York University, March 12, 1996.

28. Lourdes Portillo, phone conversation with author, October 1997, after the PBS broadcast.

29. Oscar's homosexuality was less discussed in the United States and Europe; as for Latina/o audiences, generational and cultural distinctions could also be drawn, although the Chicano students' essays that I read rarely discussed the topic.

30. By contrast, the relationship of the children and parents was much discussed at the question and answer session following the New Directors/New Films screening at the Museum of Modern Art in New York.

31. Parallels were drawn between Oscar's mysterious death and the murder of Colosio; people laughed at the newspaper headline "Corrupción en la policía," intercut with a scene in which the local detective had misplaced Oscar's file; they occasionally discussed problems linked with the irrigation of the land of Sonora or the practice of *dedazo* (handpicking one's successor), such as when a powerful politician contributed to Oscar's election as mayor. Also see below in this essay, where a Mexican spectator draws parallels between Oscar's and Salinas' lives for Anglo spectators in New York City. Read elsewhere as consciousness-raising devices, these specific references were playing with the fabric of a preexisting awareness and did not break a consensus in Latina/o spaces of exhibition. Rosa Linda Fregoso draws parallels between the family and Mexican politics in her essay "Sacando los Trapos al Sol (Airing Dirty Laundry) in Lourdes Portillo's Melodocumystery, *The Devil Never Sleeps*," in *Redirecting the Gaze: Gender, Theory, and Cinema in the Third World*, ed. Diana Robin and Ira Jaffee (Albany: State University of New York Press, 1999).

32. Toni Cade Bambara, speaking of "authenticating audiences," is quoted by B. Ruby Rich in her article on documentaries for the 1993 Biennial of the Whitney Museum, "The Authenticating Goldfish: Re-viewing Film and Video in the Nineties."

33. Lourdes Portillo, fax to author, 1997.

34. Pacific Film Archives, Berkeley, 1995.

35. The following question and answer sessions were compared: with Portillo in Berkeley (Pacific Film Archives, April 1995); in New York at Context Studios, an independent venue where the film was presented by the Latin Americanist Electa Arenal, January 1996; at the Brooklyn Museum, where the film was part of the series "Self Discoveries: A Festival of Latin American Cinema," March 1996; and at a screening organized by the Center for Media Culture and History, New York University, where the film was introduced by B. Ruby Rich and José Muñoz, March 1996.

36. Context Studios, New York, January 29, 1996.

37. Context Studios, New York, January 29, 1996.

38. Center for Media, Culture and History, New York University, March 12, 1996. It is likely that the North Americans who remembered and chose to speak about this relatively short sequence knew of Chicano laborers, in particular of the grape boycott in California. It is therefore particularly striking that they did not remember it at the screening of a film by a Chicana filmmaker.

39. "A "fiction" is neither simply false nor obviously true, but initially is merely indeterminate and nonspecific. . . . By contrast, in nonfiction no initial redescription is necessary, since we assume as starting point for our interpretation that the reference is determinate, particular, and unique (this is x: it exists as such)." Edward Branigan, *Narrative Comprehension and Film* (London: Routledge, 1992), 196.

40. Brooklyn Museum, March 12, 1996.

41. Context Studios, New York, January 29, 1996.

42. Stephen Hollden, "A Niece Rummages in a Rich and Enigmatic Uncle's Closet," *New York Times,* March 20, 1995. *The Hollywood Reporter* regretted that "the riddle of whether the lust for wealth and power caused Oscar's death remains uncertain." If the departure from the detective story was the reviewer's first concern, he nevertheless concluded by looking at Mexico—interestingly, within the United States: "Portillo's unblinking use of unadorned history gives a strong sense of the dramatic riches that lie buried beneath many of this country's Mexican roots." Laurence Vittes, TV review, *The Hollywood Reporter,* September 30, 1997.

43. Context Studios, New York, January 1996.

44. In 1983 Hal Foster attempted in *The Anti-Aesthetic* to distinguish "a postmodernism of reaction" from one of "resistance" that "seeks to question rather than exploit cultural codes, to explore rather than conceal social and political affiliations." *The Anti-Aesthetic, Essays on Postmodern Culture,* ed. with introduction by Hal Foster (Port Townsend, Wash.: Bay Press, 1983), xii. More than fifteen years later, the controversy is still ongoing within the Left and was certainly present in the minds of some spectators, particularly those viewing the film in the context of documentary festivals.

45. Rosa Linda Fregoso pointed out to me the allusion to the Mexican patriarchy in 1998, when I had only underlined a feminist reading.

46. The spectators' sympathy with Ofelia as the filmed subject was particularly apparent in the question and answer sessions with the filmmaker.

47. It is not my intention to elaborate here on the entry of a number of women into the field of documentary production in the late seventies and eighties. Recently, female detective characters have appeared on television, and Jacquie Byars remarks:

"Female-oriented television series are in a distinct minority, certainly, but even detective series—that most staunchly masculine of a television genres—occasionally show some evidence of a 'feminine voice' in both characters and plot." Jacquie Byars, "Gazes/Voices/Power: Expanding Psychoanalysis for Feminist Film and Television Theory," in *Female Spectators: Looking at Film and Television,* ed. Deirdre Pribam (London: Verso, 1988), 126. She analyzes programs such as *Spenser for Hire* (ABC) and *Cagney and Lacey.*

48. Context Studios, New York, January 1996.

49. Les Etats Généraux du Documentaire, Lussas, France, 1997. Unplanned for, the debate began in the theater at a spectator's request and was pursued outside by a small group. Discussions have their own dynamics; those who strongly objected to the film shaped an important part of the debate. I focused here on the argument made by the man who opened the discussion.

50. Fregoso, *The Bronze Screen,* 118. Although *La Ofrenda,* documenting the Day of the Dead in a rural Mexican town and in San Francisco, does not address the issue directly, it gives an important role to cross-dressers and raises questions about gender, sexuality, and AIDS. *The Devil Never Sleeps,* in reminding us of the ongoing AIDS crisis, is oblique as well; set in a family context, the topic brought reactions from Mexican audiences, but was less discussed in the United States, France, and other countries.

51. Fregoso draws an interesting parallel between feminist cinema's "conscious effort to address its spectator as female," in the words of De Lauretis, and substitutes the term "Chicana" for "female." Fregoso, *The Bronze Screen,* 129.

52. Ibid., 118.

53. Gabriela Lopez Sarasua, "*El diablo nunca duerme,* una obra de Lourdes Portillo" (unpublished student essay, University of Buenos Aires, 1997).

54. Two women at Context Studios, New York, January 1996. Another spectator proposed, in response to a controversy about the ethics of the film: "This 'ethical vacuum' is the tragedy of the portrait that she has created of Oscar. And she might want it extrapolated to present cultural conditions in Mexico and in the United States."

55. Bill Nichols, in *Representing Reality,* provided a historical typology of documentary modes: expository, observational, interactive, and reflexive. He locates the performative documentaries in the eighties and nineties (with ancestors) in *Blurred Boundaries* (Bloomington: Indiana University Press, 1994), 95.

56. Thomas Waugh offers a discussion of performance and performativity in queer and documentary theory, with references to Judith Butler and Bill Nichols. He notes the number of gay, lesbian, and queer "performative documentaries" proposed by Bill Nichols, such as films by Pratibha Parmar, Isaac Julien, and Marlon Riggs. Thomas Waugh, "Walking on Tippy Toes," in Holmlund and Fuchs, eds., *Between the Sheets.*

57. "Social subjectivity transforms desire into popular memory, political community, shared orientation, and utopian yearning for what has not yet come to be." Nichols, *Blurred Boundaries,* 97.

58. Ibid., 104.

59. "Performative documentaries: stress subjective aspects of a classically objective dis-

course. Possible limitations: loss of referential emphasis may relegate such films to the avant-garde; 'excessive' use of style." Nichols, *Blurred Boundaries,* 95.

60. Mayne, *Cinema and Spectatorship,* 172.

61. "Instead, spectatorship needs to be treated as one of these ordinary activities, and theorizing this activity can open up spaces between seemingly opposing terms, thus leading us to attend more closely to how stubbornly our pleasures in the movies refuse any rigid dichotomies." Ibid.

62. The ritualized screenings and reception of home movies are analyzed in Roger Odin, "Le film de famille dans l'institution familiale," in *Le Film de famille: Usage privé, usage public,* ed. Roder Odin (Paris: Meridiens Klinskieck, 1995).

63. Not entirely "by" or "about," but in placing itself rather in the interval, *The Devil Never Sleeps* enables several discourses to emerge. I borrow this thought from Trinh T. Minh Ha: "To me, the most inspiring works of art are those that cut across the boundaries of specific art forms and specific cultures, even in their most specific aspects." Trinh T. Minh Ha, "She of the Interval," in *When the Moon Waxes Red,* ed. Trinh T. Minh Ha (London: Routledge, 1991), 93.

Chapter Seven

1. Interviews with the three discussion groups were carried out in Tijuana between January and March of 1999. The first group was made up of youths who were born in Tijuana or who had lived most of their lives there and had some contact with Mexican-American and Mexicans in the United States. In this group only one man participated and the female majority determined the tone and the direction of the discussion. The participants were between twenty-three and twenty-eight years old. The second group was of mixed origin and with the exception of one Mexican-American from San Diego, no one from this group had ever been in a border city. They ranged in age between twenty-five and thirty years old and had been residing in Tijuana for three or four months. The third group was very similar to the second group, with the exception of one young man, Ciudad Juárez, who had had the experience of living on the U.S.–Mexican border.

Chapter Eight

1. By "conventional documentary structure," I mean that *Las Madres* follows what could loosely be termed an expository documentary model. It employs a "voice-of-God" commentary (although the voice is female). This commentary is nonsynchronous and "explains" the images to the viewer. Its story is organized according to a point/counterpoint unfolding of information, and its narrative proceeds along a linear cause-and-effect historical trajectory. A history is traced, and the involvement of the viewer solicited, around a need for the solution to a "problem," etc. See Bill Nichols, *Representing Reality: Issues and Concepts in Documentary* (Bloomington: Indiana University Press, 1991), 38.

2. See Avery F. Gordon, *Ghostly Matters: Haunting and the Sociological Imagination* (Minneapolis: University of Minnesota Press, 1997), 103.

3. Chela Sandoval, "US Third World Feminism: The Theory and Method of Oppositional Consciousness in the Postmodern World," *Genders 10* (spring 1991): 1–24.

4. In *Camera Lucida*, Roland Barthes elaborates his notions of "punctum" and "studium," two terms that are useful in understanding the importance of the visual language of portraiture in *Las Madres* history. "Studium," says Barthes, means "study" and "derives from an average effect." It relates to "training" and "culture." "Punctum," on the other hand, is whatever breaks or interrupts the studium: it "shoots out of it like an arrow and pierces me." Barthes uses "punctum" to describe the private, connotative impact of certain photographic *details* within the overall, denotative public meaning (the studium) of the photograph as an entire image. In Barthes' usage, "studium" has the characteristic of ongoingness and "punctum" of piercing, punctuation, and rupture. The terms are suggestive in conceptualizing the relationship between moving and still images in a general sense, insofar as analogies can easily be drawn between film and studium as a moving, ongoing temporal environment on one hand, and the stopped image (or photograph) and punctum on the other. See Roland Barthes, *Camera Lucida* (New York: Hill and Wang, 1981), 23–60. In *Las Madres* history, the photographic portrait became a form of punctum with which the mothers pierced the ongoing studium of political oppression. See Gordon, *Ghostly Matters*, 108–111.

5. Elaine Scarry, *The Body in Pain* (New York: Oxford University Press, 1985), 5.

6. Barthes, *Camera Lucida*, 85.

7. See Rosa Linda Fregoso, *The Bronze Screen* (Minneapolis: University of Minnesota Press, 1993), 112. Fregoso says the film juxtaposes three discourses: a documentary or "literal" discourse; a formal structure that initiates a discourse of identity politics; and a discourse on gender and sexuality contained in the coded images of the film.

8. Fregoso, *The Bronze Screen*, 114–116.

9. See Kaja Silverman, *The Acoustic Mirror* (Bloomington: Indiana University Press, 1988), Ch. 2–3.

10. See Michel Foucault, "Of Other Spaces," *Diacritics* 16, no. 1 (summer 1986): 22–27.

11. Jennifer Gonzalez and Michelle Habell-Pallan, "Heterotopias and Shared Methods of Resistance: Navigating Social Spaces and Spaces of Identity," in *Enunciating Our Terms: Women of Color in Collaboration and Conflict*, Inscriptions 7 Series, ed. María Ochoa and Teresia Teaiwa (Santa Cruz: Center for Cultural Studies, University of California, Santa Cruz, 1994).

12. Foucault, "Of Other Spaces," 25.

13. Jennifer Gonzalez, *How Things Mean: Objects and Identity* (unpublished qualifying essay) (Santa Cruz: History of Consciousness Board, University of California, Santa Cruz, 1993). Pierre Nora, "Between Memory and History: Les Lieux de memoires," *Representations* 26 (spring 1989): 31–59.

14. Gonzalez, *How Things Mean*, 50.

15. Fregoso, *The Bronze Screen*, 110–118.

16. Ibid., 112.

17. Fregoso, *The Bronze Screen*, 96–105.

18. Stuart Hall, "Cultural Identity and Diaspora," in *Identity: Community, Culture, Difference*, ed. Jonathan Rutherford (London: Lawrence and Wishalt, 1990), 222.

19. Stuart Hall, "Deviance, Politics, and the Media," in *The Lesbian and Gay Studies Reader,* ed. Henry Abelove, Michele A. Barale, and David M. Halperin (London: Routledge, 1993), 64.

20. In "The Third Meaning," Roland Barthes describes the photographic or stilled image in film as the indicator of an alternative ("unspeakable") narrative that intersects (and interrupts) the dominant, forward-moving one. This "third meaning" is articulated in sexually evocative language that suggests a latent but emphatic homosexual content. See Roland Barthes, "The Third Meaning," in *Image, Music, Text* (New York: Hill and Wang, 1977).

21. In "Desire and Narrative," Teresa de Lauretis describes the operations of film narrative in the following way: "In the narrative film the spectator's movement or passage is subject to an orientation, a direction—a teleology, we might say. . . . Film narrative . . . is a process by which the text-images distributed across the film . . . are finally regrouped in the two zones of sexual difference, from which they take their culturally preconstructed meaning: mythical subject and obstacle, maleness and femaleness" (138). Here the "culturally preconstructed meaning" of "maleness and femaleness" presume a heterosexual narrative model. See Teresa de Lauretis, "Desire in Narrative," in *Alice Doesn't* (Bloomington: Indiana University Press, 1984).

22. Barthes describes the "third meaning" contained in the privileged halted cinematic moment (which is the photograph by formal necessity) in the following way: "It intersects the narrative movement of the story at a slightly more than perpendicular angle"; it is "discontinuous with and indifferent to the 'story.' It disturbs and sterilizes the critical language by which the story is understood"; it forms a "counter-narrative" and "counter-temporality"; it has "something to do with disguise"; it is a "signifier without a signified, hence the difficulty in naming it . . . it does not copy anything"; it has a "de-naturing effect . . . with regard to the referent"; it maintains "a state of perpetual erethism, desire not finding issue in that spasm of the signified which normally brings the subject voluptuously back into the peace of nominations." The third meaning is, then, the referent that cannot speak its name and does not reproduce. It represents a deviant textual practice with clear sexual connotations that Barthes proclaims a "new—rare—practice affirmed against a majority practice . . . obtuse meaning appears necessarily as a luxury, an expenditure with no exchange." Barthes' third meaning, which attaches to the stilled cinematic image, represents a form of signification either outside the heterosexual reproductive and representational economy, or intersecting and contradicting it. He describes it finally as "this other text" that tends to erode the "strong system" of forward-moving narration, causing it to slip "away from the inside." Barthes, "The Third Meaning," 52-68.

23. Raymond Bellour, "The Film Stilled," *Camera Obscura* 24 (spring 1989): 109.

24. See Gilles Deleuze, *Cinema 1: The Movement Image* (Minneapolis: University of Minnesota Press, 1986), 5-7, for a discussion of how the impression of cinematic movement is produced from "equidistant instants selected so as to create an impression of continuity." The individual photographic moments of film function in much the same way that Judith Butler claims "iterative performance" does in rela-

tion to gender identity. "If every performance repeats itself to institute the effect of identity, then every repetition requires an interval between the acts, as it were, in which risk and excess threaten to disrupt the identity being constituted (see Judith Butler, "Imitation and Gender Insubordination," in *Inside/Out,* ed. Diana Fuss [New York: Routledge, 1991], 14). The still photograph, within this analogy, introduces the interruption of identity here postulated: the moment of "risk and excess" in which both the formal identity of cinema and the identificatory investments of the spectator are "threatened." In Portillo's films, the photograph works as a "meta-trope" (in this case, a trope defined in terms of its general formal relation to the moving image rather than its local signifying operations). It signifies a moment of alternative narration, while also representing specific, situated identities.

Appendix

1. See Rosa Linda Fregoso, "Diablos y fantasmas, madres e inmigrantes: Una retrospectiva crítica del trabajo de Lourdes Portillo" (this volume).
2. Los tres grupos de discusión se llevaron a cabo en Tijuana entre enero y marzo de 1999. El primer grupo estuvo constituido por jóvenes que habían nacido o habían vivido la mayor parte de su vida en Tijuana, y que por lo tanto tenían contactos y experiencias de vida con méxico-americanos y mexicanos en Estados Unidos. En este grupo sólo participó un hombre, y la mayoría femenina marcó el tono y la dirección del discurso. Los participantes a este grupo tenían entre veintitrés y veintiocho años de edad. El segundo grupo fue mixto, y todos, con excepción de una méxico-americana de San Diego, nunca habían vivido en una ciudad fronteriza. Tenían entre tres y cuatro meses de residir en Tijuana al momento de llevar a cabo el grupo de discusión y sus edades iban de veinticinco y treinta años. El tercer grupo tuvo características muy similares al segundo, con la excepción de que en este último participó un joven de Ciudad Juárez, quien tenía por lo tanto la experiencia de vivir en una ciudad de la frontera norte de México.

Notes on Contributors

Norma Iglesias Prieto is a professor in the Department of Chicana/o Studies at San Diego State University and a researcher at the Colegio de la Frontera Norte in Baja California. Her published books include *Entre yerba, polvo, y plomo: lo fronterizo visto por el cine mexicano* (1991); *Medios de comunicación en la frontera norte* (1990); and *La flor más bella de la maquiladora* (1985; English translation, *Beautiful Flowers of the Maquiladora,* 1996), and *Miradas de mujer* (co-edited with Rosa Linda Fregoso, 1998). Her work focuses on questions of gender in transnational media and border culture. Currently she is conducting an ethnographic study of audience reception of chicana/o cinema.

Barbara McBane has worked as a sound editor and designer for many years. Her credits include several academy award winning or nominated films (*Apocalypse Now, Amadeus, Terminator 2, Contact, The Talented Mr. Ripley,* and others) as well as documentaries, experimental films, and installations. She edited the sound for Lourdes Portillo's *The Devil Never Sleeps,* and is currently pursuing graduate studies in the History of Consciousness program at the University of California, Santa Cruz.

Kathleen Newman is an Associate Professor who teaches Latin American and Chicano Cinema at the University of Iowa. She is one of the co-authors of *Women, Culture and Politics in Latin America* (1990) and publishes regularly on Chicana/o and Latin American cinemas.

B. Ruby Rich is a San Francisco-based independent scholar and cultural critic. She has served as the Associate Director of the Film Center at the School of the Art Institute of Chicago and as Director of the Electronic Media and Film Program of the New York State Council on the Arts. She contributed regularly to the *Village Voice* in the eighties and to *Sight and Sound* and *Elle* in the nineties. Currently, she is an adjunct Associate Professor in Film Studies at the University of California, Berkeley. She is also a member of the selection advisory committee of the Sundance Film Institute. She continues to contribute to media, popular, and scholarly presses.

Sylvie Thouard is a French-born documentary producer and author who has lived in New York since 1980 when she came to the United States as the recipient of a Fulbright Fellowship. In the United States she has worked for the French channels Antenne 2 and FR3, the European television ARTE, as well as for American independent filmmakers. She has been a correspondent for the FIFARC (Festival International du Film d'Architecture), consultant for les Etats généraux du Documentaire de Lussas, curator, and teacher. She has also authored several articles on documentaries and is currently on the editorial board of La Revue Documentaires. Her Ph.D. dissertation for La Sorbonne Nouvelle (Paris) examines the production and reception of documentaries in the United States, now a "post civil-rights" society where such categories as nation or identity are redefined by worldwide migrations and globalization.

Yvonne Yarbro-Bejarano is Professor of Spanish & Portuguese and Chicana/o Studies at Stanford University. She is the author of *Feminism and the Honor Plays of Lope de Vega* (1994), co-editor of *Chicano Art: Resistance and Affirmation* (1991), and has published numerous articles on Chicana/o literature and culture. Her most recent book is *The Wounded Heart: Writing on Cherríe Moraga* (University of Texas Press, forthcoming). Her research, teaching, and writing center on the representation of race, sexuality, and gender. Her next book project involves an interdisciplinary analysis of representations of race, gender, and sexuality in Chicana/o, Puerto Rican, and Cuban American cultural production. Since spring 1994 she has been developing a digital archive called "Chicana Art," which will soon be accessible on the Internet. "Chicana Art" features over 2,000 images by leading Chicana artists, as well as information about Chicano art. Yvonne was director of the Chicana/o Fellows Program and the Chicana/o Studies program in Stanford's new Center for Comparative Studies in Race and Ethnicity. Currently, she is chairing the Department of Spanish & Portuguese.

Index